Ownership and Governance of Enterprises

Studies in Development Economics and Policy
General Editor: **Anthony Shorrocks**

UNU WORLD INSTITUTE FOR DEVELOPMENT ECONOMICS RESEARCH (UNU/WIDER) was established by the United Nations University as its first research and training centre and started work in Helsinki, Finland, in 1985. The purpose of the Institute is to undertake applied research and policy analysis on structural changes affecting the developing and transitional economies, to provide a forum for the advocacy of policies leading to robust, equitable and environmentally sustainable growth, and to promote capacity-strengthening and training in the field of economic and social policy-making. Its work is carried out by staff researchers and visiting scholars in Helsinki and through networks of collaborating scholars and institutions around the world.

UNU World Institute for Development Economics Research (UNU/WIDER)
Katajanokanlaituri 6B, FIN-00160 Helsinki, Finland

Titles include:

Ricardo Ffrench-Davis and Stephany Griffith-Jones (*editors*)
FROM CAPITAL SURGES TO DROUGHT

Aiguo Lu and Manuel F. Montes (*editors*)
POVERTY, INCOME DISTRIBUTION AND WELL-BEING IN ASIA DURING THE TRANSITION

Robert J. McIntyre and Bruno Dallago (*editors*)
SMALL AND MEDIUM ENTERPRISES IN TRANSITIONAL ECONOMIES

Vladimir Mikhalev (*editor*)
INEQUALITY AND SOCIAL STRUCTURE DURING THE TRANSITION

E. Wayne Nafziger and Raimo Väyrynen (*editors*)
THE PREVENTION OF HUMANITARIAN EMERGENCIES

Laixiang Sun (*editor*)
OWNERSHIP AND GOVERNANCE OF ENTERPRISES
Recent Innovative Developments

Studies in Development Economics and Policy
Series Standing Order ISBN 0–333–96424–1
(*outside North America only*)

You can receive future titles in this series as they are published by placing a standing order. Please contact your bookseller or, in case of difficulty, write to us at the address below with your name and address, the title of the series and the ISBN quoted above.

Customer Services Department, Macmillan Distribution Ltd, Houndmills, Basingstoke, Hampshire RG21 6XS, England

---

Ownership and Governance of Enterprises

Recent Innovative Developments

Edited by

Laixiang Sun

School of Oriental and African Studies, University of London
International Institute for Applied System Analysis, Laxenburg
Guanghua School of Management, Peking University, Beijing

in association with the United Nations
University/World Institute for Development
Economics Research

First published 2003 by
PALGRAVE MACMILLAN
Houndmills, Basingstoke, Hampshire RG21 6XS and
175 Fifth Avenue, New York, N.Y. 10010
Companies and representatives throughout the world

PALGRAVE MACMILLAN is the global academic imprint of the Palgrave Macmillan division of St. Martin's Press, LLC and of Palgrave Macmillan Ltd. Macmillan® is a registered trademark in the United States, United Kingdom and other countries. Palgrave is a registered trademark in the European Union and other countries.

ISBN 1–4039–1633–0

This book is printed on paper suitable for recycling and made from fully managed and sustained forest sources.

A catalogue record for this book is available from the British Library.

Library of Congress Cataloging-in-Publication Data
Ownership and governance of enterprises: recent innovative developments / edited by Laixiang Sun.
    p.   cm. — (Studies in development economics and policy)
    Includes bibliographical references and index
    ISBN 1–4039–1633–0
    1. Corporate governance—Case studies.   2. Stock ownership—Case studies.
    3. Corporation—Case studies.   4. Industrial management—Case studies.
    I. Sun, Laixiang, 1957 II. Series.
    HD2741.O87 2003
    338.6—dc21   2003050456

10   9   8   7   6   5   4   3   2   1
12 11 10 09 08 07 06 05 04 03

Printed and bound in Great Britain by
Antony Rowe Ltd, Chippenham and Eastbourne

Contents

List of Tables — vi
List of Figures — vii
Preface — viii
Acknowledgements — x
Notes on the Contributors — xii
List of Abbreviations — xiii

1 Adaptive Efficiency and the Evolving Diversity of Enterprise
Ownership and Governance Forms: An Overview
Laixiang Sun — 1

2 Institutional Investors, Corporate Ownership and Corporate
Governance: Global Perspectives
Stuart L. Gillan and Laura T. Starks — 36

3 New Institutional Arrangements for Product Innovation in
Silicon Valley
Hirokazu Takizawa — 69

4 Sharing Ownership via Employee Stock Ownership
James C. Sesil, Douglas L. Kruse and Joseph R. Blasi — 96

5 Hardening a Soft Budget Constraint through 'Upward
Devolution' to a Supranational Institution: The Case of the
European Union and Italian State-Owned Firms
Elisabetta Bertero and Laura Rondi — 124

6 Evolving and Functioning Mechanisms of Employee Stock
Ownership in China's Township and Village Enterprises
Laixiang Sun — 159

7 Network Externalities and Cooperative Networks: Stylized
Facts and Theory
Stephen C. Smith — 181

8 Network Externalities and Cooperative Networks:
A Comparative Case Study of Mondragón and La Lega with
Implications for Developing and Transitional Countries
Stephen C. Smith — 202

Index — 243

v

List of Tables

1.1 Number of employee ownership plans and employee participants, and the value of plan assets, early 2002   7

5.1 Italian government balances, 1980–99   139

5.2 State aid to Italian firms, 1981–96   141

6.1 Comparison of the average performance of the main ownership forms   160

6.2 Comparative models of insider control   168

8.1 Schematic view of responses to strategic issues in Mondragón and La Lega   207

List of Figures

5.1 Corporate governance of Italian public enterprises   135
5.2 Net income of public holdings, Italy, 1974–83   136
5.3 Italian public debt, 1976–96   138
5.4 State aid to enterprises, 1987–98   142
5.5 Public transfers to the industrial sector and transfers to
     public enterprises, 1980–95   143
7.1 Privately efficient cooperative density function and
     multiple cooperative density equilibia   188
7.2 The shift of the privately efficient cooperative density
     function   189
7.3 The presence of the league shifts the cooperative density
     function upwards   190
7.4 Gross payoffs and costs to members   194
7.5 Net payoffs to members and non-members   195

Preface

The renewed interest in enterprise ownership and corporate governance has been driven by a host of factors, including the diverse experiences of the centrally planned economies during their transition to market economies, the Asian financial crisis in 1997–98 and the recent corporate scandals in the United States, all of which show that the challenges to firms' ownership and governance structures have a global reach and are recurrent. In 1999 these observations spurred my colleagues at UNU/WIDER to initiate a research project called 'Property Rights Regimes, Microeconomic Incentives, and Development' with the intention of looking for innovative and successful developments in the field, exploring the forces that have driven these developments and identifying the mechanisms that underlie their dynamics.

Thanks to the dedicated efforts and professionalism of the project team, the project has contributed to the literature in three directions: theory, empirical findings and policy debates. An academic symposium with formalized analyses generated by the project has been published in the *Journal of Comparative Economics* (30, 4 [2002]: 754–863). This particular issue is oriented to general readers beyond the economist circle. In other words, all the authors have made a great effort to present their analyses in a manner that is accessible to non-economists.

This book shows that innovative developments in ownership and governance forms have typically gone far beyond the theoretical predictions. Taking China's township and village enterprises (TVEs) as an example, the recent phasing out of local government ownership in TVEs took place well before the meaningful marketization of land and bank financing, and well before a meaningful presence of the rule of law in the areas of business licensing and regulation. Even more interestingly, TVE ownership reform was largely initiated and led by local governments. The phasing out of local government ownership was widely regarded as a means of promoting, rather than a result of, marketization and the rule of law. This and similar issues discussed in this book provide the basis for further theoretical and empirical research and for fruitful policy debates.

The analyses in the book show that the nature of enterprises is changing and a diverse pattern of ownership and governance is emerging. As a consequence the boundaries of enterprises are often in flux. To understand the formation and evolution of ownership and governance structures in diverse technological and institutional environments, we need to make reference to competitive perspectives linked to the theory of enterprises and examine the interaction between the nature of enterprises and corporate governance issues under alternative circumstances. Although we are still in the process of searching for new foundations for the changing nature of enterprises, several promising perspectives have emerged, as we show in this volume. If treated in a complementary way they provide great help in understanding the fundamental trade-offs that underlie the evolving diversity of ownership and governance structures in the real world, and aid the search for adaptively efficient enterprise models in transitional economies.

Acknowledgements

The papers published in this volume form part of the outcome of a UNU/WIDER research project on 'Property Rights Regimes, Micro-economic Incentives, and Development', carried out mainly in 2000–1. The editor would like to thank UNU/WIDER for its consistent and generous support of the project and three WIDER directors – Professors Andrea Cornia, Matti Pohjola (*a.i.*) and Anthony Shorrocks – for their interest and leadership.

The staff of UNU/WIDER were of great help in providing administrative support. The editor would especially like to thank Lorraine Telfer-Taivainen for efficiently administering the entire project and the project meeting, and Adam Swallow for his expert editing and formatting of the manuscript.

The editor is most grateful to all the contributors to this volume for their input and insights. All the authors greatly appreciate their fellow project participants' stimulating discussions both during the project meeting and in follow-up communications. They are also deeply indebted to two anonymous referees for their critical comments and constructive suggestions, which were very helpful when revising the manuscript.

In addition, Stuart Gillan and Laura Starks would like to thank Terry Campbell, Joseph Fan, Douglas Fore, Ken Kim, Jennifer Ma, Raymond Schmeirer, Lelia Stroud and Kelsy Wei for their helpful comments and suggestions. Gillan began Chapter 2 while at the TIAA-CREF Institute, and stresses that the views expressed in the chapter are those of the authors and do not necessarily reflect those of the TIAA-CREF or its employees.

Elisabetta Bertero and Laura Rondi would like to thank Jonathan Leape and Waltraud Schelkle for their suggestions.

Stephen Smith would like to thank Terence Martin and Fred Freundlich for helpful discussions and their kind assistance in organizing the author's field visits to Mondragón. He would also like to thank John Bonin, Sumit Joshi, Panu Kalmi, Laixiang Sun and participants at the project meeting in Helsinki in April 2001, at the annual meeting of the Association for Comparative Economic Studies in Atlanta in January 2002, at the Northeast Universities Development Consortium Conference at Williams College in November 2002 and at a seminar at George Washington University for their helpful comments. Part of Chapter 7 draws on joint work with Sumit Joshi, whose vital contribution to the project is greatly appreciated. Special thanks go to Adrian Celeya (General Secretary of the Mondragón Co-operative Corporation) for the time and effort he generously devoted to the author's Mondragón field visits. Support from an earlier Fulbright Research Scholarship and a Jean Monet Research Fellowship, and the support provided by the European University Institute, Florence, during field visits to Italy are also gratefully acknowledged.

Notes on the Contributors

Elisabetta Bertero is Lecturer in the Department of Accounting and Finance at the London School of Economics.

Joseph R. Blasi is Professor in the School of Management and Labour Relations at Rutger University, New Jersey.

Stuart L. Gillan is Assistant Professor in the Department of Finance and the Weinberg Center for Corporate Governance at the Lerner College of Business and Economics, University of Delaware, Delaware.

Douglas L. Kruse is Professor in the School of Management and Labour Relations at Rutger University, New Jersey.

Laura Rondi is Senior Researcher for the Italian National Research Council (CNR) at CERIS, (Institute for Economic Research Centre on Firms and Growth), Torino.

James C. Sesil is Assistant Professor in the School of Management and Labour Relations at Rutger University, New Jersey.

Stephen C. Smith is Professor of Economics at George Washington University, Washington, DC.

Laura T. Starks holds the Charles E. and Sarah M. Seay Regents Chair in Finance, Department of Finance, University of Texas at Austin.

Laixiang Sun is Professor in the Department of Financial and Management Studies, SOAS, University of London; Economist at the International Institute for Applied System Analysis, Laxenburg, Austria; and Senior Research Fellow at the Guanghua School of Management, Peking University, Beijing.

Hirokazu Takizawa is Associate Professor in the Faculty of Economics at Toyo University, and a Faculty Fellow at the Research Institute of Economy, Trade and Industry (RIETI), Tokyo.

List of Abbreviations

A&D	Acquisition and Development
ACAM	Il Consorzio Nazionale Approvviggionamenti
CalPERS	California Public Employees Retirement System
CEO	chief executive officer
CFO	chief financial officer
CLP	Caja Laboral Popular
EBRD	European Bank for Reconstruction and Development
EC	European Community
EFTA	European Free Trade Association
EMS	European Monetary System
EMU	European Monetary Union
ERISA	Employment Retirement Income Security Act
ESC	endogenous sunk cost
ESOPs	employee stock ownership plans
EU	European Union
FASB	Financial Accounting Standards Board
FINEC	National Co-operative Finance Company
FTSE	Financial Times Stock Exchange
GATT	General Agreement on Tariffs and Trade
IMF	International Monetary Fund
IPO	initial public offer
IRI	Institute for Industrial Reconstruction (Italy)
IRRC	Investor Responsibility Research Center
JSCs	joint-stock cooperatives
MNC	multinational company
MEIP	market economy investor principle
MCC	Mondragón Co-operative Corporation
NAFTA	North Atlantic Free Trade Agreement
NAPF	National Association of Pension Funds (UK)
NBER	National Bureau of Economic Research
NCEO	National Centre for Employee Ownership
OECD	Organisation for Economic Co-operation and Development
PAYG	pay-as-you-go
RIETI	Research Institute of Economy, Trade and Industry
SEC	Securities and Exchange Commission (US)

SBCS	soft budget constraint syndrome
SOEs	state-owned enterprises
TIAA-CREF	Teachers Insurance and Annuity Association College Retirement Equities Fund (New York)
TVEs	Township and Village Enterprises
WTO	World Trade Organization

1
Adaptive Efficiency and the Evolving Diversity of Enterprise Ownership and Governance Forms: An Overview

Laixiang Sun

There is an extensive body of literature promoting the conventional paradigm that private investors should own the firm and that the existence of well-defined, personalized property rights is a basic precondition for the proper functioning of a market economy. The intuition underlying this wisdom is that placing property under the exclusive control of private owners makes them liable for the consequences of bad decisions but also entitles them to the rewards of good ones, thus making them more willing to motivate managers and workers.

However, reality confronts the prevailing paradigm with a rich diversity of ownership structures, even in the bastions of the free market economy: the United States and Western Europe. In the developed world, employee-owned firms are widespread in the professions including law, accounting, investment banking and medicine. Employee stock ownership is spreading in the industrial sector. Institutional investors have become the dominant shareholders of large publicly traded corporations. Farmer-owned cooperatives dominate the markets for basic agricultural products. Moreover mutual companies owned by their policyholders sell half of all life insurance and a quarter of all property and liability insurance (Hansmann, 1996; Gates, 1998). Another striking fact is that in most economies around the world, state ownership is widespread, with the state being the single most important large shareholder after individual families (La Porta *et al.*, 1999).

These facts indicate that the conventional wisdom on ownership is descriptively narrow. The claim that private investors should own the firm is not the logical consequence of free markets and free enterprise. It is of both theoretical and policy importance to examine the emergence of unconventional ownership and governance forms of enterprises across economies, to investigate the driving forces behind the evolving dynamics of these emerging forms, and to search for new paradigms on ownership and governance. This book addresses these concerns and seeks to advance the debate.

In this book five unconventional ownership forms are examined to reveal their major characteristics: institutional ownership of large publicly traded corporations; employee stock ownership in the United States; large-scale employee stock ownership in China; joint ownership and shifting governance in Silicon Valley firms; and the famous Mondragón cooperative group in Spain and the Italian cooperatives in the La Lega network. Two cases involving state ownership are also analysed and compared. They demonstrate that it is possible, in a number of alternative ways, to harden the budget constraints of state-owned enterprises (SOEs). One case is Italy's success in imposing and sustaining a hard budget constraint on SOEs by means of supranational forces; the other is the successful experience in China of hardening the budget constraints on local governments and local SOEs through fiscal decentralization and monetary centralization. In this chapter we highlight the main reasons why these new developments are unconventional, summarize the complementary theoretical perspectives developed in the search for new paradigms, and explore the policy implications of the research for developing and transitional economies.

Why are these new developments unconventional?

Institutional investors as large shareholders and information transmitters

Pension funds, mutual funds, insurance companies, foundations and university endowments – collectively known as institutional investors – have become the dominant shareholders of corporations in the United States and other developed countries. In 1999–2000, US institutional investors held securities worth twice their country's GDP (about US$17.3 trillion). Of their security holdings, over 45 per cent (US$7.8 trillion) were equity in large corporations (OECD, 1999: 26, 34; OECD, 2001: tables 1, 2). It is estimated that institutional investors as a whole now hold about 51 per cent of all outstanding shares of US corporations, up from just 16 per cent in 1965 (Blair, 1995: 45–6; OECD, 2001: tables 1, 2).

The situation is similar in the UK: by the end of 1999, institutional investors held financial assets worth more than twice their country's GDP (US$3 trillion), of which over two thirds were shareholdings in large corporations (OECD, 1999: 26, 34; 2001: tables 1, 2). In the whole OECD area, institutional investors controlled over US$29 trillion of financial assets (about 128 per cent of GDP) by the end of 1998, of which about 35 per cent were shares in large corporations (OECD, 2000: tables F.4, S.1, S.2).

The growth record of equity investment by institutional investors is spectacular. Over the period 1990–96, while the total financial assets controlled by institutional investors in the OECD area increased by an average annual rate of 9 per cent, the value of their equity investment grew by 18 per cent on average. In the United States, while the assets of institutional investors doubled during the period, the value of their equity investment almost quadrupled (OECD, 1999: 9–10, 34).

The rapid rise of institutional investors has led both to exhilaration and to anxiety among scholars, commentators and decision makers. The exhilaration has been mainly stimulated by the acceleration of innovation and institutionalization in the financial service sector and by the rise of professional fund managers in national and international financial markets. The anxiety is closely linked to the increasing disconnection between investors and corporate ownership, which is characterized by a three-way separation of ownership and control: direct shareholders (owners of shares), indirect shareholders (fund portfolio management) and executives (firm managers).

Exhilaration: conventional evolution induced by financial market development and modernization

From the perspective of financial market development and modernization, the rapid rise of institutional investors is regarded as a natural consequence of socioeconomic development, technological progress and increasing competition. Increasingly wealthy and sophisticated individual investors need advanced financial instruments to reduce firm-specific risk through fund pooling and portfolio diversification, and at the same time to avoid a significant rise in the agency costs they bear as owners of corporate equity. The rapid ageing of the population in the OECD area has increased the demand by private households for the pension products offered by various financial institutions, including pension funds, insurance companies, investment funds and banks.

On the supply side, the deregulation of the banking and securities sectors and the liberalization of the activities of institutional investors since the beginning of the 1980s have created a highly competitive and liberalized environment for the development of the financial services sector. Spectacular advances in information and communication technology have enabled in much more reliable and efficient clearing and settlements systems for securities and payments, as well as new financial instruments for risk management purposes. Professional fund managers have accumulated highly specialized knowledge and technical skills and played an increasingly active role in developing asset allocation strategies, taking investment decisions and monitoring corporate managers (Blommestein, 1998; *The Economist*, 30 October 1999: 77–8, 6 November 1999: 107–8).

Anxiety: unconventional role in corporate ownership and governance

From the perspective of corporate ownership and governance, of great concern is what it means to 'own' when ownership is institutionalized. In comparison with the highly concentrated, highly personalized, hands-on ownership of the traditional capitalist proprietor, institutional investors look more like fiduciaries or trustees than 'natural owners'. For example, although pension funds in the United States held US$7.4 trillion by the end of 1998, over 80 per cent of those assets were delegated to external fiduciaries to manage, including investment advisers, investment companies, insurance companies and banks (Monks and Minow, 2001: 110–15). Furthermore, dodging the difficulties of exercising traditional ownership rights, many institutional investors, especially the large public-sector pension funds, rely on an 'index' strategy when investing. They maintain highly diverse portfolios that are selected to match an index of companies in a given stock exchange, such as Standard & Poor's 500 index. As a consequence these institutional investors buy and sell only because a company is part of an index being tracked, not because of any knowledge about the company. For example, between 1986 and 1996 the amount of US mutual-fund money invested in the mostly widely held stock index funds increased a hundredfold to US$65 billion, a growth rate eighteen times that of the fund industry as a whole (*New York Times*, 28 January 1997: 1; Gates, 1998: 36–8, 333).

There is evidence of institutional shareholder activism. It is reported that institutional investors routinely put pressure on companies to curb excessive salaries for executives, to make boards more independent, and even to sack poorly performing managers. According to *The Economist* (30 October 1999: 77), Rakesh Khurana of the Sloan School of Management at the Massachusetts Institute of Technology has examined 1300 occasions between 1980 and 1996 when chief executives of Fortune

500 firms left their jobs. In a third of cases the person was sacked. For a similar level of performance, a chief executive appointed after 1985 is three times more likely to be fired than one appointed before that date. The California Public Employees Retirement System (CalPERS), a pension fund of more than $80 billion, compiles and publishes an annual list of 'crummy companies', judged by their stock performance and management style, and sends in people to interrogate their bosses and directors (*The Economist*, 10 August 1996: 51).

In general, however, institutional investors are passive investors. Besides the fact that regulations may prohibit some categories of institutional investor to have a direct or dominant influence over the management of a company, institutional investors are not usually interested in or capable of exercising traditional ownership rights in a direct, sustained and responsible fashion. The smaller insurance companies and pension funds typically give portfolio management mandates to outside fund management teams. The larger funds are constrained in many ways not to exercise traditional ownership rights. The main constraint is the forbiddingly high cost of acquiring firm-specific knowledge and information. For example CalPERS invests in hundreds of companies and it would be impossible for its trustees to sit on so many boards of directors, attend hundreds of shareholder meetings or evaluate thousands of quarterly financial statements in a professional manner. The US nationwide pension plan for teachers and researchers, TIAA-CREF, indexes two thirds of its stock portfolio and directly manages only about one hundred stocks. Nevertheless, even one hundred companies are a lot to monitor, apart from the problems linked to 'collective action' dilemmas, such as free riding by other shareholders (Blommestein, 1998: 36; Gates, 1998: 300).

Our view: four channels to lessen the severity of the corporate governance problem

We argue that the difference between the traditional 'natural owner' and the new institutional owner has been largely exaggerated due to popular misconceptions about the traditional natural owner, and that there are alternatives to reduce the severity of the corporate control problem linked to institutional shareholders. In a typical joint-stock company, what shareholders really own are their shares, not the corporation. When investors purchase the initial public offerings of a corporation's shares, the assets available to the corporation become the firm's property. Shareholders may sell their shares if they are dissatisfied with the performance of the firm, and in combination with other shareholders they may vote to sell the firm. What they cannot do individually is insist that the corporation buys back their shares. The inability of investors to force the firm to repurchase outstanding shares gives professional managers greater control over equity capital. The corporation as a legal person, not the shareholder, has title to the assets secured from its initial sale of stock (Monks and Minow, 2001: 10). If shareholders could reclaim these assets, the severity of the corporate governance problem would be greatly lessened. In other words, disappointed shareholders, acting individually but in large numbers, could demand payments that would strip the management of corporate assets (Demsetz, 1988: 114; 1997: 50–1). In this regard, there is little difference between natural and institutional owners, especially when there is a highly diffuse ownership structure.

As Gillan and Starks argue in Chapter 2, for companies with very diffuse shareholders, the rise of institutional shareholders would lessen the severity of the corporate governance problem in three ways. First, by pooling investment, institutional investors would be in a better position than individual investors to aggregate the ownership interest of individual investors into a controlling fraction of a corporation's stock. Second, institutional investors would be in a better position than individual investors to undertake the functions of corporate governance due to their specialization in investment and corporation control in terms of both knowledge and time. Third, large institutions would have less incentive to unload shares because unloading could cause the share price to plummet, the financial equivalent of shooting themselves in the foot. This position would make them more interested in monitoring the performance of corporations in which they have a controlling share of the total stock.

In addition, as suggested by Demsetz (1997: 51–2), financial institutions such as open-end mutual stock funds have the ability to reduce the severity of the corporate governance problem. An open-end mutual stock fund pools capital from retail investors and uses its skill to invest in the shares of other corporations. The fund's business activity does not depend on the availability and continued deployment of specialized assets, unlike the business of a manufacturing company. Capital placed at its disposal can be withdrawn by its investors without seriously compromising its commitments to others. General dissatisfaction with the management of a fund can cause investors to reclaim most of its capital, even though none of the individual investors has invested a significant sum. This disciplining force serves as a powerful mechanism to make the fund accountable. The fund can gather enough invested wealth to allow it to obtain a controlling fraction of equity in some corporations and at the same time to maintain its ability to diversify. It can act somewhat as a collectivist individualist (*The Economist* 6 November 1999: 107). Such funds might be able to play a significant role in transitional economies and developing economies in which low levels of wealth but also the egalitarian distribution of wealth have been the norm.

In short the institutionalization of corporate ownership has brought new dilemmas in the field of corporate governance. However, in comparison with individualized ownership of a company with a broad shareholding, it represents historical progress in terms of creating new opportunities for innovations and improving corporate governance.

Employee stock ownership and the increasing desire for shared ownership

Employees have become significant players in capital ownership worldwide, especially in the United States.[1] Table 1.1 shows the scale of four types of major employee ownership plans in the United States. It shows that in early 2002 there were about 18 500 company plans in which capital ownership was shared broadly with employees. About 30–40 million employees owned about US$1 trillion in stock through

Table 1.1   Number of employee ownership plans and employee participants, and the value of plan assets, early 2002

Type of plan	Number of plans	Number of participants[1] (million)	Value of plan assets ($ billion)
ESOPs and stock bonus plans	11 000	8.8	>400
410(k) plans	2 200	11	>160
Broad-based stock option plans[2]	4 000	8–10	(several hundred)
Stock purchase plans	4 000	15.7	(not realistic to estimate)

Notes:
1. Because many companies offer multiple plans and many employees participate in more than one plan, the sum of this column is certainly greater than the real total number of employee participants.
2. Broad-based stock option plans are those which grant stock options to 50 per cent or more of the full-time employees of the company.
Source: NCEO (2002a).

employee stock ownership plans (ESOPs), 401(k) plans, broad-based stock option plans and stock purchase plans.

While ESOPs experienced spectacular growth in the 1970s and 1980s after tax benefits and regulatory guidelines were made available in the 1970s, broad-based stock option plans have become popular only since the early 1990s. According to Geer (1997: 158), in 1997 about 30 per cent of the largest US companies had broad-based stock option plans covering more than half their employees, up from 17 per cent five years previously. Another 1997 survey of 1100 publicly traded companies, conducted by ShareData and the American Electronics Association, indicated that of those companies with 500–1999 employees, 51 per cent offered stock options to all employees: the corresponding proportion in 1994 was 30 per cent. Of those companies with 2000–4999 employees, 43 per cent offered stock options to all employees, compared with 10 per cent in 1994. Forty-five per cent of those companies with 5000 or more employees offered stock options to all employees, compared with 10 per cent in 1994 (NCEO, 2000). While the sample may have been biased in favour of stock option plans, the expansion rates revealed by the survey are extraordinary by any standard. A 1995 survey conducted by the Association for Quality and Participation found that 13 per cent of the Fortune 1000 companies offered stock options to 60 per cent or more of their employees (NCEO, 2000). In 2001 up to 10 million employees received stock options (Table 1.1). It is also reported that about 125 listed companies had at least 20 per cent employee owner-ship in 1996 (Gates, 1998: 61). In July 2002, companies with majority employee-ownership included United Parcel Service (344 000 employ-ees), Publix Supermarkets (111 000), United Airlines (98 400), Science Applications International (41 000) and Lifetouch (25 890) (NCEO, 2002b).

Broad-based stock options are now the norm in high-technology companies and are rapidly gaining popularity in other industrial sectors as part of an overall equity compensation strategy. Blasi *et al.* (2000) provide evidence that companies with broad-based stock option plans have significantly higher productivity levels and annual growth rates than public companies in general and their peers.

The rapid expansion of employee stock ownership clearly contradicts the mainstream theoretical prediction that employee ownership in general will lead to underinvestment, inefficient decision making and inadequate supervision, and thus poor performance.[2] The discrepancy between theoretical prediction and the real development of employee stock ownership has stimulated a great deal of empirical research in the past three decades. As discussed by Sesil *et al.* in Chapter 4, the empirical literature suggests that employee ownership is associated with either improved or unaffected employee attitudes and behaviour, and with better or unchanged performance. Almost no studies have found worse employee attitudes or behaviour, or worse corporate performance under employee ownership.

The research reported in this book suggests an extra reason for the existence and expansion of employee stock ownership in publicly traded companies, in addition to the traditional reasons of broadening the distribution of wealth, providing additional employee benefits, gaining tax advantages, improving firm performance and defending against potential takeover threats. With the help of information technology developments in the financial services sector, individual investors now have convenient means of avoiding the risk of being locked into the business fortunes of a specific firm and thus being liable for the consequences of its failure. We argue that the increasing weight of employee ownership and institutional ownership of a corporation may compensate for the decreasing liability of diverse individual shareholders and restore a desirable balance of power among the major corporate players. Under the new equilibrium, owners and employees would be able to keep managers' moral hazard in check, owners and managers could be protected from extortion or shirking by employees, and managers and employees could be assured that opportunistic behaviour by owners would not keep them from realizing a reasonable return on their firm-specific investments.

Joint ownership and shifting governance in Silicon Valley firms

Silicon Valley has become an icon for its success in nurturing a large number of outstanding high-tech firms and has remained the forerunner in the field of technological system innovations. The most illustrative example of the Silicon Valley phenomenon is the computer industry (Baldwin and Clark, 2000). In the United States the computer industry was virtually dominated by IBM until the mid 1970s, but from the early 1970s a group of entrepreneurial firms funded by venture capitalists began to gain ground in R&D activities. These firms did not try to compete with IBM in the production of stand-alone product systems but specialize in the development and production of modular components for product systems. The innovative way in which these firms operated drastically changed the landscape of the computer industry. New product systems are now evolutionarily formed by selecting and integrating new modular products developed by entrepreneurial firms.

Hence many new subindustries have grown out of the traditional computer industry, which was characterized by highly vertically integrated manufactures.

The Silicon Valley phenomenon includes multifaceted interactions between a cluster of entrepreneurial start-up firms and venture capitalists (including leading firms in related niche markets). Aoki and Takizawa (2002) have modelled the information-processing relationship and the incentive structure between venture capitalists and a cluster of entrepreneurial firms in Silicon Valley. The information-processing mechanism is captured in a team-theoretic model with venture capitalists and entrepreneurial firms while the incentive structure is characterized as a tournament game. Their paper provides a novel comparative perspective on ownership and governance based on the informational structure of three types of R&D organization: hierarchical R&D organization, which is typical of the traditional vertically integrated firm, interactive R&D organization, which is modelled on the Japanese chain-linked system for innovations, and the Silicon Valley model of venture-capitalist-mediated (V-mediated) information encapsulation.

A more general feature of the ownership and governance structure of Silicon Valley firms, is that human capital has become the most vital asset, in contrast with traditional firms, in which highly specialized inanimate assets are the most important resource for growth. Put differently, in Silicon Valley the essential resources for future growth are the entrepreneur's professional human capital, the firm's inanimate assets, and a web of information generation and sharing arrangements. As a consequence, property rights arrangements combine elements of joint ownership and bilateral option rights. Hence venture capitalists have the right to exit if the firm runs into bad times (that is, they have liquidation rights) while the entrepreneurs' right to the issued options is contingent on subsequent performance. With regard to control rights, there is a shifting arrangement: if the firm performs poorly the venture capitalists obtain full control; as the firm's performance improves the entrepreneur retains or obtains more control rights; if the firm performs very well the venture capitalists retain their cash flow rights but relinquish most of their control and liquidation rights (see Chapter 3; see also Kaplan and Strömberg, 2000; Aoki, 2001). This form of joint ownership and shifting governance is clearly unconventional but is characteristic of the novel institutional arrangement for technological product system innovation in Silicon Valley.

Ways to harden the budget constraints of SOEs: the cases of Italy and China

Economists have long argued that private ownership is generally preferable to state ownership, particularly in terms of providing a strong incentive to innovate and contain costs (Shleifer, 1998). Hence the privatization of SOEs is usually seen as desirable. However, even in developed economies the process of privatization has proved to be technically difficult and the precise effect of privatization on performance is still open to discussion (Boylaud and Nicoletti, 2000; Joskow, 2001). In the developing world the pace of privatization has been uneven but generally slow. According to the World Bank (1995: 34), during 1978–91 in low-income developing countries the share of SOEs in GDP was fixed at about 14 per cent; in middle-income developing countries this share oscillated between 8 per cent and 10 per cent, a level comparable to that in the developed world. According to an estimate by Ramamurti (1999: tables 2, 3), during 1988–96 only about 9 per cent of SOE assets in the developing world were divested. In large developing economies such as India, Indonesia and Nigeria, less than 7 per cent of SOE assets have been privatized.

In transitional economies such as the Czech Republic, Hungary and Russia, although the pace of privatization has been unprecedented and many studies estimate that 50 per cent or more of economic activities have been privatized, the state still accounts for 40–50 per cent of GDP. Furthermore, taking the Czech Republic as an example, almost half the shares in so-called 'privatized' firms in fact belong to the National Property Fund or to voucher funds controlled by state-owned banks (Spulber, 1997; Ramamurti, 1999). The hard reality in many developing and transitional economies is that weak market institutions are matched by equally weak legal, financial and government institutions. In such circumstances the policy issue of how to improve the performance of SOEs may be at least as pressing as privatization, if not more so. In cases where privatization often results in the large-scale closure and liquidation of SOEs rather than their revitalization, or where privatization means not only moving assets from the state to the private sector but also moving them from the formal to the informal sector, pressing for rapid privatization may amount to shooting at the wrong target and could induce social and political misery.

In the policy debate on how to improve the performance of SOEs, it has been claimed that the lack of means to establish and sustain a hard budget constraint on SOEs is one of the main reasons why the performance of SOEs in many countries is disappointing. Firms that face a soft budget constraint, irrespective of whether they are private or state owned, have little incentive to take market disciplines and financial pressures seriously (Shleifer and Vishny, 1994, 1997; World Bank, 1995; Kornai, 2001).

Numerous studies have shown that a combination of decentralizing the fiscal system (by devolving taxation and spending authority downwards to competing local governments) and simultaneously centralizing the monetary authority hardens SOEs' budget constraint because this combination creates competition and makes *ex post* renegotiation more difficult (Qian and Roland, 1998; Berglof and Roland, 1998; Maskin and Xu, 2001). In Chapter 5 Bertero and Rondi identify an alternative mechanism to harden SOEs' budget constraint and show that the market-promoting federalist structure also works with the 'upward devolution' of the monetary and key regulatory authorities. They state that the hardening of the budget constraint on Italian SOEs can be largely attributed to the financial discipline imposed by supranational EU institutions and agreements (such as European Monetary Union, EMU) on the Italian government.

Until the early 1990s SOEs were a major part of the Italian economy, accounting for around 15 per cent of non-agricultural employment, 20 per cent of value-added and 25 per cent of fixed investment (1991 data). In Italy SOEs are organized through fully state-owned holding companies with controlling interests in diverse subholdings. The subholdings may have minority private shareholders and in turn own individual enterprises. The environment in which Italian SOEs operated from the 1970s to the mid 1980s was characterized by political interference, accommodating endowment funds and large loans from accommodating state-owned banks. Consistent with the soft budget constraint that SOEs enjoyed, poor profitability, low productivity, high debt and heavy losses were the norm for SOEs during that period.

In the early 1980s a combination of three factors, mostly exogenous to Italian government policy, induced a radical shift from a soft to a hard budget constraint. These three factors were mounting public debt, EU pressure to reduce state aid and accelerate the privatization programme, and Italy's attempt to qualify for first-round participation in EMU. The existence of high and rising public debt, which included substantial transfers to SOEs, was inconsistent with the rules of participation in the European Monetary System (EMS) and led to the first wave of disciplinary fiscal and monetary policies. For example the Bank of Italy was given greater independence and encouraged to become more market-oriented. Moreover the banking system increasingly faced external market pressure from international competition and the restructuring of the European banking industry following capital market liberalization. In addition the tightening of competition policy by the European Commission put a rein on state aid to SOEs, and public opinion required harsher scrutiny of the management of state funds. As a consequence, in the late 1980s the environment in which Italian SOEs operated was characterized by increasing competition at the European level, the drying up of government endowment funds, the disappearance of soft credit from state-owned banks and the threat of privatization. In other words, SOEs now had to face a hard budget constraint. Finally, Italy's attempt to qualify for EMU gradually led to further submission of control power over monetary policy and the power to take decisions on SOE financing. In the early 1990s the government was forced into a privatization programme, although by then many SOEs had become accustomed to a hard budget constraint and had been restructured to make them palatable to private investors.

Based on a sample of 150 Italian SOEs over the period 1977–93, Bertero and Rondi (2000, 2002) empirically demonstrate that Italian SOEs made virtually no response to financial pressure during the period of soft budget constraint, but actively responded to such pressure during the period of hard budget constraint, with behaviour similar to that of private enterprises. The SOEs in the sample made a significant effort to increase their total factor productivity and reduce their staffing level. Furthermore the budget regime shift brought about an important change in the investment behaviour of SOEs, with managers losing their discretion to collude with politicians, empire build and make wasteful investments.

With regard to policy implications, the experience of Italian SOEs with the EU institutions exemplifies a mechanism that is likely to work beyond the context of this case study. The hardening of Italian firms' budget constraints through the dictates of supranational institutions provides a valuable preview of the financial pressure that will be exerted on state-owned and privatized companies in EU accession countries and other transitional economies. Other supranational organisations – such as the IMF, the World Bank and the WTO – may exert similar pressures, although perhaps less powerful, on governments, on their budgets and ultimately on SOEs. Finally, the competitive pressure of globalization in general and financial markets in particular may have a similar impact on the state-owned sector in many open economies.

The case of SOEs run by local governments in China has direct policy implications for the national government. From the early 1970s local governments at the county and city levels came to control all the small and a large proportion of the medium-sized SOEs. Unlike in the former Soviet Union and Eastern Europe, most SOEs in China are small or of medium size, and they are distributed throughout the country rather than being geographically concentrated (Gu, 1999). Therefore the ownership restructuring of these locally controlled SOEs is as significant as the restructuring of the large ones controlled by the central or provincial governments.

For decades the SOEs run by county and city governments were highly inefficient. They were often too small to apply economies of scale but too bureaucratic to exploit the advantage of their small size, which township and village enterprises (TVEs) were able to do. Their survival depended on soft taxation and other fiscal support by the local government and on soft credit from local branches of the state banks. However in 1993 and 1994 the environment started to change. In 1993 the central bank reversed the long-standing practice of monetary decentralization and deprived local governments of administrative control over local branches of the state banks. Since then local governments have had no right to supervise these branches. In 1995 the Central Bank Law was passed to give the central bank the mandate for monetary policy, independent of local government, and in 1998 the central bank replaced its 30 provincial branches with nine cross-province regional branches, as in the US Federal Reserve system. While these reforms might not have fully removed the influence of provincial governments over monetary policy and credit allocation decisions, they have certainly left little room for county and city governments to exercise their influence.

With regard to the tax and fiscal system, on 1 January 1994 China introduced major tax and fiscal reforms that were more aligned to international practices. A national tax bureau was established, a clear distinction was made between national and local taxes and a strict division of labour between the national and local tax bureaus was introduced. The reform also established fixed tax rules between the national and local governments. These reforms made it very difficult for local governments to act to reduce the national taxes, which they had done in the past. In 1995 the new Budget Law took effect. This law prohibits the central government from borrowing from the central bank and from deficit financing its current account. The law also imposes more stringent restrictions on local governments. In addition to the original requirement to balance local budgets, the law strictly controls bond issuance by local governments and restricts their borrowing in financial markets. To ensure enforcement of the Budget Law, an independent auditing system was introduced (Dong, 1997).

As a consequence of these fiscal and monetary reforms, the overall budget constraints of local governments and their local SOEs became much harder in the second half of the 1990s (Qian, 2000). Without the help of soft credit from local branches of state banks and soft taxation from the old fiscal system, local governments were no longer able to bail out loss-making SOEs. As a consequence, since then diverse means have been employed to restructure the ownership and governance of local SOEs, including selling, leasing, takeovers, mergers, restructuring through Sino-foreign joint ventures, corporatization and conversion to joint-stock cooperatives. All these moves represent a quite radical departure from traditional socialist ideology. By the late 1990s, in many cites and counties SOEs had largely disappeared and their replacements are typically characterized by hybrid ownership or fully private ownership.

The Chinese experience indicates that fiscal decentralization combined with monetary centralization can provide positive incentives to and place a hard budget constraint on local governments. Delegating control rights over SOEs to local governments that face a hard budget constraint and intense market competition induces a desirable restructuring of SOEs.

The benefits of cooperative alliance and networking: the Mondragón group in Spain and the Italian cooperatives in La Lega

Producer and worker cooperatives have existed in Western market economies since the introduction of the factory system. The attractiveness of worker cooperatives hinges not only on such ethical concerns as democratic control and quality of life, but also on their potential economic advantages. However worker cooperatives are rare in the industrial sector in the West. As summarized in Craig and Pencavel (1995), there are four economic advantages that can potentially make worker cooperatives more productive than conventional investor-owned corporate firms. First, cooperatives are able to mitigate the agency costs associated with the separation of ownership from control because worker-owners are likely to be much better informed about the actions taken by managers than are outside owners. Second, worker ownership avoids conflicts of interest between workers and owners and encourages voluntary cooperation. Third, workers in a cooperative are able to monitor each other's effort more effectively than in firms where the monitor is the owner's agent. Fourth, when workers identify their efforts with cooperative outcomes, morale is heightened, leading to more and better work. Moreover the upward flow of information from the shop floor facilitates improvements in or innovation of production methods, and lower turnovers induce the accumulation of firm-specific human capital (Bonin *et al.*, 1993; Smith, 1994).

Why are there so few worker cooperatives in the industrial sector of Western market economies? There are three primary explanations in the literature. The first has to do with the high costs associated with collective decision making. Usually, workers are far more likely than investors to differ among themselves about the firm's policies. In important decisions there is often more room for judgement and discretion in a cooperative, because unlike the situation with investors, there are no simple objective criteria to follow and workers often have different stakes in the firm's decisions on investment and relative wages (Hansmann, 1996: 89–91). In addition, managers may lack the necessary autonomy to make contingency decisions. The second explanation is that worker cooperatives have difficulty competing with investor-owned firms for capital financing. The amount of capital that can be raised from workers is bound to be limited, and external financiers with no direct say in the firm's governance will not commit significant funds without a substantial premium to mitigate the risks involved. The third reason is that cooperatives are disadvantaged in terms of risk diversification. Workers' incomes and capital are tied to the fortunes of the cooperative (Bonin *et al.*, 1993; Craig and Pencavel, 1995).

For individual worker cooperatives, if the above disadvantages can be offset by advantages they may be able to survive and compete side-by-side with other ownership forms, as in the case of the plywood cooperatives in the north-west of the United States. For a group of worker cooperatives under a corporate alliance, the network externalities discussed by Smith in Chapters 7 and 8 enable them to employ mechanisms to overcome a large number of these disadvantages while preserving their major advantages. The Mondragón cooperatives in the Basque region of northern Spain and the Italian cooperatives associated with La Lega in general and the Emilia-Romagna region in particular are excellent examples in this regard.

Since 1956 the Mondragón group has grown from a single, 25-member cooperative into a massive enterprise with 60 200 workers and annual sales of €8.1 billion (2001 figures). Over 25 per cent of their sales are exports. It also has a financial group with €8.6 billion in assets and over 300 branch banks around the Basque region (Mondragón, 2002). The group has adopted a systems approach to cooperative development.

It has combined collective ownership with the incentives of individual ownership by establishing a system of individual internal accounts with automatic loan-back.[3] The system explicitly addresses both the individual and the collective side of human motivation. While the principal of 'one worker, one vote' is institutionalized in the basic cooperatives (those with fewer than 500 members), the group adopted many mechanisms from traditional firms when it reorganized itself into the Mondragón Co-operative Corporation (MCC). These hybrid mechanisms have played a significant part in the MCC's success in the rapidly changing and highly competitive global market (Benello, 1996; Huet, 1997; Whyte, 1999; Cheney, 2000).

The success of the Italian cooperatives associated with La Lega Nazionale delle Co-operative e Mutue (the National League of Cooperatives and Mutual Aid Societies) again highlights the importance of cooperative alliances and networks. La Lega has developed a number of supporting mechanisms to promote the growth of the cooperative sector. Of these mechanisms the most significant are La Lega's financial institutions and its representative power and negotiating ability in its constant negotiations with the central and local governments (Ammirato, 1996).

In Chapters 7 and 8 Smith presents a theoretical framework and empirical evidence to show that there are network externalities in cooperative formation and survival. This means that even if other barriers to entry are overcome and a cooperative is established it may not survive, not because of intrinsic inefficiencies but simply because of the lack of other cooperative entry, and to some extent because of a lack of coordination among the cooperatives that do enter the market. In Chapter 7 he shows how cooperative leagues can help to internalize these externalities. In Chapter 8 he shows how this internalization has been accomplished in practice in Mondragón and La Lega. One of the key findings is that among the many adaptive innovations introduced in Mondragón and La Lega, the creation of the cooperative alliances and networks was the most important because virtually all of their other innovations required the existence of the networks as a necessary precondition.

Searching for new paradigms: complementary theoretical perspectives

The above discussion indicates that the nature of the firm is changing and a diverse pattern of enterprise ownership and governance is emerging.

As a result the boundaries of the firm are often in flux. To understand the formation and evolution of ownership and governance forms in different technological and institutional environments, it is necessary to refer to the underlying theory of the firm and examine the inter-action between the nature of the firm and corporate governance issues under various circumstances. Although we are still in the process of searching for new foundations to explain the changing nature of firms (Hansmann, 1996; Zingales, 2000) several promising perspectives have emerged: the growth option perspective, the contract cost perspective, the competition perspective, the market intermediation perspective and the institutional change perspective. In this section we interpret these in a manner that is understandable to non-economists. We hope that when received in a complementary rather than antagonistic way, they will be of great assistance in helping us to understand the fundamental trade-offs that underly the evolving diversity of ownership and gover-nance structures in the real world, and to search for adaptively efficient models for reforming enterprises in transitional economies.

The growth option perspective: the firm as a collection of growth options

Myers (1977) defines the firm as a collection of assets and growth opportunities. He used this definition to establish a theory on the capital structure of corporations but did not pay attention to the glue that keeps growth opportunities attached to the assets. Zingales (2000) attempts to explore this question and argues that what distinguishes the firm from the market is the web of specific investments in and around one or more of the crucial resources that are most closely tied to the best growth opportunities.[4] He suggests that the role of a corporate governance system is to ensure that the power to make decisions is allocated to the people with the best opportunities.

Following this perspective, we can say that in a traditional, capital-intensive, vertically integrated firm, highly specialized inanimate assets, ranging from plant and machinery to world famous brand names, are the most crucial resource for future growth. The firm's human capital (employees) is largely tied to these assets and the employment oppor-tunity outside the firm for this highly specialized human capital is rare. The boundaries of this type of firm are clearcut and defined by the ownership of its unique assets.

In modern human-capital-intensive firms such as those in Silicon Valley, as discussed earlier, the crucial resources for future growth are the entrepreneur's professional human capital, the firm's inanimate assets and a web of information generation and sharing arrangements. Consequently the property rights arrangements are a complex mixture of joint-ownership between the entrepreneur and a cluster of venture capitalists, with the provision of bilateral option rights. The control rights shift between these major actors, depending on the firm's performance.

For reforming SOEs and TVEs in a transitional economy such as China, the crucial resources for future growth include not only their existing assets and the human capital of entrepreneurs, but also a web of interorganizational relationships (*Guanxi*). This web is the firm's organizational and social capital. It is capable of mobilizing scarce resources from more than one channel and supplying an elastic contract mechanism to facilitate continuity and efficient adaptation, thus reducing uncertainty. In the early stage of China's reforms this web was fully embedded in the old government system, which is why joint ownership in China has involved local government as a key partner. The crucial question here is: can this web be used to facilitate market development in general and provide the basis for nurturing new market institutions? In Chapter 6 Sun provides new evidence to show that on balance the answer is yes (Naughton, 1995; D. D. Li, 1996, 1998; D. Li, 1997; Qian, 2000).

The growth option perspective also helps us to understand the corporate governance problems faced by a family firm in which agency costs and the cost of collective decision making among the owners are of minor importance. Because there is a lack of outside interest in the firm, once owner-managers fail to recognize growth opportunities, or pitfalls, there is an absence of knowledgeable outsiders' intervention. This tends to happen when there are changes in the market place or in technology. The fall of well-known firms such as Wang in the United States and Grundig in Germany can be attributed to this type of governance failure.

The contract cost perspective: market contracting versus ownership

The contract cost perspective has recently become mainstream in the ownership theory of the firm. It is now widely accepted that the firm may be considered as a nexus of explicit and implicit contracts (compare Aoki *et al.*, 1990; Hansmann, 1996; Zingales, 2000). Given that the market conditions and institutional structures are known, each of these contracts can be explicitly or implicitly specified and the corresponding cost (or relative cost) can be estimated empirically or theoretically.

It is helpful to classify these contracts into two types: 'market contracting' and 'ownership' (Hansmann, 1996). Market contracting is closely linked to the daily business operations of the firm. For example the firm may have signed contracts with the suppliers of components or services that the firm uses as inputs. It may have contracts with individuals who provide labour to the firm. It may have loan agreements with banks, bondholders and other suppliers of capital. It may also have sales contracts with purchasers of the firm's products. On the other hand, by virtue of ownership an owner, or a group of owners, exercises discretion and the other residual control rights over the firm that remain after the exercise of market contracting.

The persons or parties linked to the firm by market contracting can control the firm's behaviour only by seeking enforcement of their contract with the firm or by threatening to cease contracting with the firm, whereas the persons or parties holding ownership rights have the additional option of seeking to control the behaviour of the firm through internal governance mechanisms.

If the market is perfect and there is complete information, a firm may be fully specified by market contracting. In other words, in an ideal market the parties involved in setting up a firm can write detailed, comprehensive, long-term contracts that govern their relationship and specify everything that matters economically. Hence it could be that nothing is left to ownership. However in reality the market is far from perfect and information problems abound. This makes ideal and complete market contracting impossible and general market contracting costly. In order to minimize the total cost of transactions between the firm and all the parties engaging in the transactions, the assignment of ownership becomes desirable. All other things being equal, transaction costs will be minimized if ownership is assigned to those persons or parties for whom the problems of market contracting, namely the costs of market imperfections, are most severe. Of course ownership itself involves costs, mainly the cost of monitoring managers, the cost of collective decision making among the owners and the cost of risk bearing. Moreover the costs of ownership can vary greatly among the various parties involved in the transaction. Therefore the least costly assignment of ownership will minimize the sum of the costs of market contracting and the costs of ownership (Putterman, 1993; Hansmann, 1996: 20–2).

Market imperfection often takes different forms and varies in extent across industries, regions, countries and over time because the formation and evolution of the formal and informal rules of the game in a society are a concrete political process that takes time and is cultural and path dependent. These differences may mean that the costs of the same type of transaction will differ in different contexts. For example the worker cooperatives in plywood manufacturing in the north-west of the United States, have had a clear disadvantage in the capital market in comparison with private enterprises in the same industry and same location. The main reason for this is that credit institutions prefer to make loans to enterprises that are controlled by a small number of people whose behaviour can be easily monitored and directed, rather than to an enterprise whose ownership is spread among the entire work force (Gintis, 1990; Craig and Pencavel, 1995). In sharp contrast to the situation in the United States, joint-stock cooperatives in China, as worker cooperatives with a Chinese character, enjoy much greater trust by local communities and credit institutions than do private enterprises, even in the sense of economic accountability and creditability. As a consequence they enjoy a significant advantage over private enterprises in respect of acquiring capital (see Chapter 6; see also Zou and Sun, 2000). This and other differences in comparative transaction costs may be why cooperative firms are scarce in the United States but widespread in transitional China.

The competition perspective: competition can induce ownership evolution

The close link between imitative output competition and the allocation efficiency of resources has been well established in the neoclassical economics literature. In the central model of neoclassical economics – perfect competition – each firm takes the prices given to it by the mysterious market clearing forces, and competes with others by offering output, especially by offering output through entry. The market reaches equilibrium when neither insiders nor outsiders have an interest in changing the quantity they supply to the market. Given consumer preferences, technology and institutions, and full information for all rational actors, the perfectly competitive equilibrium obtained is the Pareto optimum, meaning that resources are allocated in such a way that no one can be better off without others becoming worse off. In this ideal economy all the necessary market institutions are in place and functioning perfectly, and therefore no market-creating activity is needed. Competition is no more or less than making profitable imitative output responses to given market prices (Demsetz, 1997: 137–8).

In terms of the everyday meaning of the word, the notion of competition goes far beyond imitative output competition and has a much broader implication than allocation efficiency. Competition is popularly viewed as rivalry behaviour and is the main driving force in Schumpeterian creative destruction. Competition causes firms and, more generally, organizations to become more efficient by sharpening their incentive to avoid sloth and slack. Competition results in efficient organizations prospering at the expense of inefficient ones, which is good for aggregate efficiency. Competition induces innovations in all areas of technology, organization and institutions, which have been the major source of gains in productive efficiency over time (Stigler, 1987; Vickers, 1995). Since the rivalry behaviour view of competition follows the tradition of Hayek and Schumpeter and pays attention to productive and dynamic efficiency, it is relevant to the study of the formation and evolution of firms' ownership structure in different technological and institutional contexts.

The significance of behavioural competition emphasized in the literature can be summarized as follows. First, competition stimulates the monitoring efforts of owners and sharpens the performance of managers. An increase in the number of players in the market enhances the possibility of performance comparisons between different organizational structures and between managers. Competition in product markets may make profits more sensitive to the efficiency of the organizational forms and the effort of managers, and this not only enables owners to relate managerial remuneration to profits in order to stimulate managerial effort, but also shows them the opportunity cost of different organizational structures. Competition by comparison also enables reputation-building efforts of managers and reduces moral hazard because the managers' efforts can be estimated with greater precision (Vickers, 1995; Hay and Liu, 1997). Second, competition can play a major part in differentiating more efficient firms from less efficient ones. When firms' costs differ, the lowest-cost firm will certainly win the competition and the highest-cost firm may have to exit due to its losses or an increase in the number of competitors. In order to win the competition or survive in a competitive environment, firms have to develop themselves by accumulating capital, improving their technology and management, and making innovations (Vickers, 1995; Liu and Li, 1998). Third, dispersed imperfect information can be aggregated in the competitive process (Hayek, 1949: 96; Grossman, 1989; Vickers, 1995). Firms and other organizations can obtain desired information through the process of competition and comparison. For example they can evaluate the opportunity costs of alternative choices of technologies, management modes and organizational structures through performance comparison and learning from rivals.

While competition provides both incentive (carrot) and pressure (stick) to stimulate the efforts of economic agents and promote innovation, there is no universal model of property rights regime and governance structure that can be employed to win the competition in all circumstances and at all times. Different models can coexist in the same circumstance, provided that each type of firm has its own enduring advantage but none clearly dominates the others in terms of overall efficiency. Organizational or institutional innovation can bring competitive advantages to the innovator in the same way as technological innovation does (see for example Chapters 7 and 8).

The intermediation perspective: market-taking versus market-making

There are two types of firm in an economy: market-taking firms and market-making firms. Market-taking firms take price signals and other market information as given. They are guided by the 'invisible hands' of the market, as emphasized in neoclassical economics. In contrast market-making firms establish and operate markets by setting prices, carrying out transactions, forming and monitoring contracts, and producing and distributing information. Their 'visible hands' guide many markets and they are typically known as market intermediaries (Spulber, 1996). The simplest example of a market-making firm is a retail or wholesale intermediary. This firm gathers demand and supply information, sets bid and ask prices for its commodities and makes profits from the mark-up between the two, some of which is used to cover the costs of information gathering and price setting. In addition it holds stocks of goods to sell to customers and holds cash on hand to buy from suppliers. This avoids the costs of mismatch between buyers and sellers in terms of the double coincidence of needs, in which buyer and seller must have both the need and the opportunity to transact with each other at the same time.

More generally, different types of market-making activities by market intermediaries correspond to different types of information imperfection in market places. As summarized in Spulber (1996), when there are random elements in demand or supply, intermediaries provide liquidity or 'immediacy' by being ready to buy and sell. Given uncertainty about trading partners' willingness to pay or opportunity costs, intermediaries coordinate transactions by matchmaking and brokering. When the characteristics of buyers or sellers are unobservable, intermediaries generate and supply market information and guarantee product quality. When the actions of buyers or sellers are costly to observe or monitor, intermediaries provide monitoring and contracting services. In these ways market intermediaries reduce or eliminate the uncertainty associated with making a satisfactory match between customer and supplier. In addition, intermediaries add to the number of potential trading partners, which increases the likelihood of encountering a trading partner and reduces the search costs for all market participants. Consolidating transactions through intermediaries can generate returns to scale in producing and distributing market information (Spulber, 1996; Che, 2000).

An understanding of the functions of market intermediaries helps us to understand the way in which the market mechanism normally functions. For example the existence of an equilibrium bid–ask spread, which separates a buyer's willingness to pay and a supplier's costs, is a consequence of transaction costs, asymmetric information between buyers and sellers and the returns to intermediating activities, rather than evidence of market failure. Just as the production of goods and services consumes resources, the establishment and operation of markets to allocate those goods and services also incurs costs.

The establishment and evolution of markets driven by market intermediaries are path dependent and technology dependent. For example the emergence of e-commerce has greatly enhanced the market-making activities of producers. It significantly lowers the cost and increases the speed of collecting data, expedites billing and invoicing, and facilitates the exchange of data on sales, inventory and marketing. It reduces economies of scale from vertical integration, and thus allows firms to eliminate the many layers of middlemen who were necessary in the past but symbolize inefficiency in the present.[5] Finally, it makes cross-border purchasing much easier and induces tax competition between countries (particularly in the EU), and thus puts pressure on governments to reduce taxes. More generally, the impressive technological advances in information and communication have enabled much more reliable and efficient clearing and settlements systems for securities and payments, and created new financial instruments for risk management purposes. This has made it possible for wealthy and sophisticated individual investors to reduce their firm-specific risk, by means of fund pooling and portfolio diversification without causing a significant rise in the agency costs they bear as owners of corporate equity. It has also contributed to the rapid rise in the number of institutional investors in the developed world (see above and Chapter 2).

The institutional change perspective: market institutions and adaptive efficiency

The establishment, operation and evolution of the market are governed by market institutions, or as North (1990, 1997) puts it, institutions are the 'rules of the game' in a society.[6] They are the rules that society establishes for shaping human interaction. Institutions reduce the uncertainty involved in human interaction by providing patterns of behaviour. Because of the set of institutions we have, most daily interactions are routine, so the implicit importance of institutions is often ignored. In a static sense institutions, together with the technology they employ, define the costs of transacting and the options that organizations in society have when capturing the gains from specialization and the division of labour. In a dynamic sense, institutions define the incentive structure under which organizations operate and determine the ability of organizations to evolve and advance technology.

The institutional framework includes three components: formal rules, informal rules and enforcement mechanisms. Formal rules are the written rules of society and include political and judicial rules, economic rules and contracts. Informal rules are the unwritten rules of society and include consensual conventions that evolve as solutions to coordination problems, norms of behaviour that are recognized standards of conduct, and self-imposed codes of conduct. Informal rules allow people to engage in everyday exchanges without needing to work out the terms of exchange. Informal rules can be so ingrained that people are not even aware of them. Rules are often ineffective if they are not enforced. For the enforcement of formal rules, an effective and impartial legal system of laws and courts is usually needed. For informal rules, societal sanctions help to enforce norms of behaviour, and strong normative personal standards of honesty and integrity undergird self-imposed standards of behaviour.

It is easy to claim that efficient markets are a consequence of institutions that provide low-cost transactions and enforce contracts at a moment in time. However the concrete institutions operating in a society are rooted in societal structures and have developed through adaptive evolution. Therefore they cannot be directly replicated across different societies. If an economy is to be dynamically efficient the institutions in that economy must be adaptively efficient; that is, capable of providing economic and political flexibility so that organizations and people can adapt to new opportunities. They must provide incentives for the acquisition of knowledge and learning, induce innovation and encourage risk taking and creative activities. They must also encourage trials and eliminate errors in a world of uncertainty where no one knows the correct solution to the problems they confront. Similarly, if an organizational structure is to be dynamically efficient it must be adaptively efficient. It must be able to find new and creative solutions to shortages of resources and other social/economic bottlenecks. If one method does not work, it must be willing to try new methods until successful outcomes are achieved.

The arguments in the previous paragraph are most relevant to transitional and developing economies. Today's mature market institutions and organizational forms first took root in developed economies many generations ago. A brief list of such institutions includes entry with low barriers and exit through well-established procedures of bankruptcy and liquidation; efficient financial and insurance institutions and organizations; antitrust legislation and its strict enforcement; rigorous accounting standards and their enforcement; a well-developed financial press; enforcement of contracts; sustainable social security nets; and so on. However for most economies at the beginning of transition there are no such market institutions and organizations because until recently the government controlled almost everything in the economy. In most developing economies, although there has been a base from which those institutions and organizations could evolve, the task of building up well-functioning market institutions is still very large and difficult to manage.

Market institutions and organizations cannot emerge from scratch, but the direct transplantation of market institutions rarely succeeds. Institutional and organizational innovation is not immediate replacement of the old structures by the new ones – it is a market-learning process, a process of dynamic transformation. New elements usually emerge in tandem with rearrangement of the existing institutional and organizational structures (Williamson, 1991, 1995). The process typically goes beyond the existing paradigms and evolves from sequences of progress in know-how, economizing behaviour in adaptation to changes, technological innovation and a multitude of cumulative and mutually reinforcing choices by numerous actors who have diverse interests and constantly evaluate alternatives and reconsider their previous views. In brief, transitional economies need transitional institutional arrangements that are adaptively efficient in the light of the fact that the transition process might be quite lengthy.[7]

Implications for developing and transitional economies

The theoretical emphasis of this book is on the relevance of the concrete institutional context, the technological environment and the regulatory set-up to the determination of ownership and governance structures of the firm, and on the rationality behind the emergence of unconventional ownership and governance structures of firms in the industrial sector. A major conclusion in this regard is as follows. Given the existing variations and foreseeing further changes in technology, the competition framework and the regulatory set-up, the major players of the corporate game, including owners, managers, employees and other stakeholders, have the incentive to calculate the comparative costs and benefits of feasible ownership and governance structures and to look for a desirable equilibrium in the power game. The basic features of this desirable equilibrium is that the firm's owners and employees will be able to keep managers' opportunistic behaviour in check, owners and managers will be protected from employee extortion or shirking, and managers and employees will be able to hold the opportunistic behaviour of owners in check and realize a reasonable return on their firm-specific investments. The means of achieving this equilibrium are not unique and alternatives are often possible.

Furthermore, provided that the technological and institutional contexts are kept stable and the firm has an opportunity to grow, the restructuring of the ownership and governance arrangements should focus on minimizing the organizational and transaction costs. However in more dynamic environments the key to success is to achieve the best growth opportunities possible from the firm's assets. Against such a dynamic background, an adaptively efficient form of ownership and governance would be characterized by its ability to organize a web of specific investments in and around one or more crucial resources that are inextricably linked to the best growth opportunities. More concretely, in a highly dynamic environment the aim of ownership restructuring is to ensure that the power to make strategic decisions is allocated to the people with the best growth potential.

In terms of policy implication, we would like to highlight several general lessons for developing and transitional economies, based on the analyses in this book. First, hybrid forms of ownership and governance structures may have greater significance in developing and transitional economies because firms have to use institutional, social and intermediary resources from different channels, formal or informal. The hybrid structure can help them to reduce uncertainty in interorganizational relationships involving bilateral or multilateral dependence and can supply them with an elastic contract mechanism to facilitate continuity and dynamic adaptation. The evolution of the ownership and governance structures of China's TVEs is the most striking example of this. In fact even in the developed world employee stock ownership has the hybrid advantages of both stock ownership and employee ownership. The Mondragón cooperative group has successfully combined the collective motivation of its members with the incentive of individual ownership of internal capital accumulation. The cooperatives in the Mondragón and La Lega groups all depend on their strategic alliances and networks to overcome the shortcomings of conventional cooperatives in the areas of capital financing, marketing and research and development. These innovative practices intend to take advantage of more than just one institutional and/or organizational resource. They are certainly instructive for decision makers and entrepreneurs in developing and transitional economies.

Second, the traditional dichotomy between 'nationally controlled SOEs' and 'conventional private ownership' is narrow in perception and harmful in practice because it leads to ignorance of the rich variety of ownership forms, which are typically linked to local innovations. While a national government typically has the power to allocate both fiscal and monetary resources, local governments in general and those at the lower level in particular are much less likely to enjoy such power, and even when they do it can be removed relatively easily, as shown by China's experience of fiscal decentralization and monetary centralization. In this regard the emergence of local government ownership in the SOE sector in Russia and other former Soviet countries may lead to the effective restructuring of locally controlled SOEs, provided that the urgently needed linkage between local fiscal revenues and local economic prosperity can be attained (Sun *et al.*, 1999: ch. 6; Zhuravskaya, 2000).

Community governments at the grass-root level deserve special attention in developing countries. These governments have no authority over credit decisions because they occupy the lowest rank of the government hierarchy. They have no power to regulate the market to keep out competition, simply because the community market is both small and limited. As a consequence these community governments are usually confronted with a hard budget constraint and tight competition discipline, and therefore their economic activities may be much more healthy and efficient than those conducted by governments at higher levels. The key question in many developing countries is how to mobilize community governments and other community-based organizations to support or even initiate local enterprises. The experience of the Chinese TVEs may be instructive in this regard.

Third, a substantial number of writers have shown that privatization is not a sufficient condition to improve SOEs' performance (Kornai, 2001; Megginson and Netter, 2001; see also the references in Chapter 5). When the main problem is a soft budget constraint it is essential to find an initial mechanism to harden the budget constraint. This is of particular relevance for transitional and developing economies. The experience of Italian SOEs shows that relinquishing economic policies to a supranational institution may be an effective way of mitigating the time inconsistency problem of national governments (by limiting their power of discretion) and constraining SOEs' budgets. Supranational pressure, such as that exerted by EU economic policies on member countries, is a mechanism that works through both macroeconomic and microeconomic channels and forces the implementation of economic and institutional reforms. This mechanism is already at work in those transitional economies which have applied to join the EU and it is forcing them to accelerate the transition process. Hardening the budget constraint of all firms, not just state-owned ones, in transitional economies is a necessary step towards enabling them to face product market competition. Creating an appropriate legal and institutional environment is another necessary step. As remarked by Svejnar (2002: 26), the transition process will be over when these countries become 'partners with the relatively advanced countries in the world in general and with Western Europe in particular', in short, 'when they fully enter the European Union'. The EU is unique in many respects. Its legislative power and related law enforcement, its political institutions and its monetary authority make EU policies a particularly effective external anchor. However supranational pressure on SOEs does not need to come just from the EU. In other parts of the world it could be exercised through, for example, the conditions attached to IMF or World Bank programmes or the rules of the WTO.

Fourth, the evolution of institutional ownership in the developed world offers meaningful and instructive lessons to developing and transitional economies. The establishment of a fully funded, privately managed, defined-contribution pension scheme has been an ideal in most transitional and developing economies since the 1980s. For those countries with an unfunded pay-as-you-go (PAYG) pension scheme, the desire to shift from the PAYG scheme to the above model has determined the nature of pension reforms (Holzmann, 1997). In the future pension funds will be a major player in institutional ownership in these countries too, as shown by the experience of Chile in the 1980s. Learning from the developed world by imitating successful innovations and avoiding the setbacks will bring advantages to less-developed countries in terms of promoting the development of financial institutions and institutional ownership and modernizing their financial markets.

Furthermore, as discussed earlier, open-end mutual stock funds possess certain features of collectivist individualism, and could play a significant role in transitional economies and some developing ones where low levels of wealth but an egalitarian distribution of wealth have been the norm. Using open-end mutual stock funds to pool capital from individual small investors and then investing this in the shares of corporations, with the help of skilled fund managers, would make a significant contribution to capital accumulation in these countries. The fact that capital placed at the disposal of an open-end mutual fund can be withdrawn by its investors without seriously compromising its commitments to others is a very desirable feature for small investors with a low level of wealth. To make this type of financial institution work in transitional and developing countries the transfer of know-how and technical assistance is essential. International financial institutions such as the World Bank and international financial investors could play an active part in this.

Fifth, scholars often depict institutions and organizational forms that are popular in the West as 'best practice institutions' and recommend that other countries adopt them as quickly and exclusively as possible, generating a degree of pessimism among scholars and the public about transition and development. We recommend a search for more effective institutions that are adaptable to the environment and responsive to changes brought about by innovation and reform. Some of these may eventually converge with the existing 'best practice institutions', some may not. Some of them may evolve into a new type at certain stages and in certain periods, but they will not stay the same forever. Some new 'best practice institutions' may emerge as hybrids of the existing ones and other less perfect institutions. Nowadays we are aware of the importance of biodiversity and genetic diversity, and there is no reason to reject a diversity of institutional and organizational forms.

Notes

1 Employee ownership in transitional economies has quite different features. This will be discussed below and in Chapter 6.
2 For critical reviews of this prediction see Bonin *et al.* (1993) and Blair (1995: 298–303).

3 The system of individual internal accounts is based on each cooperative in the group putting 70 per cent of its surplus into the system, and each member of the cooperative has an internal account. Each individual account has a record of the receipt of the surplus portion earmarked, and the corresponding amount is then automatically loaned back to the cooperative, with interest paid. Upon leaving a member receives 75 per cent of the accumulated funds credited to his or her internal account; the other 25 per cent is retained by the cooperative for capitalization. This system allows the cooperative to mobilize almost 100 per cent of its annual profits for capital financing (Benello, 1996).

4 Future investments are options that the firm can exercise at will, and as such they have to be valued. The real option approach to investments and valuation is only now spreading outside academia and becoming common, although as yet there is no standard technique. Unlike financial options, which are well-specified contracts with a clear owner and a defined payoff, real options rarely have these features, except for exploration rights. Many real-world growth options are not clearly allocated to one owner and their payoff is highly dependent on the way in which the option is exercised. In other words the payoff is endogenously determined rather than exogenously specified, as in the case of financial options.

5 The most famous example of vertical integration is the Japanese *keiretsu*, in which a series of suppliers and retailers are tied to a principal manufacturer, often through cross-shareholdings. This system worked very well for several decades, but is now seen as inefficient, expensive and outdated (*The Economist*, 1 April 2000: 72).

6 The concept of institutions adopted in the institutional change literature usually includes organizations and is more in line with the one used in daily conversation. According to North (1990, 1997), institutions are 'rules of game' and organizations are groups of individuals bound together to achieve some or other objective.

7 According to the perceptive remark of Abba Lerner: 'In the long run we just arrive at another short run' (Colander, 2002), while William Baumol (2000) states that 'All of history may be a tale of transitory behaviour and nothing else'.

References

Ammirato, P. (1996) *La Lega: The Making of a Successful Co-operative Network*, Dartmouth: Aldershot.

Aoki, M. (2001) *Towards a Comparative Institutional Analysis*, Cambridge, MA: MIT Press.

—— B. Gustafsson and O. E. Williamson (1990) *The Firm as a Nexus of Treaties*, London: Sage.

—— and H. Takizawa (2002) 'Information, Incentive, and Option Value: The Silicon Valley Model', *Journal of Comparative Economics*, 30, 4: 759–86.

Baldwin, C. Y. and K. B. Clark (2000) *Design Rules – vol. 1: The Power of Modularity*, Cambridge, MA: MIT Press.

Baumol, W. J. (2000) 'Review Out of Equilibrium', *Structural Change and Economic Dynamics*, 11: 227–33.

Benello, G. (1996) 'The Challenge of Mondragón', at http://dftuz.unizar.es/a/files/left-gen/96002.eng.html.

Berglof, E. and G. Roland (1998) 'Soft Budget Constraints and Credit Crunches in Financial Transition', *European Economic Review*, 41, 3–5: 807–17.

Bertero, E. and L. Rondi (2000) 'Financial Pressure and the Behavior of Public Enterprises under Soft and Hard Budget Constraints: Evidence from Italian Panel Data', *Journal of Public Economics*, 75, 1: 73–98.

—— and —— (2002) 'Does a Switch of Budget Regimes Affect Investment and Managerial Discretion of State-owned Enterprises? Evidence from Italian Firms', *Journal of Comparative Economics*, 30, 4: 836–63.

Blair, M. M. (1995) *Ownership and Control: Rethinking Corporate Governance for the Twenty-first Century*, Washington, DC: Brookings Institution.

Blasi, J., D. Kruse, J. Sesil and M. Kroumova (2000) 'Broad-based Stock Options and Company Performance: What the Research Tells Us', in NCEO (ed.), *Stock Options, Corporate Performance, and Organization Change*, Oakland, CA: NCEO.

Blommestein, H. (1998) 'Impact of Institutional Investors on Financial Markets', in OECD (1998): 29–106.

Bonin, J. P., D. C. Jones and L. Putterman (1993) 'Theoretical and Empirical Studies of Producer Co-operatives: Will Ever the Twain Meet?', *Journal of Economic Literature*, 31, 3: 1290–320.

Boylaud, O. and G. Nicoletti (2000) 'Regulation, Market Structure and Performance in Telecommmunications', OECD Economics Department working paper 237, Paris: OECD.

Che, J. (2000) 'Organizing Market Transactions', manuscript, Department of Economics, Stanford University.

Cheney, G. (2000) *Value at Work: Employee Participation Meets Market Pressure at Mondragón*, Ithaca and London: Cornell University Press.

Colander, D. (2002) 'Functional Finance, New Classical Economics and the Great Great Grandsons', Department of Economics, Middlebury College, Vermont: Middlebury College Discussion Paper No. 02–34.

Craig, B. and J. Pencavel (1995) 'Participation and Productivity: A Comparison of Worker Co-operatives and Conventional Firms in the Plywood Industry', *Brookings Papers on Economic Activity: Microeconomics 1995*, Washington, DC: Brookings Institution.

Demsetz, H. (1988) *Ownership, Control, and the Firm: The Organization of Economic Activity*, vol. 1, Oxford: Blackwell.

—— (1997) *The Economics of the Business Firm: Seven Critical Commentaries*, Cambridge: Cambridge University Press.

Dong, F. (1997) 'The "Budget Law" and Hardening Governments' Budget Constraints', in T. Xu and J. Li (eds), *China's Tax Reform*, Beijing: China Economics Publishing House, (in Chinese).

Gates, J. (1998) *Ownership Solution*, Reading, MA: Addison-Wesley.

Geer, C. T. (1997) 'Sharing the Wealth, Capitalist-style', *Forbes*, 1 December.

Gintis, H. (1990) 'The Principle of External Accountability in Competitive Markets', in Aoki *et al.* (1990): 289–302.

Grossman, S. J. (1989) *The Information Role of Prices*, Cambridge, MA: MIT Press.

Gu, E. X. (1999) 'Local Government and Ownership Reform of Small and Medium SOEs', in Sun *et al.* (1999): ch. 3.

Hansmann, H. (1996) *The Ownership of Enterprises*, Cambridge, MA: The Belknap Press.

Hay, D. A. and G. S. Liu (1997) 'The Efficiency of Firms: What Difference Does Competition Make?', *Economic Journal*, 107 (May): 597–617.

Hayek, F. (1949) 'The Meaning of Competition', in Hayek, *Individualism and Economic Order*, London: Routledge.

Holzmann, R. (1997) 'Fiscal Alternatives of Moving from Unfunded to Funded Pensions', Technical Papers no. 126, OECD Development Center, Paris: OECD.

Huet, T. (1997) 'Can Co-ops Go Global? Mondragón Is Trying', at www.igc.apc.org/dollars/issues/nov97/mon.html.

Joskow, P. L. (2001) 'California's Electronic Crisis', NBER Working Paper 8442, Cambridge, MA: NBER.

Kaplan, S. N. and P. Strömberg (2000) 'Financial Contracting Theory Meets the Real World: An Empirical Analysis of Venture Capital Contracts', NBER Working Paper 7660, Cambridge, MA: NBER.

Kornai, J. (2001) 'Hardening the Budget Constraint: the Experience of the Post-socialist Countries', *European Economic Review*, 45, 9: 1573–99.

La Porta, R., F. Lopez-De Silanes and A. Shleifer (1999) 'Corporate Ownership Around the World', *Journal of Finance*, 54, 2: 471–517.

Li, D. (1997) '"The Visible Hands" in the Economic Development of Wenzhou', *China's Rural Economy*, 1 (January): 41–6 (in Chinese).

Li, D. D. (1996) 'A Theory of Ambiguous Property Rights in Transition Economies: The Case of the Chinese Non-state Sector', *Journal of Comparative Economics*, 23, 1: 1–19.

—— (1998) 'Changing Incentives of the Chinese Bureaucracy', *American Economic Review*, 88, 2: 393–7.

Liu, S. and J. Li (1998) 'Beyond Property Right Argument and Enterprise Performance', *Journal of Economic Research*, 8: 3–12 (in Chinese).

Maskin, E. and C. Xu (2001) 'Soft Budget Constraint Theories. From Centralization to the Market', *Economics of Transition*, 9, 1: 1–27.

Megginson, W. L. and J. M. Netter (2001) 'From State to Market: A Survey of Empirical Studies on Pivatization', *Journal of Economic Literature*, 39, 2: 321–89.

Mondragón (2002) *Mondragón 2001 Annual Report*, Mondragón: Mondragón Group.

Monks, R. A. G. and N. Minow (2001) *Corporate Governance*, 2nd edn, New York: Blackwell.

Myers, S. (1977) 'Determinants of Corporate Borrowing', *Journal of Financial Economics*, 5, 1: 147–75.

Naughton, B. (1995) *Growing out of the Plan: Chinese Economic Reform 1978–1993*, Cambridge: Cambridge University Press.

NCEO (2000) 'Employee Stock Options Fact Sheet – The rise of broadly granted employee stock options', at www.nceo.org/library/optionfact.html.

—— (2002a) 'A Statistical Profile of Employee Ownership', at www.nceo.org/library/eo_stat.html.

—— (2002b) 'The Employee Ownership 100', at www.nceo.org/library/ eo100.html.

North, D. C. (1990) *Institutions, Institutional Change, and Economic Performance*, New York: Cambridge University Press.

—— (1997) 'The Contribution of the New Institutional Economics to an Understanding of the Transition Problem', WIDER Annual Lecture 1, Helsinki: UNU/WIDER.

OECD (1998) *Institutional Investors in the New Financial Landscape*, OECD Proceedings, Paris: OECD.

—— (1999) *Institutional Investors Statistical Yearbook 1998*, Paris: OECD.

—— (2000) *Institutional Investors Statistical Yearbook 1999* (CD-ROM), Paris: OECD.

—— (2001) *Financial Market Trends*, 80 (September), Paris: OECD.

Putterman, L. (1993) 'Ownership and the Nature of the Firm', *Journal of Comparative Economics*, 17, 2: 243–63.

Qian, Y. (2000) 'The Institutional Foundation of China's Market Transition', in B. Pleskovic and J. Stiglitz (eds), *Annual World Bank Conference on Development Economics 1999*, Washington, DC: World Bank: 289–310.

—— and G. Roland (1998) 'Federalism and the Soft Budget Constraint', *American Economic Review*, 88, 5: 1143–62.

Ramamurti, R. (1999) 'Why Haven't Developing Countries Privatized Deeper and Faster?', *World Development*, 27, 1: 137–55.

Shleifer, A. (1998) 'State versus Private Ownership', *Journal of Economic Perspectives*, 12, 4: 133–50.

Shleifer, A. and R. W. Vishny (1994) 'Politicians and Firms', *Quarterly Journal of Economics*, 109, 4: 995–1025.

—— and —— (1997) 'A Survey of Corporate Governance', *Journal of Finance*, 52, 2: 737–83.

Smith, S. C. (1994) 'Innovation and Market Strategy in Italian Industrial Co-operatives: Econometric Evidence on Organizational Comparative Advantage', *Journal of Economic Behavior and Organization*, 23, 3: 303–20.

Spulber, D. (1996) 'Market Microstructure and Intermediation', *Journal of Economic Perspectives*, 10, 3: 135–52.

Spulber, N. (1997) *Redefining the State: Privatisation and Welfare Reform in Industrial and Transitional Economies*, New York: Cambridge University Press.

Stigler, G. J. (1987) 'Competition', in J. Eatwell, M. Milgate and P. Newman (eds), *The New Palgrave*, London: Macmillan-Palgrave.

Sun, L. with E. Gu and R. McIntyre (1999) 'The Evolutionary Dynamics of China's Small and Medium-Sized Enterprises in the 1990s', *World Development Studies*, 14, Helsinki: UNU/WIDER.

Svejnar, J. (2002) 'Transition Economies: Performance and Challenges', *Journal of Economic Perspectives*, 16, 1: 3–28.

Vickers, J. (1995) 'Concepts of Competition', *Oxford Economic Papers*, 47, 1: 1–23.

Whyte, W. F. (1999) 'The Mondragón Co-operatives in 1976 and 1998', *Industrial and Labor Relations Review*, 52, 3: 478–81.

Williamson, O. E. (1991) 'Comparative Economic Organization: The Analysis of Discrete Structure Alternatives', *Administrative Science Quarterly*, 36 (June): 269–96.

—— (1995) *The Institutions and Governance of Economic Development and Reform*, Proceedings of the World Bank Annual Conference on Development Economics 1994, Washington, DC: World Bank.

World Bank (1995) *Bureaucrats in Business: The Economics and Politics of Government Ownership*, New York: Oxford University Press.

Zhuravskaya, E. V. (2000) 'Incentives to Provide Local Public Goods: Fiscal Federalism, Russian Style', *Journal of Public Economics*, 76, 3: 337–68.

Zingales, L. (2000) 'In Search of New Foundations', *Journal of Finance*, 55, 4: 1623–53.

Zou, L. and L. Sun (2000) 'Liability Sharing as a Mechanism to Improve Firms' Investment and Liquidation Decisions', *Journal of Comparative Economics*, 28, 4: 739–61.

2
Institutional Investors, Corporate Ownership and Corporate Governance: Global Perspectives

Stuart L. Gillan and Laura T. Starks

This chapter examines the role of institutional investors in financial markets and corporate governance. In many countries institutional investors have become the predominant players in financial markets and their influence is growing worldwide, chiefly due to the privatization and development of pension fund systems. Moreover foreign institutional investors are becoming a significant presence, bringing their trading habits and corporate governance preferences to international markets. In fact we argue that the primary actors prompting change in many corporate governance systems are institutional investors, often foreign institutional investors. In other countries institutional investors have only a limited role. In these countries large block-holders, often in the form of individuals, family groups, other corporations or lending institutions, are the dominant players.

This chapter presents the theoretical arguments for the involvement of investors in shareholder monitoring and a brief history of institutional ownership and activism in the USA and other countries. It also discusses studies of the efficacy of such activism, and examines differences in ownership structures around the world and the implications of these different structures for institutional investor involvement in corporate governance. Over time we might expect elements of corporate governance to become similar across countries. However the endogenous nature of the interrelation among the factors of corporate governance suggests that the evolution of the latter will vary across countries. We would expect that, eventually, institutional investors will increase the liquidity, volatility and price informativeness of the financial markets in which they participate. In turn the increased information provided by institutional trading should result in better corporate governance structures, including more effective monitoring.

Introduction

Senior executives' activities are potentially constrained by a number of factors that constitute and influence the governance of the corporations they manage. These factors include the board of directors, who set policies and monitor managerial actions, debt constraints, governmental laws and regulations, labour agreements, the market for corporate control, and even the competitive environment. Broadly speaking these can be thought of as either internal control mechanisms (such as the board) or external control mechanisms (for example the market for corporate control). An increasingly important external control mechanism that affects governance worldwide is the presence of institutional investors as equity owners. The latter can exert direct influence on management's activities through their ownership and indirect influence by virtue of their ability to trade their shares. In this chapter we consider the role of institutional investors in corporate governance, the motivation for that role, and how the role has changed in the recent past.[1]

Before assessing the role of institutional investors in corporate governance we must first define what we mean by corporate governance. Recent researchers have defined the concept in different ways. For example Gillan and Starks (1998) define it as 'the system of laws, rules, and factors that control operations at a company'. They highlight that a firm's governance comprises the set of structures that provide boundaries for the firm's operations. This set of structures includes participants in corporate activities, such as managers, workers and suppliers of capital, the returns to those participants and the constraints under which they operate. Shleifer and Vishny (1997) define corporate governance in terms of the economic interests of the participants. In particular they describe corporate governance as dealing 'with the ways in which suppliers of finance to corporations assure themselves of getting a return on their investment'. Similarly Zingales (1998) defines it as 'the complex set of constraints that shape the ex-post bargaining over the quasi-rents generated by the firm'.

The need for governance arises from potential conflicts of interest among participants (stakeholders) in the corporate structure. These conflicts of interest, which are often referred to as agency problems, arise from two main sources. First, different participants have different goals and preferences. Second, the participants have imperfect information about each others' actions, knowledge and preferences. In the 1930s Berle and Means (1932) addressed these conflicts by focusing on the separation of corporate ownership from corporate management – commonly referred to as the separation of ownership and control. Berle and Means noted that this separation, absent other corporate governance mechanisms, provides managers with the ability to act in their own self-interest rather than in the interests of shareholders.[2]

Corporate governance practices have evolved since the time of Berle and Means, primarily in response to changes in the corporate environment. The evolution of corporate governance, which has varied internationally, has been particularly strong in countries where the banking, capital markets and legal systems have undergone dramatic change. Moreover there is evidence to suggest that investor protection and corporate governance are stronger in common-law than in civil-law countries. Further, governance changes have been prevalent in countries with relatively high levels of institutional investment. We argue that the primary actors prompting change in many corporate governance systems are institutional investors, often foreign institutional investors. We recognize that corporate governance structures, including ownership structures and the role of institutional investors, are likely to arise as endogenous responses to environmental factors. Put another way, although institutional investors may drive corporate governance changes and financial liberalization in some economies, in other economies institutional ownership will change in response to government actions and changes in the regulatory environment.

The conventional view is that institutional investors play a potentially important role in developed markets but a minor one in many developing and transitional economies. Even in the context of developed markets, however, different investors play different roles. Many institutional investors, particularly index funds, have traditionally been large, low-cost and passive owners. Yet during the past two decades several of these investors have become active in the corporate governance of their portfolio companies. Some consider this to be paradoxical and unconventional.

An unconventional role for institutional investors in transitional economies would, perhaps, be one in which they are significant owners. In many cases the conventional role of institutional investors in transitional economies is upheld – they are present but other forms of ownership play a more dominant role. Yet in some cases, notably in the Czech and Bulgarian markets, institutional investors are major owners, thus their role in corporate governance is important and less conventional. Of course what constitutes an unconventional role for owners depends largely on what constitutes the basis for comparison, as well as the legal and economic factors that influence ownership structures in a given market. To establish a basis for subsequent comparisons, in this chapter we emphasize the theoretical rationale for shareholder involvement in corporate governance and empirical evidence on ownership structures in developed markets.

Rationale for institutional investor involvement in corporate governance

During the latter half of the twentieth century, institutional investors became a significant, if not a major, component of equity markets in many countries. For example in the United States institutional investment grew from 6.1 per cent of aggregate ownership of equities in 1950 to over 50 per cent by 2002 (Board of Governors of the Federal Reserve System, 2003). Assets held by institutional investors have been growing in other markets as well. For example the total financial assets held by institutions in the EU grew by over 150 per cent during 1992–99 (Conference Board, 2002). Although institutional investors have not played as prominent a role in transitional and developing economies, pension reform and privatization initiatives have started to influence the financial holdings of institutions and thus the capital markets in these economies. For example in Chile domestic pension funds are the most important minority shareholders in Chilean publicly traded corporations. They are also a major source of debt financing (Iglesias-Palau, 2000; Lefort and Walker, 2000a). Moreover investment funds are majority holders in many Bulgarian corporations (Atanasov, 2002). Given the differences in institutional ownership across markets, we shall consider the role of institutional shareholder monitoring in economies characterized by diffuse ownership and in economies characterized by dominant controlling shareholders.

The role of institutional shareholder monitoring in any economy is the subject of continuing debate. Shareholders, as the owners of the firm, have certain rights, including the right to elect the board of directors. The board, as the agent of the shareholders, is directly responsible for monitoring corporate managers and their performance. The potential for shareholder activism, particularly institutional investor shareholder activism, arises when shareholders believe that the board of directors has failed in its duty, that is, they are dissatisfied with the performance of the board (and presumably the firm). In other words the potential for activism is high when agency costs are high. In such cases shareholders can (1) 'vote with their feet', that is, sell their shares, (2) hold their shares and voice their dissatisfaction, or (3) hold their shares and do nothing. Hirschman (1971) has characterized these alternatives as exit, voice and loyalty. The question naturally arises as to what conditions lead investors to exercise their voice, as opposed to exiting or remaining loyal.

The institutional investor as a large shareholder

As Roe (1990) notes, it is not just the separation of ownership and control that gives rise to the agency problem between shareholders and managers, it is also the atomistic or diffuse nature of corporate ownership, that is, an ownership structure characterized by a large number of small shareholders. When there is a diffuse ownership structure there is no incentive for an individual owner to monitor corporate management. The rationale is that the individual owner bears the entire monitoring costs, although the benefits accrue to all shareholders. Roe's point suggests that the magnitude and nature of agency problems is related to ownership structures. Given the differences in these structures around the world, one would expect differences in the form, consequences and solutions to the shareholder–manager agency problem across countries. In countries where ownership structures are dominated by large shareholders the agency problems envisioned by Berle and Means (1932) and Roe (1990) may not be prevalent.

Indeed numerous authors have argued that an important task of large shareholders is to ameliorate agency problems by monitoring or otherwise taking control of the corporation (Shleifer and Vishny, 1986; Huddart, 1993; Admati *et al.*, 1994; Maug, 1998; Noe, 2002). These authors have also argued that, because all shareholders benefit from the actions of a monitoring shareholder without incurring the costs, only large shareholders have a sufficient incentive to monitor.[3] Put another way, large investors have a stronger incentive to undertake monitoring activities as it is more likely that the gain on their investment from monitoring will be sufficient to cover the associated costs.[4]

Empirical evidence on the monitoring role of large shareholders has supported this theory to some extent. For example Bethel *et al.* (1998) have found that company performance improves after an activist investor purchases a block of shares. Kang and Shivdasani (1995) and Kaplan and Minton (1994) claim that the presence of large shareholders is associated with increased management turnover, suggesting that these shareholders undertake a monitoring function.

Another perspective arises when the large shareholder is also a lending institution. Previous researchers have argued that lenders occupy a unique governance position, given their monitoring and control abilities. In particular it has been argued that banks have a comparative cost advantage in monitoring corporations due to their access to inside information. The bank lenders' access to superior information, relative to the information available to bond holders, reduces the potential agency costs of debt financing (Fama, 1985).

There is also evidence on the role of shareholders as lenders in countries that do not have restrictions on equity investment by lending institutions. For example in the United States, for most of the twentieth century legislation prohibited banks from holding equity in a firm. In Japan, however, banks could take large equity positions in firms, including firms to which they made loans. One implication of these different restrictions is that if institutions that are equity holders and lenders to the same firm are more effective monitors, then agency problems in Japan should be less than those in the United States, everything else being equal.

The evidence on the role of lenders in the Japanese equity markets is mixed. Prowse (1990) and Kaplan and Minton (1994) conclude that banks are an important aspect of corporate governance in Japan. More recent research, however, has questioned the effectiveness of banks in governing corporations. In the case of Japan, Morck and Nakamura (1999) argue that bank intervention serves the short-term interests of the bank rather than the interests of the firms' shareholders. Moreover Kang and Stulz (2000) report that during the 1990s bank-dependent Japanese firms experienced a worse stock price performance than other firms.[5] For Germany, Boehmer (1999) reports that banks control a substantially higher fraction of corporate voting rights than cash-flow rights (due to board memberships and control of proxy votes). Since banks typically have larger loan positions than equity investments in portfolio companies, it is unclear whether banks' voting power is used in the shareholders' interests. Indeed Boehmer provides empirical evidence that bank control appears to have only a modest association with a portfolio company's stock market performance.

The evidence from studies that compare corporate governance structures and their effects should be interpreted with caution. For example, the observed differences in bank equity holdings between Germany, Japan and the United States did not arise in isolation, and might be related to other differences in corporate governance. Moreover institutions with debt and equity interests in portfolio companies might have different goals from other types of shareholder. Thus, as the papers discussed above suggest, it is not clear that lender equity positions uniformly benefit corporate governance and firm performance.

Institutional investors, monitoring and information transmission: theory and evidence

Another potential role for large institutional investors is providing a credible mechanism for transmitting information to the financial markets, that is, to other investors (Chidambaran and John, 1997). Large institutional investors can obtain private information from the management and convey that information to other shareholders. But if such monitoring is to be credible the large shareholder will need to maintain the investment for a sufficiently long time and hold enough shares to mitigate the freerider problem. As a result, under certain conditions there will be a payoff for the institutional investor who performs a costly monitoring of managers and a payoff for the manager who cooperates. Thus Chidambaran and John argue that relationship investing is optimal for both the large investor and the management. This view of a large investor who engages in non-control-related monitoring can be compared with that of Shleifer and Vishny (1986), who envision a large shareholder who is willing to take control of the firm.

A differentiation also exists between the monitoring abilities and incentives of institutional investors versus those of large non-institutional block-holders. Gorton and Kahl (1999) argue that institutional investors might provide imperfect monitoring due to their own internal agency problems. Because there are not sufficient individual large block-holders to provide better monitoring, however, even imperfect monitoring is beneficial. Thus one would expect large institutional investors and large non-institutional block-holders to coexist.

Furthermore the abilities and incentives of institutional investors to monitor will vary. Different institutional investors have different clienteles, constraints, goals and preferences. For example Brickley *et al.* (1988) point out the difference between pressure-sensitive and pressure-insensitive institutional shareholders, arguing that pressure-sensitive institutions are more likely to go along with management decisions. The rationale is that pressure-sensitive investors might have current or potential business relations with the firm that they do not want to jeopardize.[6] The authors support their hypothesis with evidence that firms with greater holdings by pressure-sensitive shareholders have more proxy votes cast in favour of the management's recommendations, while firms with greater holdings by pressure-insensitive shareholders have more proxy votes cast against the management's recommendations.

When studying the adoption of antitakeover amendments Borokhovich *et al.* (2000) found evidence to support the hypotheses of Gorton and Kahl (1999) and Brickley *et al.* (1988). Specifically, Borokhovich *et al.* found that the market reaction to news of an antitakeover measure being adopted and the percentage of outside block-holdings depends on the identity of the block-holder. When the block-holders are individuals or pressure-insensitive institutions (investment companies or independent investment advisers), the market reaction and percentage block-holdings are positively related. When the block-holders are pressure-sensitive institutions, such as banks or insurance companies, market reaction and percentage block-holdings are negatively related.[7]

Further evidence on monitoring differences across institutions is provided by Bushee (1998) in a study of the relation between a firm's aggregate institutional ownership and its R&D investment. He suggests that institutions serve an overall monitoring role by reducing pressures for managers to behave myopically. He also suggests that the strength of this monitoring role varies between the various types of institutional investor. Institutions characterized by high turnover and momentum trading appear to encourage myopic behaviour by managers. However, when studying expenditure on R&D and property, plant and equipment, Wahal and McConnell (2000) reached a somewhat different conclusion. They argue that, regardless of the investment style of the institutional investor, there is no evidence that institutional investors contribute to managerial myopia. On the contrary, they reduce the pressures that contribute to managerial myopia.

Hartzell and Starks (2003) have found evidence to suggest that institutional investors provide a monitoring function with regard to executive compensation contracts. First, there is a positive relation between the concentration of institutional ownership and the pay-for-performance sensitivity of a firm's executive compensation. Second, there is a negative relation between the concentration of institutional ownership and excess salary. One implication of these results, which are consistent with the theoretical literature on the role of the large shareholder, is that institutions have greater influence when they have a larger proportional stake in firms. Almazan *et al.* (2003) also find that the monitoring influence of institutions is associated more with investment companies and pension fund managers (pressure-insensitive institutions) than with banks and insurance companies (pressure-sensitive institutions).

Even investors that sell their shares rather than try to instigate change in the firm can affect corporate governance. As noted by Parrino *et al.* (2003), there are several potential effects from the institutional selling of shares: downward price pressure due to supply–demand effects, information signals to other investors, and changes to shareholder composition. The first effect is supported by empirical evidence demonstrating that heavy institutional selling can put downward pressure on the stock price (see for example Brown and Brooke, 1993). Alternatively, institutional selling might be interpreted as bad news, thus triggering sales by other investors and further depressing the stock price. Finally, the composition of the shareholder base might change, for example from institutional investors with a long-term focus to investors with a more myopic view. This last effect might be important to directors if the institutions that hold the stock affect the share value or the management of the company.

Parrino *et al.* (2003) have found that firms that fire their top executives have a significantly greater decline in institutional ownership in the year prior to the CEO changeover than firms experiencing voluntary CEO changeover. This finding supports the hypothesis that institutional selling influences decisions by the board of directors – institutional investor selling increases the likelihood of a CEO being forced from office.[8] The implication is that boards care about institutional trading and ownership activity in their firms. Parrino *et al.* have also found that large decreases in institutional ownership are associated with a higher probability of an outsider being appointed to succeed the CEO. The hiring of an outsider suggests that directors are more willing to break with the current corporate management and institute change.

Although a large institutional shareholder can receive benefits from monitoring, there are also potential costs. For example concentrated ownership could reduce the level of trading activity or affect the price at which shares are sold, thus reducing market liquidity and adversely affecting the ability of investors to sell their shares (Holmstrom and Tirole, 1993). This link between liquidity and monitoring (or control) has been addressed in a number of studies, including those by Coffee (1991), Bhide (1994), Maug (1998) and Kahn and Winton (1998). One view is that liquidity and control are antithetical (Coffee, 1991; Bhide, 1994). Historically, institutional investors have preferred liquidity to control because the ability to exercise control over corporate management entails a sacrifice of liquidity – a sacrifice that is deemed an unacceptable cost by many institutional investors (Coffee, 1991). For example in the United States, while extensive regulation has promoted liquidity it has also promoted diffuse, arm's length stock holding (Bhide, 1994). This in turn has detracted from the establishment of close relations between owners and managers. Corporate and pension fund managers are reluctant to receive private information from managers because the receipt of such information could compromise their fiduciary responsibility to protect the liquidity of their portfolio. Put another way, insider trading and disclosure rules that enhance liquidity for passive shareholders adversely affect governance by limiting liquidity for active shareholders.

The Securities and Exchange Commission (SEC) has reinforced this perspective by the issuance of new disclosure regulations ('Regulation for Fair Disclosure'). In addition, institutional investors tend to stay below the 10 per cent ownership level lest they trigger federal regulations pertaining to short-term and insider trading. Bhide (1994) also suggests that diversification rules in the United States have led to institutional investors holding only small amounts of any one firm, which in turn compounds the freerider problem. As such, many of the shareholders that could play an active role in the governance of the corporation instead remain passive.

Bhide's view contrasts with the more recent work by Maug (1998), Kahn and Winton (1998) and Noe (2002). Maug argues that the alleged trade-off between liquidity and control does not exist. Liquid markets in which shares can be traded easily without adverse price effects make it less costly to sell a large stake, but make it easier for investors to accumulate large stakes and capitalize on shareholder activism. He concludes that the impact of liquidity on corporate control is unambiguously positive.

Kahn and Winton (1998) focus on how firm characteristics affect an institutional shareholder's decision to intervene in a corporation's decision-making process and the implications of this intervention for the firm's ownership structure. They show that the intervention decision depends on the benefits to be gained from increasing the value of the existing stake in the firm and the effects on the institution's trading profits.

Noe (2002) demonstrates that a core group of institutional investors can develop naturally with the goal of monitoring the corporation and preventing managers from engaging in opportunism. In his model a wide range of institutions exist, from small to large, not all of which will be motivated to monitor. Some will choose to be passive, but there is not a monotonic relation between size of shareholding and incentives. Noe also shows that there is not a monotonic relation between concentration and liquidity.

In summary, the consensus in the literature is that there are many shareholder costs associated with shareholder activism and increased ownership concentration. Moreover the existing regulations impair governance by encouraging diffuse ownership and liquidity while simultaneously discouraging active investing. Despite these barriers to shareholder action, there has been an increased degree of non-control-related monitoring in the recent past by large block-holders and institutional investors.

Institutional investor activism across countries

The US experience

Given the growing influence of institutional investors in the financial markets, it is perhaps not surprising that they have become more active in their role as shareholders. The activism by these investors has been both private and public, with public activism perhaps being most visible in the United States.[9]

Regulation in the United States has strongly influenced institutional investors' choice between exit, voice or loyalty. In the early 1900s insurance companies, mutual funds and banks became active in corporate governance, that is, exercised voice. In all cases, however, laws were passed to limit the power of financial intermediaries and to prevent them from playing an active role in corporate governance (Roe, 1990). In particular banks were prohibited from directly owning equity. Thus the corporate governance system in the United States has historically differed from that in other countries, such as Germany and Japan where, by design, institutions (particularly banks) have played a large role in the ownership and monitoring of corporations.

The position of US government agencies on institutional activism has changed in recent years. This change is apparent in the Labor Department's encouragement of pension funds actively monitoring and communicating with corporate management if these activities are likely to increase the value of the funds' holdings.[10] It is also apparent in the 1992 decision by the Securities and Exchange Commission (SEC) to allow shareholders to communicate freely with each other without the prior approval of the SEC, and in the 1999 repeal of the Glass–Steagall Act, which ended the restriction on direct ownership of US equity by banks.

Despite the legal and regulatory impediments there is evidence that some US institutional investors have become more active in corporate governance in recent years. In the mid 1980s, for example, public pension and union funds started to submit shareholder proposals to companies, both individually and in collaboration with each other.[11] Later they changed their strategy somewhat by negotiating directly with corporate management and by publicly targeting corporations through the media.

In addition to public pension funds, private pension and mutual fund advisors have become more active in the corporate governance of firms in which they hold investments (although their activism has tended to be less publicized). For instance some money managers have purportedly influenced high-profile decisions to replace top managers (Myerson, 1993; *Pensions and Investments*, 1993). Others, such as the Lens Fund and Relational Investors, have specifically targeted companies that are performing poorly and are perceived to have a poor governance structure. Pressure for reform is exerted on these firms. According to Ettorre (1996), 'Fifteen years ago, the CEO and CFO did not know major holders and really didn't care. CEOs are now more accessible to money managers.' This change in attitude demonstrates the growing import-ance of institutional investors.[12]

Although there has been activism on the part of private US pension funds, and the US Labor Department has encouraged such activities, corporate pension funds in general have been reluctant to engage in activism against other corporations. One explanation of this reluctance is the fear that activism could result in retaliation. Because of business relations with the corporation, pressure-sensitive institutional investors might be compelled to vote with the management even if this were contrary to their fiduciary interests (Pound, 1988; Brickley *et al.*, 1988). Hence there is a presumption that corporate pension funds have a conflict of interest in monitoring management at other corporations. Romano (1993) cites a widely held hypothesis that public pension funds are more effective monitors of management because they vote their own shares, in contrast to private pension funds, which typically delegate their voting to external money managers. However she can find no evidence that this hypothesis is valid. According to a survey of institutional investors from the Investor Responsibility Research Center, there is no significant difference in voting policy between public and private pension funds; both groups have supported management over the survey period.

One other study has attempted to determine whether there are differences between institutional investors with regard to shareholder activism. In a survey of the 40 largest pension funds, 40 largest investment managers and 20 largest charitable foundations, Useem *et al.* (1993) found large differences between institutions, even institutions of the same type, with regard to their opinions on and responses to shareholder activism. For example it might be expected that index funds are more likely to engage in activism because they cannot withdraw their investments in the company. Index fund managers who are unhappy with a firm are constrained to giving voice. However the survey conducted by Useem *et al.* shows that this is not the case – some index fund managers are highly active while others engage in no activism.

The efficacy and appropriateness of activism by institutional investors has been the subject of debate. Those in favour of institutional investor activism maintain that it results in improved corporate governance and that it has positive externalities because the monitoring benefits all shareholders. They also argue that institutional monitoring has an added benefit: it provides an incentive for managers to extend their short-term focus to the firm's longer-term prospects, thus counteracting a tendency towards managerial myopia.

However others contend that institutional investors should not have a role in corporate governance. For example some argue that portfolio managers lack the expertise to advise corporate management. (This argument is essentially the same as that behind the passage of early twentieth century laws limiting control by institutional investors. The legislators did not want Wall Street to direct 'Main Street'.) Opponents to institutional shareholder activism also maintain that activism detracts from the primary role of pension funds: managing money for the beneficiaries. Moreover Murphy and Van Nuys (1994) question the idea that public pension fund managers have an incentive to undertake such activities. Indeed these authors contend that the incentive structure of public pension funds is such that it is surprising that they engage in this activity at all. Woidtke (2002) tests this hypothesis by comparing the relative value of firms held for public versus private pension funds. She reports that relative firm value is positively related to private pension fund ownership and negatively related to (activist) public pension fund ownership. She interprets these results as supporting the view that the actions of public pension fund managers might be motivated more by political or social influences than by firm performance. Finally, Monks (1995) makes the point that public pension funds have a more natural role as valuable allies for activism by other investors, rather than engaging in primary activism themselves.

The effectiveness of institutional investor activism

Measuring the effectiveness of shareholder activism is problematic. First, it is difficult to determine the outcome of activism and whether it has had positive consequences for the firm. For example, if a shareholder proposal has been submitted we can explore whether subsequent changes in the firm's governance structure reflect the intentions of the activists. That is, whether the firm repeals its antitakeover amendments, changes its compensation plans or changes the structure of its board of directors. But then there is the problem of determining whether any changes that are made have been caused by the activism and whether they are beneficial, that is, whether they result in economic improvements. For example, one major goal of shareholder activists has been to increase the independence of the board. Although we can observe whether the number of independent directors has increased, it is difficult directly to attribute this increase to shareholder activism. More importantly, it is difficult to assess whether changing the composition of the board in this way results in economic changes for the corporation.[13]

A second problem is that much of the activism is conducted behind the scenes in private negotiations with no external observers. For example the California Public Employees Retirement System (CalPERS) submitted a shareholder proposal to Texaco calling for the creation of an advisory committee of major shareholders to work with the management. After direct negotiations with Texaco an agreement was reached that the management would nominate a pro-shareholder candidate to its board of directors, at which point CalPERS withdrew its shareholder proposal (Parker, 1989).[14] More recently the Teachers Insurance and Annuity Association College Retirement Equities Fund (TIAA-CREF) pressured companies to remove the 'dead-hand' provision from poison-pill antitakeover measures. The dead-hand provision allowed only those directors who had put a poison pill in place to remove it, thus potentially delaying a new board's decision to sell the company. Since 1998, when the TIAA-CREF began its focus on poison pills, 56 of the 60 corporations approached have removed their dead-hand provision or removed their pills altogether.[15] Such activities have not been included in most studies of shareholder activism. An exception is the paper by Carleton *et al.* (1998) on direct negotiations between the TIAA-CREF and targeted companies during 1992–96. The authors state that of the 45 firms contacted by the TIAA-CREF, 71 per cent reached a negotiated settlement prior to a vote on the shareholder proposal. The remaining 29 per cent resisted the TIAA-CREF's pressures and the shareholder proposal was put to the vote. This suggests that academic studies might substantially understate the effects of shareholder activism because they do not observe the full set of (potential) shareholder proposals and their effects.

The empirical evidence on the influence of shareholder activism is mixed. Although some studies have found some form of short-term market reaction to the announcement of certain types of activism, there is little evidence of improvement in long-term stock market performance or operating performance after the activism. A number of studies have found some change in the real activities of firms subsequent to shareholder pressure, but it has been difficult to establish a causal relationship between the pressure and the changes.

Institutional investor monitoring in other countries

The relatively active role played by institutions in the United States contrasts with that of institutional investors in other countries. For example, although it is estimated that institutional investors own between 65 per cent and 80 per cent of the equities in the UK, historically they have not voted their shares.[16] Mallin (1995) notes that in a survey of 250 large UK companies, 90 per cent reported voting levels of less than 52 per cent. The Report of the Committee of Inquiry into UK Vote Execution (sponsored by the National Association of Pension Funds, NAPF) reported that voting levels at UK companies were as low as 20 per cent in 1990, increasing to 50 per cent by 1999.[17] This increase might be attributable to external pressure on institutions to vote their shares. During 1998 the UK trade and industry secretary used the 'bully pulpit' to pressure institutional investors to vote their shares, threatening legislative action in the absence of any improvement. Indeed this appeared to spark the NAPF to encourage its members to vote. Although a voting turnout of 50 per cent represented an increase, it was low by US standards. In the United States, voting turnout, the proportion of votes cast at the annual meeting, can easily reach 70–80 per cent at many companies (Bethel and Gillan, 2002.)

The differential between voting turnout in the United States and the UK might be partly due to differences between the institutional and regulatory environments in the two countries. For example in the United States the Department of Labor mandates that pension funds regulated by the Employment Retirement Income Security Act (ERISA) should vote their proxies. Although there has been increased pressure for institutional investors in the UK to vote their shares, voting has not been mandated by regulation. In fact part of the recent increase might be attributable to the NAPF's recommendation that its members vote in order to forestall regulatory intervention. It appears, however, that changes are on the horizon for UK institutions and companies. The Myners Report, commissioned by HM Treasury, advocated the adoption of standards analogous to those under ERISA, 'articulating the duties of managers to intervene in companies – by voting or otherwise – where there is a reasonable expectation that doing so might raise the value of the investment'.[18] In the March 2001 budget speech the chancellor of the exchequer supported the Myners Report and the possibility of legislation mandating governance reforms.

This is not to imply that there is a complete absence of active monitoring in the UK. For example in response to the Myners Report eight major institutional investors, representing over 5 per cent of the UK stock market, wrote to the CEOs of 750 UK companies requesting that they voluntarily put their compensation reports to a shareholder vote. More systematic evidence is provided by Dahya and Travlos (2002), who report that CEO turnover increased after the issuance of proposed corporate governance reforms in the 1992 Cadbury Committee's code of best practice, and that sensitivity of turnover to performance was concentrated in firms that adopted the code. Moreover Dahya and McConnell (2002) demonstrate that boards dominated by outsiders are more likely to appoint an outside CEO.

Also of note is the fact that Hermes Pensions Management Limited (Hermes), which is wholly owned by the British Telecommunications Pension Scheme, established a fund in October 1998 to 'invest in companies whose businesses are fundamentally strong, but where concerns about the company's direction mean that its shares are underperforming'. The manager of the fund, Hermes Focus Asset Management (HFAM), met with directors and shareholders in an attempt to resolve governance concerns and enhance long-term shareholder value. HFAM has over £600 million invested in UK focus funds. In the fourth quarter of 2001 Hermes announced a plan to expand its activities with the proposed launch of a fund to invest in underperforming European equities.

The influence of the legal environment

A further influence on the role of institutional shareholders is the legal system. For example the ability to monitor by means of voting might be limited due to features of the national legal and regulatory environments. In some European countries the voting system entails 'share blocking', which requires investors who wish to vote to hold their shares on the day of the annual meeting (in contrast with the United States, where a record date is set and holders from the date of record are permitted to vote at the annual meeting). This highlights the potential trade-off between liquidity and control, as blocking the shares effectively prohibits the investor from trading prior to the annual general meeting. Share blocking probably also contributes to low voting turnout at some companies.

The case of the French company Vivendi Universal provides an illustration of how governance structures and the legal environment affect shareholders' rights and their ability to vote. At the 2000 annual meeting Vivendi shareholders approved a resolution curbing voting rights. The resolution permitted the company to scale back the voting power of blocks above 2 per cent, contingent on the level of voting turnout. Given the company's historical 30 per cent voting turnout, it was argued that the resolution would prevent block-holders from exerting a disproportionate degree of influence on the company. Investors in France and elsewhere condemned the action. Not only would such voting caps limit shareholders' voting rights, they also had the potential to entrench management and exacerbate agency problems.

More generally, differences between countries' legal and financial systems have led to a disparity between their corporate governance systems. For example La Porta *et al.* (1997) argue that investor protection and corporate governance are stronger in countries where the legal system is based on common law rather than civil law. Roe (1990) contends that in the early part of the twentieth century, institutions in the United States were active in corporate governance but the federal government curtailed their participation. In contrast the roles of institutional investors in other countries differ due to differences in their development and in the laws that govern their behaviour. It has been suggested that these laws are the major reason for the evolutionary differences between the corporate governance systems in the United States and those in other countries, such as Germany or Japan. By design, institutions, particularly banks, have played a large role in the ownership and monitoring of corporations in Germany (the *Hausbank*) and Japan (the *Keiretsu*).[19]

Shareholder protection measures also affect the ability of a firm to raise capital, including capital from institutional investors. As the demand for funds increases in transitional markets, foreign institutions demand stronger legal protection and stronger corporate governance. Moreover financial liberalization and the ensuing development of pension systems and other domestic institutional investment may act as catalysts for improved legal protection and corporate governance. More generally, as alluded to above, the protection of shareholders, particularly minority shareholders, is important for corporate governance and the continued ability of firms in transitional markets to attract external capital (La Porta *et al.*, 1997).

Ownership structures

Differences between ownership structure across countries

In many economies large shareholders and concentrated ownership, as opposed to institutional ownership, are important factors in a firm's governance structure. As noted earlier, the agency problems between managers and shareholders envisioned by Berle and Means (1932) and Roe (1990) might not be prevalent in economies where ownership structures differ. Indeed La Porta *et al.* (1998) conclude that in many economies the primary agency problem is restricting the expropriation of minority shareholders by the controlling shareholders, rather than restricting the activities of professional managers who are unaccountable to shareholders. Put another way, controlling block-holders may enjoy private benefits of control at the expense of other shareholders.

Striking evidence on the variation of ownership structures internationally is provided by Majluf *et al.* (1998), who report that although the largest shareholders in Chile control 40 per cent of the shares of the largest companies, this drops to 22 per cent for Germany and 7 per cent for Japan. These findings contrast with the situation in the United States, where there is substantially more dispersion in share ownership and the largest shareholder often controls as little as 5 per cent of the voting rights. La Porta *et al.* (1998) report that, for a sample of large publicly traded firms around the world (the largest 20 firms in each country), 36 per cent were widely held, 30 per cent were family-controlled, 18 per cent were state-controlled and the remaining 15 per cent had a variety of other ownership structures. The authors found little use of differential voting rights but widespread use of pyramidal structures to control firms. Some 26 per cent of their sample had pyramidal structures (multiple layers of corporate ownership that permit the control of voting rights with relatively low levels of investment). In the average country, the ultimate or top family owners on average controlled 25 per cent of the value of the largest 20 firms. Finally, other than in Germany, La Porta *et al.* found little evidence of control by single financial institutions, such as banks, and little evidence of cross-shareholdings by other corporations.

In the case of West European firms, Becht and Roell (1999) provide evidence of dominant block ownership of firms domiciled in Austria, Belgium, France, Germany, Italy, Spain and the Netherlands (there is less evidence of dominant block ownership in the UK). In many of these countries the largest voting stake for the median firm in their sample exceeded 50 per cent. The authors conclude that in much of continental Europe there exist large block-holders who can and do exercise control over management. Consistent with La Porta *et al.* (1998), Becht and Roell also conclude that the main conflict of interest lies between controlling shareholders and minority shareholders, as opposed to dispersed owners and professional managers as in the United States.

The East Asian environment has a number of parallels to that of Western Europe. Claessens *et al.* (2002) argue that the separation of voting from cash-flow rights in East Asian corporations is associated with the potential expropriation of minority shareholders and lower market values. However Faccio *et al.* (2001) argue that East Asian capital markets generally appear to be capable of containing expropriation within tightly controlled groups by requiring that higher dividends be paid to corporations affiliated with such groups. In contrast capital markets fail to extract more dividends from corporations in groups with intermediate levels of control; that is, a greater discrepancy between ownership and control is associated with lower dividend rates.

With regard to Latin America, there are both similarities with and differences from the other regions. Claessens *et al.* (2000) compared group affiliation in seven East Asian countries and Chile, and found that 75 per cent of the listed firms in their East Asia sample were associated with business groups, compared with 40 per cent in Chile. Valadares and Leal (2000) have found a high degree of ownership concentration in publicly traded companies in Brazil. Similar to the concentration found in Chile, the major shareholder owns an average 41 per cent of the equity capital.[20]

Thus ownership structures, the legal environment and the role of institutional investors differ between major market economies. As we shall discuss below, the same is true in transitional economies.

Ownership in transitional economies

The preliminary evidence on ownership structure and control in transitional economies and emerging markets is increasing as new data sets become available. In this section we shall first focus on several multi-country studies and then review evidence on a number of specific markets as illustrations of how ownership structures in transitional economies compare.

Large differences in ownership structure exist between transitional economies. Djankov (2000) reports that the differences between the ownership structures in six newly independent state countries – Georgia, Kazakhstan, the Kyrgyz Republic, Moldova, Russia and Ukraine – appear to be driven by each country's choice of privatization programme. Companies in Georgia and Ukraine, where managers were favoured in the privatization process, are characterized by high managerial ownership (53 per cent and 46 per cent respectively). In contrast markets where mass privatization dominated, such as Kazakhstan and the Kyrgyz Republic, have higher levels of outside ownership (37 per cent and · 21 per cent respectively). In Russia, privatizing firms primarily chose 51 per cent insider ownership, with the remaining shares being given to investment funds or retained by the state. In each of these markets the state still has significant ownership of many companies. A further factor is the low level of foreign ownership, which in 1999 ranged from 0.9 per cent in Ukraine to 6.8 per cent in Kazakhstan. Djankov suggests that these low levels of foreign ownership are due to governance mechanisms external to the firm, including foreign ownership restrictions, the legal framework and the lack of secondary capital markets.

Frydman *et al.* (1999) report that previously state-owned companies in the Czech Republic, Hungary and Poland are typically characterized by four types of owner: insiders (25 per cent of their sample), foreign investors (25 per cent), privatization funds (20 per cent) and the state (15 per cent). More recently Lins (2003) studied equity ownership in a sample of 1448 firms in 18 emerging markets[21] and found that control in emerging markets is more concentrated than reported in earlier studies. On average management groups held 30 per cent of the control rights in the firms studied. Also of note is that non-management block-holders on average held 20 per cent of the control rights. This suggests that control by unaffiliated block-holders can have an important monitoring function in transitional economies. Of the 1821 block-holders in the sample, 66 per cent were management, 20 per cent were other companies, 6 per cent were government and less than 8 per cent were mutual funds, pension funds or insurance companies.

Illustrative of many other countries is the case of the Czech market after privatization. Claessens and Djankov (1999) report that increased ownership concentration in Czech firms is associated with improved performance. Although a breakdown of firms by ownership type is not reported, the authors suggest that ownership type appears to be important. Ownership by foreigners with a strategic interest in the firm and ownership by non-bank funds are associated with improved performance. Also noteworthy is the fact that by the end of privatization, bank and non-bank funds were the dominant owners. Using an updated data set, Cull *et al.* (2002) also show that the state, foreigners, bank funds and non-bank funds are important owners in the Czech market. However the authors argue that firms dominated by fund owners perform poorly (irrespective of whether or not the fund is bank sponsored). More generally, the authors argue that the privatization process was flawed in that it allowed managers to strip firms' assets and channel them into firms or accounts controlled by the managers. The authors go on to suggest that environmental considerations – including weak laws and law enforcement in respect of disclosure, and the protection of minority shareholders – might have contributed to flaws in the privatization process. Specifically, vouchers were widely distributed and ownership concentration was limited by law, which effectively prohibited the emergence of large shareholders.

Other studies provide interesting perspectives on the different types of owner. Similar to the Czech situation, Atanasov (2002) reports that by the end of the privatization process in Bulgaria, funds owned 75 per cent of the vouchers issued and individuals owned the remaining 25 per cent. Of note here is the fact that the Bulgarian government created privatization funds to promote investor diversification and encourage the development of large shareholders that would monitor portfolio companies. Although the author does not examine performance effects, he does note that individual shareholders may have suffered somewhat in the process in that share trading dried up in the case of firms where funds accumulated a block, and stock prices fell.

Funds also appear to have been important in the Romanian context. Earle and Telegdy (2002) note that in Romania several different approaches to privatization were implemented, including employee buyouts, mass privatization and sales to outside block-holders. For 40 per cent of their sample the firms' shares were given to a state fund (70 per cent of the firms' shares) and to five private ownership funds under state control (30 per cent of the firms' shares). Five years after privatization the state fund held shares in more than 75 per cent of corporations, with an average holding of 46 per cent and majority ownership of just under 50 per cent of all companies. The private funds had an interest in approximately 40 per cent of companies, with an average ownership level of 20 per cent. Although private funds had majority control of only a few companies, they were important minority shareholders. Approximately 36 per cent of the sample firms – those which were part of the employee buyout process – could be characterized as employee-owned. The latter situation is similar to that in Ukraine, where insiders own about 51 per cent of firms, with 8 per cent being held by managers and 43 per cent by workers (Estrin and Rosevear, 1999). Outsiders, including banks and institutions, foreign firms and private individuals, hold 38 per cent, while the state holds the remaining 11 per cent. Estrin and Rosevear have found little evidence that form of ownership is linked to improved performance, although there is evidence that privately owned firms, particularly those with insider control, undertake more restructuring.

In China, as in many other countries, the state is an important shareholder and ownership by institutions is limited. Xu and Wang (1999) report that in the case of Chinese stock companies in 1995, domestic individuals, domestic institutions and the state were the three main types of shareholder. Each of these groups held about 30 per cent of total outstanding shares. Employees and foreign investors together held less than 10 per cent of outstanding shares. Moreover ownership concentration was high, with the five largest shareholders accounting for 58 per cent of outstanding shares.[22] For 826 Chinese companies with large shareholders, Tian (2001) found that in 1998 the most important block-holders were the state (43.9 per cent of firms), domestic companies (39.2 per cent), domestic institutions (10.9 per cent) and foreigners (5.1 per cent). Qi *et al.* (2000) focus on the ownership and performance of firms listed on the Shanghai Stock Exchange from 1991 to 1996. They state that firm performance is positively related to the proportion of ownership by domestic companies but negatively related to the proportion of shares owned by the state. Moreover firm performance increases with higher levels of corporate ownership relative to state ownership. The authors have found no evidence that the level of ownership by other shareholders, foreign or domestic, is associated with firms' performance.

On balance these studies support the contention that institutional investors, foreign or domestic, currently play a limited role in many transitional equity markets. However in some cases, such as the Bulgarian and Czech markets, institutions are important. The influence of foreign investors also appears to be limited, although they have the potential to become a large component of some markets. Indeed questions have been asked about how the entry of foreign institutional investors may affect financial market operations and valuations. Several authors have studied this issue. For example Bekaert *et al.* (1999) have found that after stock market liberalization, capital flows to the stock market increase by an annual rate of 1.4 per cent of market capitalization for three years, and then the increase slows down. They have also found evidence of a permanent price pressure effect from these capital flows, but they propose that the actual return effect is not solely due to price pressure. Finally, they suggest that capital tends to leave more quickly than it arrives. Choe *et al.* (1999) have examined whether foreign investors have a destabilizing effect on the Korean stock market and conclude that they do not. Similarly, in a review of the literature Stulz (1999) concludes that opening a country to international investors decreases firms' capital costs without adversely affecting the securities market. Specifically, he states that there is no evidence that volatility, contagion or destabilization increase following the liberalization of a country's financial markets.

Interaction among ownership structures

The trade-off between the concentration and dispersion of ownership raises further questions. The first concerns the extent to which diverse types of equity owner (for example domestic institutional investors, employees, large block-holders and foreign institutional investors) will participate in corporate ownership. The second question is how the interaction of these investors will affect corporate governance structures. The third is whether the increased presence of institutional investors (domestic or foreign) will cause corporate ownership in general to become more dispersed, changing firms' corporate governance structures. Finally, there is the question of whether dispersed ownership will lead to more efficiently managed firms or whether agency problems will become magnified in the absence of large block-holders with an incentive to monitor.

Hence these are important questions about how ownership structures and the interrelations among different types of investor will affect markets. Since the relative roles of institutional investors and large block-holders are not well understood, this too is an important issue to consider. Although their roles can overlap, as mentioned previously, there is only modest evidence that when an institutional investor takes on the role of an activist block-holder there is a change in the corporation. On the other hand there is evidence that corporate performance improves after an activist block purchase. Of course, as discussed earlier, corporate governance structures, including ownership structures and participation by institutional investors, are likely to emerge as endogenous responses to environmental factors. From the policy perspective, the goal should not necessarily be to encourage one form of ownership over another. Rather it should be to facilitate the efficient use of capital. Legal and regulatory approaches that advocate disclosure, transparency, investor protection and the establishment of property rights are likely to prove central to encouraging capital investment by many types of shareholder.

Regardless of the interaction between different types of owner, research shows that the presence of institutional investors should lead to more informative prices, and consequently lower monitoring costs for all investors. Hence the outcome should be better monitoring of managers and better corporate governance.

The evolving environment

It can be speculated that increased ownership by foreign institutional investors will be an important influence in many economies, particularly transitional economies, as the demands for capital in these countries increases. Some countries have already experienced an influx of capital, primarily from foreign institutional investors. According to a recent IMF report, emerging markets' issuance of bonds, equity and syndicated loans increased by 32 per cent during 2000 to some US$216 billion. Of this, approximately US$86.7 billion of debt was raised by private sector entities. Emerging market equity issuance increased by 80 per cent between 1999 and 2000 to US$41.8 billion, the highest level ever. Moreover China accounted for about 50 per cent of new issues during 2000 (Mathieson and Schinasi, 2001).[23]

Due to the increased globalization of their investments during the past decade, foreign investors have had, and can be expected to continue to have, a large influence on some transitional economy stock markets and the firms traded in these markets. Such influence will affect the firms' corporate governance either through direct intervention or through indirect supply–demand effects. Examples of direct intervention include the efforts of investors such as CalPERS and TIAA-CREF to improve the corporate governance systems in their holdings, both domestic and foreign. However there are impediments to institutional investor intervention: the costs of intervention, the limited number of institutions that choose to intervene, and restrictions on activities (including ownership and voting rights) of foreign institutions. In some cases foreign institutions may exert a significant influence due to their large presence in the markets, particularly when they hold more shares than domestic institutions. For example in the late 1990s Mexico's stock markets had over 30 per cent foreign investment, while its domestic mutual fund industry held about 1 per cent of outstanding equity (Cervantes, 1999).

Institutions also use their option to exit from a particular firm or market, particularly in transitional economies. Karmin notes the problem that some markets now have with attracting foreign institutional investors: 'unless companies start paying more attention to corporate governance, emerging markets could remain stuck in the backwaters of global finance for years to come. Many investors say it is easier to "vote with their feet" and simply abandon many of these markets.'[24] Indeed CalPERs recently eliminated its public equity investment positions in Indonesia, Malaysia and Thailand, a move that at least in part can be attributed to poor corporate governance.[25] The question now arises as to whether or not indirect supply – demand effects could lead to improved governance. That is, will firms change their corporate governance structure in order to attract capital from foreign investors? To some extent this may already be taking place. For example Mitton (2002) suggests that during the East Asian financial crisis more focused firms and firms with higher quality disclosures and more concentrated outside ownership performed better. Consistent with these findings, Klapper and Love (2002) argue that firm-level governance provisions are more important in countries with weak legal environments. Thus firms that improve their governance and credibly commit to protecting shareholders can compensate for a weak legal environment.[26]

Despite the ability of shareholders to sell and firm-specific actions to improve corporate governance, pressure for governance reform remains strong in many markets. For example Anthony Neoh, senior adviser to the China Securities Regulatory Commission, has stated that China must improve the corporate governance of enterprises (Deutsche Presse-Agentur, 2001). Similar sentiments aimed at attracting and retaining capital appear to underlie the promulgation of corporate governance codes of best practice in many markets. The development of governance codes, often with legislative backing, is taking place in developed countries such as Hong Kong, Singapore and the UK, and in emerging markets such as Brazil, India and Thailand, among others. Moreover recent events in the United States, including the failure of Enron and Worldcom, have sparked a wave of regulatory reforms to address corporate governance concerns.[27]

A further example of the indirect influence of a firm's corporate governance structure in attracting capital is the development of corporate governance ratings services. In Europe, Déminor provides research on corporate governance practices in the top 300 index companies on the Financial Times Stock Exchange (FTSE), covering 17 countries. Déminor's ratings are based on corporate governance criteria spanning four main areas: the rights and duties of shareholders, the absence of takeover defences, disclosure, and board structure.

Similar ratings services exist elsewhere. For example in Russia the Institute of Corporate Law and Corporate Governance evaluates Russian companies for corporate governance efficiency and provides corporate governance ratings. Likewise Standard & Poor's has developed a corporate governance rating system for transitional economies and emerging markets,[28] a system that is being extended to the United States. Meanwhile the Emerging Markets Division of Credit Lyonnais Securities Asia has released corporate governance rankings for 495 companies in 25 countries. Finally, during recent months no fewer than five rating services have been announced for US firms: the Corporate Library, Governance Metrics, Institutional Shareholder Services, the Investor Responsibility Research Center, and Standard & Poor's. The existence of such services reflects the desire of institutional investors to have corporate governance information in order to make investment decisions.

Conclusions

This chapter has examined the role of institutional investors in financial markets and the governance of corporations. Previous research tells us that institutional investors are the predominant players in some countries' financial markets and are therefore important in corporate governance. Yet ownership structures and other governance characteristics differ across markets. These differences are partly attributable to legal and regulatory systems and partly to the manner in which the market has evolved. For example the interrelation between institutional investors and other factors of corporate governance, such as the market for corporate control, the board of directors, large block-holders, lenders and employees, may affect their importance in a particular market. Furthermore ownership structures may change for many reasons, including the development of pension systems, financial liberalization, the investment policies of foreign institutional investors, privatization initiatives, the establishment of stronger shareholder protection, or other environmental, legal and regulatory changes.

Despite these differences across markets, because of the growth of institutional ownership and influence, institutional investors worldwide have the opportunity to play an important role in many markets. Research has shown that because of the costs involved, only large shareholders are able to engage in extensive monitoring of management. Whether institutions, as large shareholders, should or will provide such monitoring will depend in part on the constraints to which they are subject, their objectives and their preferences for liquidity. These characteristics will continue to vary between countries, leading to differences in the role and influence of institutional investors in corporate governance.

On balance, we expect that institutional investors will increase the liquidity, volatility and price informativeness of the markets in which they invest. In turn, the increased information provided by institutional trading should result in better monitoring of corporations and better corporate governance structures. In some cases financial liberalization and aspects of government policy will be the major engines of change, suggesting that the role of institutional investors will be a minor one. In other cases institutional investors, foreign and domestic, will play a major role, particularly given the capital they control.

Notes

1   Denis and McConnell (2002) provide a comprehensive review of other governance issues.
2   For more recent discussions see Jensen and Meckling (1976), Fama and Jensen (1983), and Jensen (1993).
3   That is, the existence of a large shareholder can provide a partial solution to the free-rider problem that is inherent in diffusely owned companies, as pointed out by Grossman and Hart (1980).
4   However, as pointed out by Shleifer and Vishny (1986), because the large shareholder can only reap the gains from his or her own shares, despite the existence of a monitoring shareholder there will still be too little monitoring.
5   See Anderson and Campbell (2003) for a more detailed discussion of Japanese bank governance.
6   For example an insurance company that underwrites a corporate client may feel pressure to vote with the corporate management in order not to lose the insurance business.
7   Borokhovich *et al.* (2000) use the terms affiliated and unaffiliated rather than pressure-sensitive and pressure-insensitive.
8   As noted by the Parrino *et al.* (2003), these results also support the hypothesis that institutional investors are better informed than other investors, and thus become net sellers over the period prior to forced turnovers, when these firms typically experience negative market-adjusted returns.
9   For surveys of shareholder activism see Black (1998), Gillan and Starks (1998) and Karpoff (1998).

10 The Labor Department has oversight responsibility for corporate pension funds through ERISA.

11 The major issues raised by these proposals dealt with corporate governance, particularly, the problems arising from the misalignment of the interests of managers and those of shareholders.

12 For a more complete discussion of management's view of institutional investor activism see Martin and Kensinger (1996), who interviewed a number of executives whose firms had been targeted by institutional investor activists.

13 For an analysis of whether board independence results in improved performance for firms see Bhagat and Black (1998a). For a more general survey of empirical evidence on the relation between the composition of the board of directors and firm performance, see Bhagat and Black (1998b).

14 See also Gillan and Starks (2000) and Del Guercio and Hawkins (1999).

15 http://www.tiaa-cref.org/siteline/siteline_article_5_528_38329.html

16 See also Ersoy-Bozcuk and Lasfer (2000).

17 The NAPF is the principal UK body representing the interests of occupational pension funds. With more than £450 billion of pension fund assets, its membership includes companies, local authorities and public sector bodies.

18 http://www.hm-treasury.gov.uk/docs/2001/myners_report0602.html

19 In other markets, family or business groups appear to be dominant players. See Campbell and Keys (2001) and Ferris *et al.* (2003) for a discussion of the *chaebol* in South Korea and Khanna (2000) for business groups more generally.

20 For further discussion of the effects of institutional investors on corporate governance in Latin America see Starks (2000).

21 Argentina, Brazil, Chile, the Czech Republic, Hong Kong, Indonesia, Israel, Malaysia, Peru, Philippines, Portugal, Singapore, South Africa, South Korea, Sri Lanka, Taiwan, Thailand and Turkey.

22 During the sample period Class B shares were only for foreign investors.

23 The remaining debt issues were public sector debt or sovereign debt.

24 C. Karmin, 'Corporate-Governance Issues Hamper Emerging Markets – Stalled Changes Push Some Shareholders To Abandon the Field, *Wall Street Journal*, 8 November 2000, C1.

25 The decision to change allocations was based on a review of a number of factors on each market, including market liquidity and volatility, market regulation and investor protection, capital market openness, settlement proficiency and transaction costs (accounting for 50 per cent of the review). Political stability, financial transparency and labour standards accounted for the remaining 50 per cent.

26 In a related work Carlin and Mayer (2000) argue that corporate governance systems are strongly related to economic development. Lefort and Walker (2000b) examine the effects of economic and political shocks on the development of corporate governance systems.

27 See Gillan and Martin (2002) for a discussion of Enron.

28 A. Cullison, 'S&P Rates Russian Firms on Governance – McGraw-Hill Unit Gauges Shareholder Treatment In Land of Lax Laws', *Wall Street Journal*, 29 November 2000, A23.

References

Admati, A., P. Pfleiderer and J. Zechner (1994) 'Large Shareholder Activism, Risk Sharing, and Financial Market Equilibrium', *Journal of Political Economy*, 102, 6: 1097–130.

Almazan, A., J. Hartzell and L. Starks (2003) 'Active Institutional Shareholders and Executive Compensation', working paper, University of Texas at Austin.

Anderson, C. W. and T. L. Campbell (2003) 'Corporate Governance of Japanese Banks', *Journal of Corporate Finance*, corrected proof 24 April.

Atanasov, V. (2002) 'Valuation of Large Blocks of Shares and the Private Benefits of Control', working paper, Babson College, MA.

Becht, M. and A. Roell (1999) 'Blockholdings in Europe: An International Comparison', *European Economic Review*, 43: 1049–56.

Bekaert, G., C. Harvey and R. Lumsdaine (1999) 'The Dynamics of Emerging Market Equity Flows', *Journal of International Money and Finance*, 2002, 21: 295–350.

Berle, A. and G. Means (1932) *The Modern Corporation and Private Property*, New York: Macmillan.

Bethel, J. and S. L. Gillan (2002) 'The Impact of the Institutional and Regulatory Environment on Shareholder Voting', *Financial Management*, 31, 4: 29–54.

—— J. Liebeskind and T. Opler (1998) 'Block Share Purchases and Corporate Performance', *Journal of Finance*, 53: 605–35.

Bhagat, S. and B. S. Black (1998a) 'Board Independence and Long-term Performance', working paper, University of Colorado and Stanford University.

—— and —— (1998b) 'The Uncertain Relationship Between Board Composition and Firm Performance', in K. Hopt, M. Roe and E. Wymeersch (eds), *Corporate Governance: The State of the Art and Emerging Research*, Oxford: Oxford University Press.

Bhide, A. (1994) 'Efficient Markets, Deficient Governance: US Securities Regulations Protect Investors and Enhance Market Liquidity. But Do They Alienate Managers and Shareholders?', *Harvard Business Review*, 72: 128–40.

Black, B. S. (1998) 'Shareholder Activism and Corporate Governance in the United States', in P. Newman (ed.), *The New Palgrave Dictionary of Economics and the Law*, London and New York: Palgrave-Macmillan and St. Martin's Press.

Board of Governors of the Federal Reserve System (2003) *Flow of Funds Accounts of the United States: Annual Flows and Outstandings*, Washington, DC.

Boehmer, E. (1999) 'Corporate Governance in Germany: Institutional Background and Empirical Results', working paper, University of Georgia.

Borokhovich, K., K. Brunarski and R. Parrino (2000) 'Variation in the Monitoring Incentives of Outside Blockholders', working paper, University of Texas at Austin.

Brickley, J., R. Lease and C. Smith (1988) 'Ownership structure and voting on antitakeover amendments', *Journal of Financial Economics*, 20: 267–92.

Brown, K. and B. Brooke (1993) 'Institutional Demand and Security Price Pressure: The Case of Corporate Spin-offs', *Financial Analysts Journal*, September–October: 53–62.

Bushee, B. (1998) 'The Influence of Institutional Investors on Myopic R&D Investment Behavior', *The Accounting Review*, 73: 305–33.

Campbell, T. L. and P. Y. Keys (2001) 'Corporate governance in South Korea: the *chaebol* experience', *Journal of Corporate Finance*, 8, 4: 373–91.

Carleton, W., J. Nelson and M. Weisbach (1998) 'The Influence of Institutions on Corporate Governance through Private Negotiations: Evidence from TIAA-CREF', *Journal of Finance*, 53, 4: 1335–62.

Carlin, W. and C. Mayer (2000) 'International Evidence on Corporate Governance: Lessons for Developing Countries', *ABANTE*, 2: 133–60.

Cervantes, M. (1999) 'What Explains the Returns in the Mexican Stock Market?', dissertation, Instituto tecnologico y de Estudios Superiores de Monterrey, EGADE.

Chidambaran, N. and K. John (1997) 'Relationship Investing and Corporate Governance', working paper, Tulane University and NYU.

Choe, H., B. Kho and R. Stulz (1999) 'Do Foreign Investors Destabilize Stock Markets? The Korean Experience in 1997', *Journal of Financial Economics*, 54, 227–64.

Claessens, S. and S. Djankov (1999) 'Ownership Concentration and Corporate Performance in the Czech Republic', *Journal of Comparative Economics*, 27, 3: 498–513.

—— —— J. P. H. Fan and L. Lang (2002) 'Disentangling the incentive and entrenchment effects of large shareholdings', *Journal of Finance*, 57, 6: 2741–71.

—— —— and L. Klapper (2000) 'The Role and Functioning of Business Groups in East Asia and Chile', *ABANTE*, 3: 91–107.

Coffee, J. (1991) 'Liquidity versus Control: The Institutional Investor as Corporate Monitor', *Columbia Law Review*, 91: 1277–368.

Conference Board (2002) 'Equity Ownership and Investment Strategies of US and International Institutional Investors', *Institutional Investment Report*, 4.

Cull, R., J. Matesova, and M. Shirley (2002) 'Ownership and the Temptation to Loot: Evidence from Privatized Firms in the Czech Republic', *Journal of Comparative Economics*, 30, 1: 1–24.

Dahya, J. and J. J. McConnell (2002) 'Outside Directors and Corporate Board Decisions', working paper, Purdue University, IN.

—— —— and N. G. Travlos (2002) 'The Cadbury Committee, Corporate Performance, and Top Management Turnover', *Journal of Finance*, 57, 1: 461–83.

Del Guercio, D. and J. Hawkins (1999) 'The Motivation and Impact of Pension Fund Activism', *Journal of Financial Economics*, 52.

Denis, D. K. and J. J. McConnell (2002) 'International Corporate Governance', working paper, Purdue University, IN.

Deutsche Presse-Agentur (2001) 'Securities adviser urges transparency in China's financial markets', 21 March.

Djankov, S. (2000) 'Ownership Structure and Enterprise Restructuring in Six Newly Independent States', *Comparative Economic Studies*, 41, 1: 75–86.

Earle, J. S. and Á. Telegdy (2002) 'Privatization Methods and Productivity Effects in Romanian Industrial Enterprises', *Journal of Comparative Economics*, 30, 4: 657–82.

Ersoy-Bozcuk, A. and M. A. Lasfer (2000) 'Changes in Shareholder Groups' Holdings and Corporate Monitoring: The UK Evidence', working paper, City University Business School, London.

Estrin, S. and A. Rosevear (1999) 'Enterprise Performance and Corporate Governance in Ukraine', *Journal of Comparative Economics*, 27, 3: 442–58.

Ettorre, B. (1996) 'When Patience is a Corporate Virtue', *Management Review*, 85, 11: 28–32.

Faccio, M., L. Lang and L. Young (2001) 'Dividends and Expropriation', *American Economic Review* 91, 1: 54–78.

Fama, E. (1985) 'What's Different about Banks?', *Journal of Monetary Economics*, 15: 29–39.

—— and M. Jensen (1983) 'Separation of Ownership and Control', *Journal of Law and Economics*, 26 (June): 301–25.

Ferris, S. P., K. A. Kim and P. Kitsabunnarat (2003) 'The Costs (and Benefits?) of Diversified Business Groups: The case of Korean chaebols', *Journal of Banking and Finance*, 27, 2: 251–73.

Frydman, R., C. Gray, M. Hessel and A. Rapaczynski (1999) 'When Does Privatization Work? The Impact of Private Ownership on Corporate Performance in Transition Economies', *The Quarterly Journal of Economics*, 114, 4: 1153–92.

Gillan, S. L. and J. D. Martin (2002) 'Financial Engineering, Corporate Governance, and the Collapse of Enron', working paper, University of Delaware Weinberg Center for Corporate Governance and Baylor University.

—— and L. T. Starks (1998) 'A Survey of Shareholder Activism: Motivation and Empirical Evidence', *Contemporary Finance Digest*, 2, 3: 10–34.

—— and —— (2000) 'Corporate Governance Proposals and Shareholder Activism: The Role of Institutional Investors', *Journal of Financial Economics*, 57, 2: 275–305.

Gorton, G. and M. Kahl (1999) 'Blockholder Identity, Equity Ownership Structure and Hostile Takeovers', NBER working paper 7123, Cambridge, MA: NBER.

Grossman, S. and O. Hart (1980) 'Takeover Bids, the Free Rider Problem, and the Theory of the Corporation', *Bell Journal of Economics*, 11: 42–64.

Hartzell, J. C. and L. T. Starks (2003) 'Institutional Investors and Executive Compensation', *Journal of Finance*, forthcoming.

Hirschman, A. (1971) *Exit, Voice and Loyalty: Responses to Decline in Firms, Organizations, and States*, Cambridge, MA: Harvard University Press.

Holmstrom, B. and J. Tirole (1993) 'Market Liquidity and Performance Monitoring', *Journal of Political Economy*, 101: 678–709.

Huddart, S. (1993) 'The Effect of a Large Shareholder on Corporate Value', *Management Science*, 39: 1407–21.

Iglesias-Palau, A. (2000) 'Pension Reform and Corporate Governance: Impact in Chile', *ABANTE*, 3: 109–41.

Jensen, M. C. (1993) 'The Modern Industrial Revolution, Exit, and the Failure of Internal Control Systems', *Journal of Finance*, 48: 831–80.

—— and W. Meckling (1976) 'Theory of the Firm: Managerial Behavior, Agency Costs, and Capital Structure', *Journal of Financial Economics*, 3: 305–60.

Kahn, C. and A. Winton (1998) 'Ownership Structure, Speculation, and Shareholder Intervention, *Journal of Finance*, 53: 99–129.

Kang, J. K. and A. Shivdasani (1995) 'Firm Performance, Corporate Governance, and Top Executive Turnover in Japan', *Journal of Financial Economics*, 38, 1: 29–59.

—— and R. Stulz (2000) 'Do Banking Shocks Affect Firm Performance? An Analysis of the Japanese Experience', *Journal of Business*, 73: 1–23.

Kaplan, S. and B. Minton (1994) 'Appointments of Outsiders to Japanese Boards: Determinants and Implications for Managers', *Journal of Financial Economics*, 36: 225–58.

Karpoff, J. (1998) 'The Impact of Shareholder Activism on Target Companies: A Survey of Empirical Findings', working paper, University of Washington.

Khanna, T. (2000) 'Business Groups and Social Welfare in Emerging Markets: Existing Evidence and Unanswered Questions', *European Economic Review*, 44: 748–61.

Klapper, L. F. and I. Love (2002) 'Corporate Governance, Investor Protection, and Performance in Emerging Markets', working paper 2818, Washington, DC: World Bank.

La Porta, R., F. Lopez-de-Silanes and A. Shleifer (1998) 'Corporate Ownership Around the World', *Journal of Finance*, 54, 2: 471–517.

—— —— and R. Vishny (1997) 'Legal Determinants of External Finance', *Journal of Finance*, 52: 1131–50.

Lefort, F. and E. Walker (2000a) 'Ownership and Capital Structures of Chilean Conglomerates: Facts and Hypotheses for Governance', *ABANTE*, 2: 3–27.

—— and —— (2000b) 'The Effects of Economic and Political Shocks on Corporate Governance Systems in Chile', *ABANTE*, 2: 183–206.

Lins, K. V. (2003) 'Equity Ownership and Firm Value in Emerging Markets', *Journal of Financial and Quantitative Analysis*, forthcoming.

Majluf, N., N. Abarca, D. Rodriguez and L. Fuentes (1998) 'Governance and Ownership Structure in Chilean Economic Groups', *ABANTE, Estudios en Direccion de Empresas*, 1: 111–39.

Mallin, C. (1995) 'Voting and Institutional Investors', *Accountancy* (London), 116, 1225 (September): 76.

Martin, J. D. and J. W. Kensinger (1996) 'Relationship Investing: Active Institutional Investors Want from Management', monograph, Financial Executives Research Foundation, Inc., New Jersey.

Mathieson, D. J. and G. J. Schinasi, (2001) 'International Capital Markets Developments, Prospects, and Key Policy Issues', World Economic and Financial Surveys, Washington, DC: IMF.

Maug, E. (1998) 'Large Shareholders as Monitors: Is There a Trade-off between Liquidity and Control?', *Journal of Finance*, 53: 65–98.

Mitton, T. (2002) 'A Cross-firm Analysis of the Impact of Corporate Governance on the East Asian Financial Crisis', *Journal of Financial Economics*, 64: 214–41.

Monks, R. (1995) 'Corporate Governance and Pension Plans: If One Cannot Sell, One Must Care', unpublished manuscript, Washington, DC.

Morck, R. and M. Nakamura (1999) 'Banks and Corporate Control in Japan', *Journal of Finance*, 54: 319–39.

Murphy, K. and K. Van Nuys (1994) 'State Pension Funds and Shareholder Inactivism', working Paper, Harvard University.

Myerson, A. (1993) 'Wall Street, the New Activism at Fidelity', *New York Times*, 8 August, Section 3: 15.

Noe, T. (2002) 'Institutional Activism and Financial Market Structure', *Review of Financial Studies*, 15: 289–319.

Parker, M. (1989) 'It's Almost Spring, and That Means Proxy Fever', *New York Times*, 5 March, Section 3: 8.

Parrino, R., R. W. Sias and L. T. Starks (2003) 'Voting with Their Feet: Institutional Investors and CEO Turnover', *Journal of Financial Economics*, 68, 1.

Pensions and Investments (1993) 'The Value of Activism', 22 February: 12.

Pound, J. (1988) 'Proxy Contests and the Efficiency of Shareholder Oversight', *Journal of Financial Economics*, 20: 237–65.

Prowse, S. (1990) 'Institutional Investment Patterns and Corporate Financial Behavior in the United States and Japan', *Journal of Financial Economics*, 27: 43–66.

Qi, D., W. Wu and H. Zhang (2000) 'Shareholding Structure and Corporate Performance of Partially Privatized Firms: Evidence from Listed Chinese Companies, *Pacific-Basin Finance Journal*, 8, 5: 587–610.

Roe, M. (1990) 'Political and Legal Restraints on Ownership and Control of Public Companies', *Journal of Financial Economics*, 27: 7–41.

Romano, R. (1993) 'Public Pension Fund Activism in Corporate Governance Reconsidered', *Columbia Law Review*, 93: 795–853.

Shleifer, A. and R. Vishny (1986) 'Large Shareholders and Corporate Control', *Journal of Political Economy*, 94: 461–88.

—— and —— (1997) 'A Survey of Corporate Governance', *Journal of Finance*, 52: 737–75.

Starks, L. (2000) 'Corporate Governance and Institutional Investors: Implications for Latin America', *ABANTE*, 2: 161–81.

Stulz, R. (1999) 'International Portfolio Flows and Security Markets', working paper, Ohio State University.

Tian, L. (2001) 'State Shareholding and the Value of China's Firms', working paper, London Business School.

Useem, M., E. Bowman, J. Myatt and C. Irvine (1993) 'US Institutional Investors Look at Corporate Governance in the 1990's', *European Management Journal*, 11, 2: 175–89.

Valadares, S. and R. Leal (2000) 'Ownership and Control Structure of Brazilian Companies', *ABANTE*, 3: 29–56.

Wahal, S. and J. McConnell (2000) 'Do Institutional Investors Exacerbate Managerial Myopia?', *Journal of Corporate Finance*, 6, 3: 307–29.

Woidtke, T. (2002) 'Agents Watching Agents? Evidence from Pension Fund Ownership and Firm Value', *Journal of Financial Economics*, 63, 1: 99–131.

Xu, X. and Y. Wang (1999) 'Ownership Structure and Corporate Governance in Chinese Stock Companies', *China Economic Review*, 10, 1: 75–98.

Zingales, L. (1998) 'Corporate Governance', *The New Palgrave Dictionary of Economics and the Law*, London and New York: Palgrave Macmillan.

3
New Institutional Arrangements for Product Innovation in Silicon Valley

Hirokazu Takizawa

Introduction

Silicon Valley has long been successful in bringing a lot of outstanding entrepreneurial firms into existence, including high-tech firms such as Hewlett-Packard, National Semiconductor, Intel, Advanced Micro Devices, Apple, Sun Microsystems, Silicon Graphics, Oracle, 3Com and Cisco Systems. More recently leading firms in Internet/web services, such as Netscape, Yahoo and e-Bay, have been funded and nurtured in Silicon Valley. Compared with other high-tech industrial districts such as Cambridge in the UK, Silicon Valley is undoubtedly the forerunner in product system innovation.[1]

The recent dot com bubble and crash seem to have reduced the previous enthusiasm for Silicon Valley. It should be noted, however, that the mechanism for product system innovation in Silicon Valley had shown its effectiveness well before those events, and the crash just returned things to the way they had been before. The mechanism still invites serious interest from policy makers around the world who want to create a mechanism for nurturing entrepreneurial firms, and thus it deserves to be elucidated. What is the mechanism that makes Silicon Valley a major driving force in product system innovation, especially in the information and communications industry? Is it fully understandable within the framework of traditional economic theories? What lessons can we draw from it for other industries/localities? The purposes of this chapter are to analyze the working of this mechanism and to explore the implications deduced from the analysis. This chapter does not constitute a wholly new contribution, but draws a more complete picture of the mechanism and its implications, based mainly on the work by Baldwin and Clark (2000), Aoki (2001) and Kaplan and Strömberg (2002).

The institutional arrangement for product system innovation in Silicon Valley has several characteristics that go beyond traditional economic principles. First, venture capital contracts in Silicon Valley are characterized by complicated patterns in the allocation of control rights among entrepreneurs and venture capitalists. This is in contrast with the conventional wisdom that the exclusive control right that comes with ownership is the premise for proper functioning of the market economy. Second, the informational arrangement in Silicon Valley is unique in that there are substantial degrees of decentralized information sharing among competing entrepreneurial firms on the one hand, and information hiding (encapsulation) on the other (Saxenian, 1994). Understanding these ostensibly contradictory phenomena seems to be the key to understanding the Silicon Valley model. Third, the nature of product system innovation in Silicon Valley is now sparking serious interest in the part played by the patent/copyright system in innovation. It has come to be recognized that, while incumbent firms lobby for a strengthening of the current intellectual property rights, this could reduce new innovators' incentive to innovate. Although many ideas remain debatable, the allocation and perfect enforcement of exclusive property rights over them may not necessarily ensure the social efficiency of economic activities.

The chapter is organized as follows. It first presents the background facts on the mechanism for product system innovation in Silicon Valley, and then focuses on the venture capital contracts that govern the relationship between entrepreneurs and venture capitalists. A close look at real-world venture capital contracts reveals a complex allocation of various rights between entrepreneurs and venture capitalists. The chapter then goes on to explore another important aspect of the Silicon Valley model: modularity in the architecture of product systems. Based on Baldwin and Clark (2000), this section explores the non-incentive aspects of modular architecture and argues that modular architecture is complementary to the organizational arrangement found in Silicon Valley – the unique mixture of information sharing and information encapsulation. The final focus is on the incentive to innovate in modular environments.

The Silicon Valley model

The strikingly innovative nature of Silicon Valley is best exemplified by the computer industry. Between its birth in the 1940s and the mid 1970s the computer market was virtually dominated by IBM. However in the mid 1970s a group of entrepreneurial firms, mostly small or of medium size and funded by venture capitalists, were set up and immersed themselves in R&D activities. A common feature among these firms was that they usually specialized in the development and production of modular components of a product system, instead of competing with IBM by producing a stand-alone product system. Thus many sub-industries were formed within the domain of the traditional computer industry. Various R&D activities previously conducted by IBM came to be conducted independently by small entrepreneurial firms. Although the main product of the industry has since shifted from mainframe to minicomputer, personal computer and network computing, the decentralized structure that emerged in the 1970s still persists.

Along with these changes in the industrial organization of the computer industry came new product system innovations. Today new product systems are formed by selecting and combining modular component products developed by entrepreneurial firms. In this sense we could say that a novel and unique economic institution has emerged in the domain of product system innovation. Aoki (2001) calls the theoretical conceptualization of this mechanism the 'Silicon Valley model' after the place that embodies the mechanism.[2]

In Silicon Valley there are networks of people and institutes to help start-up firms, including universities, research institutes, specialized suppliers, lawyers, accountants, head-hunters and venture capitalists. These actors play an important part in nurturing start-up firms by providing a smooth environment for product system innovation. However at the heart of the entrepreneurial process in Silicon Valley is the relationship between entrepreneurs, who have promising ideas but lack the money to develop them, and venture capitalists, who seek promising investment projects.[3]

When an entrepreneur comes up with a new idea it is highly uncertain whether it can create any value in the market. A venture capitalist, faced with the would-be entrepreneur, judges the idea's marketability based on a consideration of the entrepreneur's personality, talent, the originality of the idea, recent trends in technology and so on. Thus the venture capitalist plays a screening role, where the processing of tacit knowledge is especially important. The relationship between entrepreneur and venture capitalist begins when the venture capitalist judges the idea to be promising. It should be noted that a venture capitalist often funds a number of entrepreneurs in the same niche market, which results in a tournament-like situation among the entrepreneurs. If the project turns out to be successful, the entrepreneurial firm will either go public or be acquired by a leading firm, bringing the entrepreneur and the venture capitalist huge rewards. At this stage most of the tacit knowledge on the business of the firm is turned into codified knowledge that is accessible to the public. Thus the process of venture capital financing is, simply put, that of transforming tacit knowledge into codified knowledge.[4]

The part played by venture capitalists *vis-à-vis* entrepreneurs in this process is not confined to funding and they usually provide a wide range of services. First, they play an important part in the governance of the firms they fund, which are mainly structured by a venture capital contract. At the time of start-up, venture capitalists usually provide only a fraction of the capital needed to complete the project (called 'seed money'), with additional financing being made available in stages, contingent upon the project proceeding smoothly. This is what Sahlman (1990) calls staged capital commitment. This arrangement enables venture capitalists to refuse additional financing if the project proves to be unpromising, while entrepreneurs can increase their ownership share if certain performance objectives are met. Venture capitalists are well represented on the boards of directors of start-up firms and play a conventional role in structuring their governance, often firing the founder-manager if needed. It is not at all rare for founder-managers to lose their managerial position.

Second, venture capitalists provide a wide range of advisory and consulting services to the senior managers of start-up firms, help to raise additional funds, review and assist with strategic planning, recruit financial and human resource managers, introduce potential customers and suppliers, and provide public relations and legal specialists. The commitment of venture capitalists can be so deep and wide-ranging that their contribution is sometimes regarded as essential to a company's success.[5]

Third, and related to the second, venture capitalists provide entrepreneurs with the most recent technological information. Venture capitalists are often successful entrepreneurs themselves and have enough technological expertise to provide such a service. Since speed is important for their business, the informal exchange of technological information that is not yet available to the public is often crucial. The agglomeration of universities, research institutes and specialized suppliers in Silicon Valley provides venture capitalists and entrepreneurs with a great advantage in this regard.

Recent start-up firms tend to become targets of acquisition by leading firms, which are often grown-up entrepreneurial firms that have been successful in assuming leadership of their niche markets. The purpose of acquisition is usually either to remove a potential challenger or to strengthen the market position by shortening the period of in-house R&D through A&D (acquisition and development). Acquiring firms also seek to bundle complementary technologies in order to create a new product market.

This practice is strongly connected to the nature of technological development in the information and communication industries. Since the advent of IBM's System/360, new generations of computers have been defined by a definite platform or architecture, which has enabled various niche markets to be formed within the traditional computer industry. For the acquisition mechanism to work well, it is important for each platform to have open and standardized interfaces among modular component products, through which firms engaged in component production can coordinate their designs. Nowadays firms often try to propose new interfaces based on the current architecture/platform, leading to increased uncertainty in technology. Hence there is a strong need for information sharing, which is realized by means of decentralized information exchanges between entrepreneurs and venture capitalists. However most of the detailed information on the development of modular products is encapsulated and/or hidden within the firms concerned. This is the unique mixture of decentralized information sharing and information encapsulation that Saxenian (1994) regards as the key to understanding the innovative nature of Silicon Valley firms.

In earlier times standardized interfaces were defined and controlled by a single dominant firm, such as IBM. Nowadays, however, there are fierce struggles among several leading firms for leadership in standard setting. This is because a market for a new product can now be formed by adding a new modular component to the existing product system, by bundling existing modular components or by unbundling an existing modular component. Standardized interfaces are thus formed evolutionarily in the interaction between firms, large and small. In this process too, venture capitalists play an important role by dispersing necessary information among the entrepreneurial firms.

The governance of Silicon Valley firms through venture capital contracts

With regard to how entrepreneurial firms in Silicon Valley are governed, a recent work by Kaplan and Strömberg (2002) provides stylized facts and analyses on venture capital contracts based on a sample of 213 venture capital investments in 119 portfolio companies by 14 venture capital partnerships. About 42 per cent of the portfolio companies in their sample are in the information technology and software industries, while 13 per cent are in telecommunications.

These stylized facts can be summarized as follows:[6]

1. Venture capital contracts separately allocate cash-flow rights, voting rights, board rights, liquidation rights and other control rights.
2. Venture capitalists use various securities to fine-tune these rights. Convertible preferred stock is most frequently used. Even when common stock is used, venture capitalists obtain a different class of common stock with different rights from those of the entrepreneurs.
3. Cash-flow rights, voting rights, control rights and future financing are often contingent on observable measures of financial and non-financial performance.
4. If the firm performs poorly the venture capitalists obtain full control. If the firm's performance improves, the entrepreneur retains/obtains more control rights. If the firm performs very well, the venture capitalists relinquish most of their control rights and retain only cash flow rights.
5. Venture capital contracts usually include non-compete and vesting provisions in order to make it more expensive for the entrepreneur to leave the firm. The vesting provision dictates that the entrepreneur's shares vest over time, while the non-compete provision prohibits the entrepreneur from working for another firm in the same industry for a certain period of time.
6. In general, venture capitalists have more control in later rounds of financing.

It is worth noting that while cash-flow rights, board rights, voting rights, liquidation rights and other control rights are allocated separately as independent instruments, these arrangements seem to be far more complex than the conventional wisdom of property rights suggests. An investment project here can be regarded as jointly owned by an entrepreneur and a set of venture capitalists, and the control rights shift between them as the project proceeds and its performance varies.

Kaplan and Strömberg (2002) use their survey data to test the validity of recent financial contracting theories and conclude that the theories are doing a fairly good job, although real-world financial contracting is far more complex than predicted by the theories. The model by Aghion and Bolton (1992) seems better able to capture the real-world situation faced by entrepreneurs and venture capitalists: a would-be entrepreneur has a promising project idea but lacks sufficient wealth, while a venture capitalist seeks a promising investment project. The venture capitalist has a strong incentive to maximize the project's value and is less concerned with the private benefits of control, while the entrepreneur may privately benefit from controlling the firm. There is a fundamental need to draw up an elaborate contract to align their diverse incentives.[7]

Another dimension that can be added to the discussion is the perspective suggested by Rajan and Zingales (2000). Traditional firms, which have been extensively studied in the corporate governance literature, typically owned and controlled a large quantity of highly specialized inanimate assets, such as plant, machinery and well-known brand names. Since these assets were hard to replicate and thus were unique, they defined the boundary of the firm in both legal and economic terms. Human capital was closely tied to these assets and was immobile. The ownership of unique inanimate assets was a primary source of power in the corporation.

Recent trends however, show that, the nature of the firm is changing. In many leading industries, inanimate assets are becoming less and less important, while easily appropriated assets such as information and human capital are becoming increasingly important. In the new types of enterprise the ownership of inanimate assets can no longer be used as a lever to exert power over employees, so a new governance mechanism is required. Rajan and Zingales argue that it is important to identify the critical resource of the firm, and to induce employees to make a firm-specific investment by giving them privileged access to that resource.[8]

The typical entrepreneurial firm in Silicon Valley seems to fit well with Rajan and Zingales' characteristics of the new enterprise. In most venture capital contract settings, inanimate assets are unimportant in comparison with those in traditional firms, whereas the founder's project idea is the critical resource of the firm, or at least in the start-up stage. Thus it is important to tie the entrepreneur to the firm, but allowing the entrepreneur to accumulate too much power is dangerous from the financing point of view. The complicated nature of this requires very complicated financial contracting. On the one hand, stock options that vest over time are used to tie the entrepreneur to the firm. On the other hand a contingent shift in control rights is included in the contract to make sure that the management of the firm is professionalized. The fact that venture capitalists have more control in later rounds of financing can also be explained from this perspective. When the project is nearing completion, the decision about the timing of going public or selling the firm to a larger firm is critical for maximizing value and requires the professionalism of the venture capitalist. Note that here the ownership of the firm is utilized less for having residual control rights over plant assets, but more offers an incentive that motivates the entrepreneur.

Since more than 50 per cent of the firms in Kaplan and Strömberg's (2002) sample are concentrated in the information and communication industries, one might doubt the relevance of the above insight to developing countries. However the general lessons drawn from the analyses can be useful even for emerging markets. First, our discussion deals with the situation in which a wealth-constrained entrepreneur with a promising project idea seeks funding by an investor. This is ubiquitous even in developing countries. Second, some countries may have laws that do not accommodate aspects of venture capital contracts. Indeed US laws seem to be more flexible in respect of devising a complex and subtle incentive design than are Japanese commercial laws. To the extent that venture capital contracts in the United States are successful, other countries could learn from them and improve their legal environment.

The power of modularity

Modular architecture

Another important aspect of the Silicon Valley model is that most innovation occurs within the framework set by the modular architecture of a product system. Modularity has been particularly effective in the information and communication industries, however its broader implications have been explored since the 1990s, and the insights into the modular environment may be useful to industries other than information and communications.

Simply put, a module is a quasi-autonomous subsystem that consists of a complicated system or process combined with similar subsystems. The way in which these subsystems are combined is often referred to as a connective rule or interface rule. Modularization involves decomposing a complex system or process into modules that can be designed independently. The best example is a computer system, which is composed of a CPU, an LC monitor, a hard disk drive, an OS and so on. Almost all communication systems are modularized because they are usually a combination of component technologies.

It was probably Herbert Simon who first pointed out the importance of the concept of modularization, although he did not use exactly the same term (Simon, 1962). He used the construction of a watch to illustrate a generic principle to cope with complexity. Suppose that two watchmakers combine 100 parts to make a watch. Their work may be interrupted by such things as phone calls. One watchmaker combines the 100 parts in a straight run, whereas the other starts by making intermediate parts, each of which is composed of 10 parts, and then completes the job by combining the 10 intermediate parts. The production system of the latter watchmaker is certainly more efficient than that of the former when random events disturb the continuity of work process. Obviously in this example each intermediate part can be regarded as a module. As this example illustrates, modularization is the mechanism with which boundedly rational humans cope with the complexity of a product system.

This naturally leads to the question: why the renewed interest in modularity? Perhaps the main reason is that we have only recently come to produce and consume very complex systems on a large scale. Furthermore each of the modules that constitute a complex system has itself become increasingly complex. Second, as the power of modularity has come to be widely recognized, firms have adapted themselves to the new business environment that modularization entails.

In a context that is most relevant to us, Baldwin and Clark (2000) provide an operational definition of 'modularization in design' and examine the detailed process of designing an artefact. They define the design of an artefact as a complete description of the artefact, which can be broken down into smaller units called design parameters. For example the design of a cup has to specify such parameters as material, colour, height, weight, diameter, whether or not it has a cap, the diameter of the cap if it has a cap, and so on. Usually there are intricate interdependencies among these parameters. In the above example, the diameter of a cap has to be specified only when the design designates that the cup is to have a cap (hierarchical dependency). When the cup has a cap, the diameter of the cup and that of the cap must be consistent with each other (lateral dependency). The combination of the dependencies is called a design structure.

Dependency between two design parameters implies that some coordination is necessary between those who determine the parameters. Thus in general a design structure with complicated dependencies will make the cost of coordination expensive. Therefore it will pay to reduce the number of dependencies. According to Baldwin and Clark, it is possible to eliminate intricate dependencies among several parameters by setting a 'design rule' that simultaneously determines those parameters. Carrying out this process repeatedly results in a modular design, in which there are relatively independent blocks, but in each block there remain intricate dependencies among the design parameters. Across blocks, however, there are few if any dependencies. Thus each of these blocks may be regarded as a module.

Of course the process of modularization incurs costs. Baldwin and Clark illustrate this with a case study of IBM's System/360, which they identify as the first platform with a modular design. It is very difficult to foresee and enumerate all dependencies *ex ante*. Thus carrying out modularization is a costly investment, but this is sunk once the modular design is set. The modular structure of a product system can be reused across generations of the system. A platform or architecture is an invariant property of the product system, which can be described as a combination of modular structures and interfaces among modules. With a fixed platform, new modular components are successively brought forth, resulting in generations of the product system.

As the above discussion suggests, the main purpose of modularizing a design is to rationalize the design process for a complex product system so as to reduce the coordination costs and be able to reuse the modular architecture over generations of products. This was certainly the case with IBM's System/360. However modularization brings other benefits as well, to which we shall now turn.

Option value

Modularization offers the following benefits. First, it enables the design tasks for modular parts to be conducted in parallel, that is, concurrent engineering is possible (Brooks, 1995). Second, it enables designers to concentrate on their own modular part without having to pay much attention to what is happening with the other parts. In addition to these benefits, there is the benefit of being able to aggregate small improvements in each module, rather than adopting a completely new product system each time. In one of the most important contributions to the theory of modularization, Baldwin and Clark (2000) analyze this benefit of modularization by regarding the results of R&D activity as 'real options'.

Suppose that an organization is engaged in R&D of a product system as a whole, the value of which is expressed by a stochastic variable, X. Suppose that $X \sim N(0, \sigma^2)$, where zero is interpreted as the default value of the current product system. The expected value of the R&D activity in the current period may be lower or higher than the default value. However the result of the R&D in the current period will be adopted if and only if its expected value is higher than the default value. Thus the expected value of the product system at the end of the current period is:

$$E(X_+) = \int_0^\infty x\phi(x)dx = \frac{\sigma}{\sqrt{2\pi}} \qquad (3.1)$$

where $X_+ = \max(0,X)$ and ϕ denotes the probability distribution function of $N(0, \sigma^2)$.

Next suppose that the product system is now divided into n modular parts, and at any moment before the adoption of the R&D result the value of the whole system is the sum of the values of those modular parts.[9] Let the result of the R&D on the ith module be denoted by X^i and, to make the comparison easier, assume that $X^i \sim N(0, \sigma^2/n)$. That is, $X = X^1 + X^2 + \ldots + X^n$. Again, the result of the R&D on each module will be adopted if and only if it is higher than the default value. The expected value of the ith module at the end of the period is thus $E(X^i_+)$. Then it follows that for $n > 1$

$$E(X^1_+) + \ldots + E(X^n_+) = \frac{\sqrt{n}\sigma}{\sqrt{2\pi}} > E(X_+) \qquad (3.2)$$

This implies that the expected value of a modularized product system is higher than that of a non-modularized product system. Observing that the left-hand side of the above inequality increases in proportion to the square root of n, it is easy to see that the finer the partitioning of a product system, the higher the expected value of the new system. This is what Baldwin and Clark call the 'splitting operator' effect.

Coordination cost reduction

In Baldwin and Clark's (2000) account of modularization it is presumed that setting a design rule automatically eliminates interdependencies and thus reduces the coordination costs. Then, in view of the other benefits of modularization, the finest possible partition will result in any modular design. However this is hardly the case in reality, so it is necessary to examine a more general, not necessarily modularized, setting and analyze what modularization brings to a design organization.

The first attempt to extend Baldwin and Clark's model was made by Schaefer (1999), who identifies specialization as a benefit of partitioning a design organization (the second benefit in the previous subsection), unlike Baldwin and Clark. With regard to cost, he assumes that the statistical correlation between the results of R&D on two design parameters will be lower if these design tasks are allocated to different teams in a design organization. Thus as the partition becomes finer, the statistical correlation of R&D activities becomes lower, and the expected value of the whole product system will be lower since the value function of the whole product system is assumed to be supermodular in the values of the respective designs.[10]

On the other hand Takizawa (2002) states that the benefit of partitioning an organization is that it brings many smaller real options, following Baldwin and Clark, while the cost of partitioning arises from the increased incidence of interteam coordination under finer partitioning. It is interesting that, although their models are different, both Schaefer (1999) and Takizawa (2002) obtained almost the same comparative static results. Here I shall present the intuitions underlying my model.

Consider an organization that is engaged in the design of a product system. Suppose that the design is not necessarily modular, so there may be intricate interdependencies among its design parameters. Given a design structure, consider the problem of partitioning the set of design parameters and allocating elements of the partition (subsets of the set of all the design parameters) to different teams. Suppose that there is dependency between two design parameters and that some coordination is necessary between them. It would be natural to assume that the cost of coordination will be higher when the two interdependent parameters are allocated to different teams than when they are handled by the same team. Thus having a finer partition increases the incidence of interteam coordination and the total coordination cost will increase. On the other hand it is assumed that each team is a decision-making unit in respect of the adoption of a new design. Under this assumption, having a finer partition means having a larger number of smaller options, and is therefore beneficial.

By using the comparative static technique developed by Topkis (1998) it can be shown that the optimal partition becomes finer when the cost of interteam coordination becomes lower, the cost of intrateam coordination becomes higher and the degree of uncertainty in the results of R&D becomes higher. These results confirm those obtained by Schaefer (1999). Further analysis can be conducted by endogenizing the cost of interteam coordination. Members of the same team are likely to have frequent face-to-face contact, but interteam coordination will require such communication devices as faxes, phones, and the Internet. It can be supposed that the design organization will try to lower the cost of interteam coordination by installing these devices, so lower-cost interteam coordination corresponds to a higher level of information and communication technology investment. It can be shown that higher-cost interteam coordination, lower-cost intrateam coordination and coarser partitioning are complementary to one another in the design organization's objective function.[11] Therefore if the cost of intrateam coordination is low the organization will tend to rely more on intrateam coordination, and as a result will have a coarser partition, which will in turn lead to higher-cost interteam coordination, that is, lower information and communication technology investment. Conversely if the cost of intrateam coordination is high, the organization will increase its information and communication technology investment and choose a finer partition.

Recall that this analysis relates to a very general design structure and therefore does not address the situation in which the design of the product system is modularized, in the sense outlined by Baldwin and Clark (2000). However it does have some implication for the effect of modularization on the design organization. Specifically, it can be shown that modularization sets an upper bound for the coarseness of the optimal partition. In this sense modularization works to make the partitioning of a design organization finer. Since finer partitioning is complementary to lower-cost interteam coordination, this implies that modularization induces greater investment in information and communication technology.

Admittedly the situation analyzed by Schaefer (1999) and Takizawa (2002) is an optimization problem faced by a single organization. However we can suppose that the problem is being faced by a quasi-organization that comprises multiple firms, and that each team in the model represents an independent firm.[12] Then the result of the analysis can be interpreted as follows. Given the design structure of a product system, the size of each firm will be smaller if the cost of interfirm coordination becomes lower, the cost of intrafirm coordination becomes higher and the degree of uncertainty in development becomes higher. This prediction coincides with the finding by Brynjolfsson *et al.* (1994) that information and communication technology investment has led to smaller firm size in the United States.

This finding is also instrumental in understanding Saxenian's (1994) interesting comparison of industrial firms in Silicon Valley and Route 128. She observes that Silicon Valley firms are characterized by high worker mobility, frequent communication and a substantial degree of information sharing among firms, in marked contrast to Route 128 firms. Hence it is natural to assume that the cost of interfirm coordination is substantially lower in Silicon Valley than in Route 128. Combined with the above analysis, this may explain why there are a large number of small independent firms in Silicon Valley, while large integrated firms dominate in Route 128.

That higher-cost interteam coordination, lower-cost intrateam coordination and coarser partitioning are complementary to one another has another interesting implication. By adopting modular designs the information and communication industries have developed at an amazing pace, possibly through increased option values. This has resulted in huge increases in the value of product systems in these industries as well as lower information and communication technology investment, which in turn might have induced a finer partitioning of product systems or smaller firm size in other industries.

Parallel experiments

When the design of a product system is modularized over a quasi-organization and the interfaces among modular parts are put to tender, multiple firms may be engaged in each modular product, competing with one another in development. Baldwin and Clark (2000) model this situation as one in which $n(>1)$ independent stochastic trials are held in parallel for each modular product, and the result with the highest value, if it is higher than the default value, is adopted. Mathematically the value created in this process is the expected value of the first order statistics of a sample with size n, and of course increases in n. They call the value thus created the 'substituting operator' effect, and show that it can create a large value when combined with the 'splitting operator' effect.

It seems more natural, however, to regard the above situation as one in which a set of tournament games are being held and each of the firms involved with the same modular component are competing with one another. We shall consider such a model later.

The informational arrangement for modularity

Baldwin and Clark's (2000) argument for the power of modularity prompts several questions. First, one wonders how the arrangement for product system innovation emerged and evolved in Silicon Valley. Baldwin and Clark identify IBM's System/360 as the first conscious application of the concept of modularity. Three IBM engineers – Gene Amdahl, Gerrit Blaauw and Fred Brooks – marshalled the whole process of modularization, and while this took time and incurred substantial costs the System/360 platform brought IBM enormous success. IBM managed to retain control over the system for generations of new products. However it eventually had to relinquish control over its modular products, especially in the software and peripherals sector, because of the US government's antitrust policy (Bresnahan, 1999). Later it even had to concede control over its PC platform to companies such as Intel and Microsoft. Thus the mechanism is formed and reproduced by a complicated interplay among several competing firms. We shall return to this in the next section.

Second, although modularity in design, as defined by Baldwin and Clark, is *prima facie* a technological matter, it could have a profound impact on economic institutions, especially in respect of the organization of firms. This section explores this question, especially from the information-systemic viewpoint. It is easy to see that the modularization of a product system would have an impact on the way in which information flows in the design organization; a modular design will enable information flows in the design process to be hierarchical as well as encapsulated. Suppose there are two design parameters, a and b, and that these are interdependent. Designers who work on these design parameters will have to exchange information on shocks arising in their own tasks. However if a design rule is set that determines both design tasks, it is possible to make an informational arrangement in which these designers only have access to the relevant design rule and do not laterally exchange information.

What information arrangement would be the fittest for the modular architecture of a product system? Aoki (2001) and Aoki and Takizawa (2002) analyzed this problem by using Marschak and Radner's (1972) team-theoretic framework, in which all team members are assumed to have a common payoff function, that is, the incentive problems are abstracted away. Suppose that a generic R&D organization – composed of a development manager, M, and two design teams, T_i ($i = a, b$) – is engaged in the development of a product system. M is responsible for formulating a development strategy, allocating R&D funds and so on, while the two T_i's are respectively engaged in the R&D for components a and b. They coordinate their activities so as to maximize the value of the product system in uncertain environments. The environments affecting their activities are segmented as follows:

1. A systemic segment, E_s, that affects the activities of all members (M and the T_i's).
2. Engineering segments that affect the activities of the T_i's, which are further divided into the following segments.

2a. An engineering environment, E_e that affects both T_i's.
2b. An idiosyncratic engineering environment, E_i ($i = a, b$), that affects each T_i individually.

The members of the organization observe stochastic parameters arising in these environments with some error, and adjust their activity accordingly. Obviously there will be various patterns, depending on who observes what information and who share the observation.[13] Different patterns of information sharing generate different types of R&D organization that exhibit different informational efficiency in different sets of parameters. The types of R&D organization identified by Aoki and Takizawa (2002) are as follows.

Hierarchical R&D organization

In this type of R&D organization M is an R&D manager of an integrated firm, while the T_i's are project teams in the firm. Inserted between them is an intermediating agent, say a systems engineer, denoted by IM. M is specialized in observing the stochastic parameter, γ_s, arising in E_s and transmitting the observation of γ_s, denoted by ξ_s, to the T_i's through IM. IM is engaged in observing the stochastic parameter, γ_e arising in E_e, the observation of which, ξ_e, is communicated to the T_i's. The T_i's observe γ_i's arising in their own idiosyncratic engineering environments. The observation of γ_i is denoted by ξ_i. Thus M chooses his or her activity level based upon ξ_s, while the choice variables of the T_i's depend on $\xi_s + \epsilon_{si}, \xi_e + \epsilon_{ei}$, and ξ_i, where ϵ_{si} and ϵ_{ei} are the communication errors on the side of the T_i's. This type of R&D organization reflects the essential aspects of the R&D organization of a large, traditional, hierarchical firm, sometimes referred to as the 'waterfall' model (Klein and Rosenberg, 1986; Aoki and Rosenberg, 1989).

Interactive R&D organization

In this type of R&D organization M is an R&D manager and the T_i's are interactive development teams. All of them share information on the systemic environment through interaction and communication. The T_i's also share information on the systemic engineering environment, but they independently observe the stochastic parameter, γ_i, arising in their idiosyncratic environment. Thus M's activity level depends on ξ_s (common to M and the T_i's), while that of the T_i's depends on ξ_s, ξ_e (common to the T_i's), and ξ_i (idiosyncratic to each T_i). The characteristic of this type of R&D organization is that the assimilation of information is realized through the feedback of information across the various levels of the organization and between the teams on the same level. This type of R&D organization is sometimes referred to as the 'chain-linked' model of innovation (Klein and Rosenberg, 1986; Aoki and Rosenberg, 1989).

V-mediated information encapsulation

In this type of R&D organization, information on the systemic environment is shared among M and the T_i's, as in interactive R&D organization. However unlike in the latter situation the T_i's independently observe the systemic engineering environment and the idiosyncratic engineering environment. Thus the activity level chosen by M depends on ξ_s, while those of the T_i's depend upon ξ_s (common to M and the T_i's), ξ_e (common to all T_i's) and ξ_i (idiosyncratic to a T_i). There are two interpretations of this type of R&D organization: it can be interpreted as consisting of highly autonomous project teams within an integrated firm; or it can be interpreted as reflecting the unique mixture of decentralized information sharing and information encapsulation observed in the relationship between venture capitalists and entrepreneurs in Silicon Valley.

The objective function of the R&D organization comprises not only the stochastic parameters listed above, but also constant parameters that are related to the degree of complementarity among the activity levels of the members.[14] Suppose that, once the R&D organization has selected the prefered type of organization, the members coordinate their activity levels according to the second-best decision rules. Then different types of R&D organization are shown to be optimal in different sets of stochastic parameters and constant parameters. Within this framework, Aoki (2001) and Aoki and Takizawa (2002) show that, of the three types of R&D organization, V-mediated information encapsulation is the most efficient type if the idiosyncratic engineering environment is important (its variance is large) relative to the systemic engineering environment, and/or the complementarity between both project teams is low. This proposition has the following implications in the present context.

First, modularization partitions a complex product system into multiple modules so that the modules are relatively independent. Hence the way of partitioning cannot be arbitrary. Albeit in a somewhat different context, Crémer (1980) shows that an organization is optimally partitioned when the statistical correlation among the units created by the partitioning are minimized. This means, in the current context, that the whole design task should be divided into two tasks so that the systemic engineering environment is unimportant relative to the idiosyncratic engineering environment. Thus the viability of V-mediated information encapsulation, as observed in Silicon Valley, is enhanced by the 'good' modular architecture of a product system. Second, all the modules created through the process of partitioning have to be compatible with each other and work together in a smooth manner. In order to ensure such compatibility, the interfaces among the modules have to be clearly and explicitly determined in the process of modularization. Thus modularization enables the R&D on the respective modules to be conducted in parallel and to be later combined. This means that modularization reduces the technological complementarity between the two teams, which will generally exhibit some degree of complementarity. Therefore the standardization of interfaces also makes V-mediated information encapsulation a viable organizational arrangement.

On the other hand, as the complementarity between the two tasks is reduced, the value function will be almost additively separable, meaning that improvement of the entire product system stems from that of each modular product, rather than from the coordinated and simultaneous improvement of several modular products. This sets the technological basis for a product system to evolve by combining new modular products *ex post*. Thus the two aspects of modular architecture – partitioning a product system and standardizing the interfaces – are complementary to the mixture of decentralized information sharing and information encapsulation that is unique to the organizational arrangement in Silicon Valley.

This observation is also helpful in understanding why most of the successful firms in Silicon Valley are found in the information and communication industries. In fact the technological developments in the information and communication industries have been fostered by setting standards for various interfaces that arise in information and communication systems: IBM's System/360, IBM-PC compatibles, the Internet and so on. Once good architecture is set, innovations usually take place in individual modules, and architecture and interfaces change less frequently. In such an environment, complementarity between modular products and/or the degree of uncertainty in the systemic engineering environment will be reduced, which makes V-mediated information encapsulation more viable as an organizational arrangement.

The above argument also sets a general framework for understanding what is happening in the car industry. In general the design of cars is said to exhibit a strong complementarity between various task units. Hence, the interactive R&D organization will be the most efficient type of R&D

organization, as often observed in the Japanese car industry. Indeed many management scientists have reported that the design/production processes for cars necessarily require *'suriawase'* (tight coordination) across the various task units (Fujimoto, 1997). However the present landscape of the car industry around the world is somewhat intricate: while Japanese car manufactures are reluctant to adopt general-purpose modular parts, their European and American counterparts have opted to outsource modular parts. This may be evidence that technology is determined endogenously by the organizational conventions in each country's economic system. The above model assumes that technology determines the information system of R&D organization, but the different kinds of information-processing activity in different information systems may require corresponding skills. Hence the current distribution of relevant skills in a country may affect the adoption of technology.

Modularization and incentives

We examined earlier how a venture capital contract is structured to motivate an entrepreneur, who is not necessarily in a modular environment. The modularization of a product system adds a new dimension to the entrepreneur's incentive to innovate. However one of the most striking characteristics of modularization is its impact on the incentive to innovate, to which we now turn.

Open interfaces and competition

A modular design can create a new industrial arrangement in which a large number of firms are independently engaged in the development of modular parts for a product system – a phenomenon observed among entrepreneurial firms in Silicon Valley. As the example of IBM's System/360 illustrates, the standardization of interfaces among modules is not sufficient alone to attract new firms into the development of modules. The interfaces have to be somehow open to tender.[15]

We have already seen how Baldwin and Clark's (2000) 'substituting operator' captures the value-enhancing aspect of such an arrangement. However their model abstracts away incentive issues, which may be important in this situation. Formulating this situation as a 'VC tournament game', Aoki (2001) explicitly considers the incentive effect of this mechanism on the participants in cases where there are just two participants. Since only one of the two participants in the tournament can win the prize, this mechanism necessarily entails social costs in the duplication of R&D activities. Aoki shows that this mechanism can nonetheless create more value than the social cost because it can encourage a very large effort by the participants if the prize is sufficiently large and the ability of venture capitalists precisely to determine the winner is sufficiently high.

In Silicon Valley, winning entrepreneurs can expect a huge prize as their successful firms will either be put on the IPO markets or will be sold to a leading firm. Furthermore venture capitalists are specialized in relatively small technical segments and are very capable of evaluating a new technology. These facts suggest that entrepreneurs have sufficient incentives to participate in the tournament game in Silicon Valley and that the mechanism may be socially efficient. Aoki's analysis also provides us with an important insight: the presence of competent venture capitalists is essential if the mechanism for product system innovation in Silicon Valley is to be transplanted to other regions and/or industries.

Aoki and Takizawa (2002) have extended Aoki's model by endogenizing the number of tournament participants as a choice variable for a venture capitalist. Their model can also be seen as an extension of Baldwin and Clark's (2000) 'substituting operator' in that it captures the benefit of having multiple experiments for the same modular product. The findings are as follows:

1. An increase in the number of tournament participants will lower the incentive for each participant in equilibrium. On the other hand, with their effort levels given, the higher the number of participants, the more value is created. Thus the optimal number of participants is determined by the trade-off between these two countervailing factors.
2. An increase in marketing uncertainty will decrease the equilibrium effort level, while an increase in technical uncertainty increases the equilibrium effort level.[16]
3. A decrease in the cost of start-up financing for each project will increase the optimal number of tournament participants.

The above propositions have some interesting implications for the dot com bubble, in which most of the entrepreneurial firms concerned were engaged in e-commerce business. Although the dot com bubble and crash might have been caused primarily by erroneous expectations about profitability (Baldwin and Clark, 2001), the above observation indicates that the number of entrants into Internet/web services was very large because the start-up costs were low. This observation suggests that the large number of entrants might have adversely affected the incentive of entrepreneurs. Furthermore it is often said that the technology involved in these businesses was not strikingly innovative, and only new business models had to be contrived. Indeed most of the basic technologies used by e-commerce businesses and the Internet auction have long been known in experimental economics. Thus most e-commerce businesses had low technological uncertainty as well as high marketing uncertainty, which might have also adversely affected entrepreneurs' incentive.

Ex post evolutionary formation of a product system and the role of innovation commons

It is well known that IBM managed to retain control of its System/360 but had to concede its control of the PC platform to Intel and Microsoft, which resulted in the so-called 'Wintel' platform. Thus as a hitherto dominant firm lost its exclusive control over the direction of innovation, another possibility emerged in the form of the modularized product system. Modularized product systems could now continually evolve in a fairly complex manner. Firms that aimed to assume leadership tried to change the product system by proposing their own interfaces, out of which *the* interface was evolutionarily formed. Aoki (2001) coined the term '*ex post* evolutionary formation of a product system' to express an aspect of this complicated process, which is almost equivalent to what Bresnahan (1999) calls 'divided technological leadership' or 'vertical competition'.

Baldwin and Clark (2000: 228) identify the following modular operations, which can be applied to various points of a given product system:[17]

1. Splitting a module into multiple modules.
2. Substituting one module for another.
3. Augmenting the system by adding a module with new functions at a particular interface.
4. Excluding a module from the system.
5. Inverting a recurrent design element in several modules into an independent module.
6. Porting a module to another system.

It should be emphasized that a single firm no longer controls the whole process of innovation. The complexity of a product system often involves fierce competition for technological leadership. The modular architecture of a product system has ceased to be a well-defined static partitioning of the design tasks and there is fertile ground for the continuing evolution of the system, the process of which might gradually change the original architecture. Thus we could say that the current architecture of the product system is playing the role of 'innovation commons', where the opportunity to innovate and build upon the current platform is open to anyone (Lessig, 2002).

Lessig argues that any process of innovation can be regarded as a production function that produces a new idea, with old ideas and the innovator's human capital being inputs. This highlights that there are two countervailing powers acting on innovators' incentive to innovate. On the one hand the protection of intellectual property rights enhances innovators' incentive since it enables them to reap a reward. On the other hand, making intellectual property rights too stringent can damage new innovators' incentive because it makes it too costly to try a new idea. Hence, striking the right balance between these two factors is especially important. While making some resources freely available may seem to damage innovators' incentive, there are various ways to reap what they sow. Lessig's point is best illustrated by the Internet and IBM-PC compatibles, where various technologies have flourished through innovation commons. The existence of an innovation commons can, and actually has, encouraged more new innovators to innovate, resulting in rapid technological development but also increased uncertainty about the direction of innovation.

As already argued, modularization is conducive to open architecture or open interfaces. However the openness of an architecture or interface *per se* does not necessarily guarantee the existence of an innovation commons, because the firm with a patent on the current technology may file a lawsuit against others to prevent them from changing the technology. It was just such a process that made the IBM-PC architecture an innovation commons. In some cases, however, abandoning a proprietary strategy may enable an innovator to earn a higher profit, because the pie to be shared will be huge if his or her technology assumes the position of *de facto* standard and successfully meets consumers' needs (Kokuryo, 1999). Although many issues remain to be resolved, the commons argument tells us that fine-tuning various rights, as in a compulsory licence arrangement, may enhance social efficiency instead of simply strengthening intellectual property rights.

Conclusion

This chapter has examined the new arrangement of product system innovation from Silicon Valley. The main focus has been on the complex venture capital contracts that structure the governance of entrepreneurial firms, and the modular architecture of product systems. On the one hand it has been argued that a complex allocation of rights is utilized in venture capital contracts, and that this goes beyond the perspective of the traditional property rights framework. On the other hand the recent development of the information and communication industries has been largely due to the adoption of modular designs for product systems. Modularization has markedly increased the productivity of R&D efforts, created a new industrial structure where clusters of small firms are engaged in developing modular products, and opened the door to the evolutionary formation of product systems, often contributing to the creation of new product markets. In short, modularization has changed the way we do business wherever a product system has been modularized.

While this chapter has been mainly concerned with the information and communication industries in Silicon Valley its arguments are relevant to developing countries. First, since the situation in which capital-constrained entrepreneurs seek funding for their project ideas is ubiquitous, the analysis of real-world venture capital contracting provides a basis for the development of institutional environments in developing countries. Second, an increasing number of developing countries are now involved in the production of modular products. For example most of the production of hard disk drives had been transferred to South-East Asia by the late 1990s, although most of the design process still takes place in Silicon Valley. Knowledge transfers would have occurred with this shift of production, and understanding the nature of modular environments can be very important. Third, the dissemination of knowledge about the nature of product system innovation in Silicon Valley has sparked serious interest in the role of the patent/copyright system in innovation. It has come to be widely recognized that, while incumbent firms are lobbying for a strengthening of the current intellectual property rights, this could damage new innovators' incentive to innovate. Although much remains to be debated, it seems that when it comes to ideas the allocation and perfect enforcement of exclusive property rights over them may not necessarily guarantee the efficiency of an economic system.

The information and communication industries are still changing so rapidly that it is extremely difficult to extract the novel parts of the observed arrangements. In this sense, this chapter is just a cornerstone for the illumination of some aspects of the emerging arrangements. Of course a considerable number of issues remain to be explored. Two of the most pressing research needs are to advance the comparative industrial study of modularization, and to explore the applicability of modularization beyond the information and communication industries. Theoretical studies on property rights are also needed. As the analysis of venture capital contracts and the argument for innovation commons suggest, property rights are a bundle of various rights, the allocation of which can be designed more freely.

Notes

1 In what follows we refer to the goods or services that form a system (for example a computer or the various Internet/web services) as a 'product system'. As will be argued, product systems have a huge implication for economic activities and very complex product systems have today become objects of mass production/consumption.

2 Bresnahan (1999) also uses the term 'Silicon Valley model' to express the emerging mechanism of product systems. This is in contrast to the 'IBM model', in which an integrated firm completely controls a platform and has an exclusive role in the coordination of innovations. According to Bresnahan, 'In the "Silicon Valley" form, distinct technologies are advanced by a wide number of different firms. Interface standards, cross-company communication, and markets have been used when supply is by a group of vertically disintegrated specialty technology firms' (ibid.: 225).

3 In purely financial terms, venture capitalists are financial intermediaries who channel a large amount of capital from other financial institutions into entrepreneurial firms. Legally, venture capital funds involve two classes of partner: general and limited. General partners accept personal responsibility and legal liability for fund management, while limited partners provide most of the funds but are not involved in their management. Although funds are usually maintained only for a fixed period of time, venture capital companies are often formed by general partners to maintain managerial continuity. To be more precise, venture capitalists do not usually fund entrepreneurial firms in the early stage of their development; instead angel investors meet the need for small amounts of start-up capital. (See Mayer, 2001, for a discussion of how angel investors and venture capitalists differentiate their working fields.) However in Silicon Valley there is a very close relationship among angel investors, venture capital funds and venture capital companies. Hence I will not explicitly distinguish between them and will refer to them all simply as 'venture capitalists'.

4 In the process of transforming tacit knowledge into codified knowledge, relational financing is more effective than arm's-length financing. See Aoki (2001, ch. 12).

5 See Lee *et al.* (2000, ch. 13) for examples. Venture capitalists even engineer mergers between start-up firms in their own portfolio, as Kleiner Perkis did with Excite and @Home.

6 Hart (2001) provides a similar summary, but he states that venture capitalists have less control in later rounds of financing.

7 Some may suppose that the Aghion–Bolton model lies within the framework set by Grossman and Hart (1986) and Hart and Moore (1994), that is, the incomplete contract approach. While this is true, the only asset involved in the Aghion–Bolton model is a project idea, not a physical asset, and this

makes a great difference. Concentrating on a physical asset allows the traditional property right models to identify ownership with (residual) control rights.

8   See Rajan and Zingales (1998) for a more technical argument.
9   One might think that this is too strong an assumption. However in most cases modularization allows the value of the whole product system to be expressed as the sum of the value of its modular components. For a more detailed discussion of this assumption, see the next section.
10 If the value is expressed by a supermodular function, it is more beneficial to have all the variables move in the same direction, even if this is the wrong direction. See Milgrom and Roberts (1994) for the argument.
11 More precisely, the objective function is supermodular in those variables.
12 Strictly speaking, interpreting each team in the model as an independent firm implies that the boundary of a firm is determined by the ease of coordination. Brynjolfsson *et al.* (1994) explain this assertion by broadly treating coordination costs as general transaction costs.
13 However we shall assume that, in any mode of R&D organization, M is only engaged in the observation of E_s, and the E_i's are only observed by the T_i's.
14 Assuming that the activity levels of members are aligned linearly, the objective function common to all the members can be expressed as the following quadratic function:

$$V(x, y_a, y_b) = \gamma_s x + (\gamma_s + \gamma_e + \gamma_a)y_a + (\gamma_s + \gamma_e + \gamma_b)y_b$$

$$-\frac{A}{2}x^2 + Dx(y_a + y_b) - \frac{K}{2}(y_a + y_b)^2 - \frac{L}{2}(y_a - y_b)^2$$

where x is M's choice variable, the y_i's are the T_i's choice variables ($i = a, b$). As noted in the text, this objective function has two kinds of parameter. First there are stochastic parameters: γ_s is a parameter exhibiting the uncertainty arising in the systemic segment of the environment, γ_e is a parameter indicating the uncertainty arising in the systemic segment of the engineering environment, and the γ_i's are parameters showing the uncertainty arising in the idiosyncratic engineering environments. Second, K and L are constant parameters: $\partial^2 V/\partial y_a \partial y_b = L - K$ shows the degree of complementarity between the activity levels of the T_i's. Namely, the choice variables of T_i's are complementary if $K < L$, while they are substitutive if $K > L$. We assume that the activity levels of M and the T_i's are complementary, so that $\partial^2 V/\partial x \partial y_i = D > 0$ holds.
15 Open interface is not a sufficient condition for the market for the modular product to be competitive. A firm with a monopolistic position in some modular part may use that position to control the innovations occurring in a platform. Intel in the CPU market and Microsoft in the OS market are example of this. Bresnahan and Greenstein (1999) explain the fact that there have been only a few platforms in the computer industry by applying Sutton's theory. According to Sutton (1991), if the expenditure by firms to improve their product has the following properties of endogenous sunk cost (ESC), then the market necessarily has a concentrated structure. The necessary conditions for the expenditure to be ESC are as follows: (1) it has to be sunk, (2) it must have no upper limit and (3) a large proportion of potential customers must respond to it. Bresnahan and Greenstein apply this theory to the

market structure of the computer industry by replacing the firm in Sutton's theory with a platform. They also assert that once established a platform has persistency, because both seller and buyer have to invest much in it.

16   According to an observation by an experienced venture capitalist, marketing uncertainty tends to be low (high) when technological uncertainty is high (low). Investment in Silicon Valley used to be concentrated in projects with high technological uncertainty and low marketing uncertainty. However the trend has reversed recently due to an increase in the number of entrepreneurial firms engaged in e-commerce. Venture capitalists, of course, have to consider different properties of the risks when building up their portfolios. See Lee *et al.* (2000).

17   This list of modular operations includes 'splitting' and 'substituting' operations. Note that these can be applied to modular parts of an existing product system.

References

Aghion, P. and P. Bolton (1992) 'An Incomplete Contracts Approach to Financial Contracting', *Review of Economic Studies*, 59, 3: 473–94.

Aoki, M. (2001) *Towards a Comparative Institutional Analysis*, Cambridge, MA: MIT Press.

—— and N. Rosenberg (1989) 'The Japanese Firm as an Innovating Institution', in T. Shiraishi and S. Tsuru (eds), *Economic Institutions in a Dynamic Society*, New York: Macmillan, 137–54.

—— and H. Takizawa (2002) 'Incentives and Option Value in the Silicon-Valley Tournament Game', *Journal of Comparative Economics*, 30: 759–86.

Baldwin, C. Y. and K. B. Clark (2000) *Design Rules (volume 1): The Power of Modularity*, Cambridge, MA: MIT Press.

—— and —— (2001) 'Commentary to "Managing in an Age of Modularity"', in R. Garud, A. Kumaraswamy and R. Langlois (eds), *Managing the Modular Age: Architecture, Networks and Organizations*, Oxford: Blackwell, 161–71.

Bresnahan, T. (1999) 'Computing', in D. C. Mowery (ed.), *US Industry in 2000*, Washington, DC: National Academy Press, 215–44.

—— and S. Greenstein (1999) 'Technological Competition and the Structure of the Computer Industry', *The Journal of Industrial Economics*, 47, 1: 1–40.

Brooks, F. P. J. (1995) *The Mythical Man-Month: Essays on Software Engineering*, Reading, MA: Addison-Wesley.

Brynjolfsson, E., T. W. Maline, V. Gurbaxani and A. Kambil (1994) 'Does Information Technology Lead to Smaller Firms?', *Management Science*, 40: 1628–44.

Crémer, J. (1980) 'A Partial Theory of the Optimal Organization of a Bureaucracy', *Bell Journal of Economics*, 11: 683–93.

Fujimoto, T. (1997) *Seisan System no Shinkaron: Toyota Jidosha ni miru Soshiki Nouryoku to Souhatu Process* (An Evolutionary Theory of Production Systems: Organizational Capability and Emergent Processes in the Toyota Corporation), Tokyo: Yuhikaku.

Grossman, S. J. and O. D. Hart (1986) 'The Cost and Benefit of Ownership: A Theory of Lateral and Vertical Integration', *Journal of Political Economy*, 94: 691–719.

Hart, O. D. and J. Moore (1994) *The Governance of Exchanges: Members' Cooperative versus Outside Ownership*, Manuscript, Cambridge, MA: Harvard University.

—— (2001) 'Financial Contracting', *Journal of Economic Literature*, 39: 1079–100.

Kaplan, S. N. and P. Strömberg (2002) 'Financial Contracting Theory Meets the Real World: An Empirical Analysis of Venture Capital Contracts', *Review of Economic Studies*, forthcoming.

Klein, S. and N. Rosenberg (1986) 'An Overview of Innovation', in R. Landau and N. Rosenberg (eds), *The Positive Sum Strategy*, Washington, DC: National Academies Press.

Kokuryo, J. (1999) *Open Architecture Strategy*, Tokyo: Diamond (in Japanese).

Lee, C., W. F. Miller, M. G. Hancok and H. S. Rowen (eds) (2000) *The Silicon Valley Edge: A Habitat for Innovation and Entrepreneurship*, Stanford, CA: Stanford University Press.

Lessig, L. (2002) *The Future of Ideas: The Fate of the Commons in a Connected World*, New York: Vintage Books.

Marschak, J. and R. Radner (1972) *The Theory of Teams*, New Haven, CT: Yale University Press.

Mayer, C. (2001) 'Financing the New Economy: Financial Institutions and Corporate Governance', WIDER Discussion Paper no. 2001/04, Helsinki: UNU/WIDER.

Milgrom, P. and J. Roberts (1994) 'Complementarities and Systems: Understanding Japanese Economic Organization', *Estudios Económicos*, 9, 1: 3–42.

Rajan, R. and L. Zingales (1998) 'Power in a Theory of the Firm', *Quarterly Journal of Economics*, 113, 2: 387–432.

—— and —— (2000) 'The Governance of the New Enterprise', in X. Vives (ed.), *Corporate Governance*, Cambridge: Cambridge University Press, 201–27.

Sahlman, W. (1990) 'The Structure and Governance of Venture Capitalist Organizations', *Journal of Financial Economics*, 27: 473–521.

Saxenian, A. (1994) *Regional Advantage: Culture and Competition in Silicon Valley and Route 128*, Cambridge, MA: Harvard University Press.

Schaefer, S. (1999) 'Product Design Partitions with Complementary Components', *Journal of Economic Behavior and Organization*, 38: 311–30.

Simon, H. (1962) 'The Architecture of Complexity', *Proceedings of the American Philosophical Society*, 106: 467–82.

Sutton, J. (1991) *Sunk Costs and Market Structure*, London: MIT Press.

Takizawa, H. (2002) 'Coordination Costs and the Optimal Partition of a Designing Organization', Working Paper Series no. 25, Tokyo, Center for Research of Global Economy, Toyo University.

Topkis, D. (1998) *Supermodularity and Complementarity*, Princeton, NJ: Princeton University Press.

4

Sharing Ownership via Employee Stock Ownership

James C. Sesil, Douglas L. Kruse and Joseph R. Blasi

Introduction

There is considerable focus at the moment on equity ownership. According to an article in *The Economist*,[1] in 2001 over 50 per cent of the adult population in the United States owned equity. This was a 100 per cent increase since the time of the market correction in 1987. Equity ownership is not only a growing phenomenon in the United States but is also occurring worldwide. More than 50 per cent of Australians and 20 per cent of Germans own shares, and equity ownership is growing in virtually every major Western country.[2] Equity ownership, in the form of stocks or property, plant and equipment, has always been an important element of the wealth of upper-income people in Western societies. However the recent rise of equity ownership has occurred in the context of four major developments. First, equity markets have grown as a way of raising funds and have prospered as a result of general business expansion, the rise of world capital markets and the wide diffusion of information technology in financial markets.

Second, among Western nations, and this has been very clear-cut in the United States, there has been a decline in the ability of the average worker to increase his or her standard of living solely through wage increases adjusted for inflation. These increases have been generally flat or within conservative ranges since 1980, while increases in pension benefits and social security benefits have been very modest. Companies have increasingly offered their workers equity, partly as a response to this reality. Some companies simply supplement wages with equity compensation, others reduce fixed wages and benefits and trade these reductions for equity. As a result of the fact that fixed state pension schemes can no longer deliver retirement income security, some governments have created various pension savings schemes that private companies can offer and many of these – such as the widely imitated US 401(k) plan – hold employer stock.

Third, governments in Western Europe, Latin America and transitional economies have used the privatization of state assets to jumpstart their public stock markets. Virtually all of these cases have included some form of broad worker equity. While there have been wide variations in terms of success, this has popularized the stock market in some of these countries. Fourth, the rise of high technology companies in an atmosphere of tight labour markets for skilled labour has led to a move to increase the equity incentives offered to knowledge workers. In the last few years public policy discussions in the EU, Latin America and Asia have included soul-searching discussions about whether conservatism in their property-sharing and equity-participation regimes has served to moderate their ability to nurture high-tech sectors. Certainly one of the problems associated with any examination of shared property ownership by employees and any objective assessment of the research literature is that so many different manifestations of employee ownership have emerged in the last two decades. The past decade has also seen growth in the use of broad-based stock option plans. While employees do not directly own shares with employee ownership plans, broad-based stock option plans are similar in that they represent an employee equity stake in the company, where employee compensation is tied to the firm's stock price and employees are likely to develop greater interest in firm performance.

What lessons have been learnt from the accumulated evidence on employee equity stakes in companies? Do they improve outcomes for workers and firms, or does the evidence confirm the views of detractors who point to excessive worker risk and other possible dangers? While no economies have been fundamentally structured around employee ownership, many Western industrialized economies have a substantial share of firms embodying these concepts in some form, and a number of transitional economies are experimenting with employee ownership. This has provided the basis for over 70 empirical studies on the causes and consequences of employee ownership.

This chapter presents an overview of evidence on employee ownership and broad-based stock options, and a discussion of further research needs. Employee ownership is defined broadly as any ownership of company stock by employees, whether directly through stock purchase plans or indirectly through employee stock ownership plans (ESOPs), 401(k) plans or other pension plans. A stock option, in contrast, is the right to buy a share of stock in the future at a fixed price (generally after a vesting period), which can then be resold at the market price or retained by the employee. Broad-based stock options plans make stock options available to over half of non-management employees. The following sections provide an overview of relevant economic theory, discuss the incidence, company characteristics and determinants of share ownership, and consider the evidence on firm performance (profitability, productivity, firm survival and employment stability) and employees' attitudes and behaviour.

As will be seen, one broad generalization that can be made from the many studies on the subject is that employee ownership and broad-based stock options do not automatically improve outcomes for workers or firms, although they are more often associated with better outcomes than with worse ones. This broadly supports the case that there may be benefits – and there are unlikely to be adverse consequences – from expanding employee equity stakes in companies, although clearly the results cannot be preordained and depend on a number of factors. The findings also create a strong case for further research in this area, in order to gain better insights into the conditions that underlie positive and negative outcomes when employees have significant equity stakes in their companies.

Theoretical overview

Principal–agent theory

Many advocates of employee ownership focus on how the latter can serve as a collective incentive to improve workplace cooperation and performance. This is founded on the idea that workers' motivation is improved by giving them a direct stake in the firm's future by tying compensation and/or wealth more closely to performance. While there are a variety of methods that employers can use to encourage optimum performance by workers (for example close supervision, piece rates, deferred compensation, efficiency wages), collective incentives can complement or substitute for these methods under certain conditions. Piece rates, for example, may be difficult to implement and can discourage innovation and cooperation, and centralized monitoring may be more costly and less effective than 'horizontal monitoring' done by coworkers (Nalbantian, 1987). This can be especially true in current modular team production settings (Applebaum and Berg, 2000).

A theoretical objection to the positive productivity effects of employee ownership concerns managerial incentives to supervise workers. The objection is that, by reducing the share of economic surplus going to owners, the owners (and their agents, the managers) will have less incentive to monitor workers effectively, leading to poorer performance (Alchian and Demsetz, 1972). This argument relies on several assumptions, including the absence of principal–agent problems between owners and managers, and that the reduced monitoring by management will not be accompanied by an increase in workers monitoring each other. Putterman and Skillman (1988) note that the argument is based on 'incentives to monitor but not on the ability to observe accurately', and the lack of accurate observation can offset the theorized incentives for management monitoring. Nalbantian (1987) points out that

> Employees engaged in the routine day-to-day fulfilment of a task are usually in a position to detect inefficiencies in operations that diminish productivity. They are also likely to acquire important information concerning the actual productive contributions of their co-workers. The information derived from such activity is potentially very valuable to the firm as an input to production. Yet such information transfers will not be induced under an individual performance-based rewards system since it does not affect his own performance measures.

But under the group system the appropriate incentives are much more likely to be present. If positive externalities are associated with these information inputs and all the relevant group members are subject to the same incentives, then there is reason for employees to identify their own interests with those of the firm and to furnish the inputs required for the firm's success (ibid.: 26). In analyzing the theory that optimal monitoring requires concentrated residual rights, Putterman and Skillman (1988: 118) conclude that 'closing the story which says that a particular assignment of residual rights will best elicit the desired monitoring effort remains a difficult challenge, especially if monitoring is itself difficult to observe and there are reasons why the monitor or monitors might want to misrepresent their information'. It is possible for management monitoring costs to be lower in employee ownership firms if employees reach a consensus to monitor each other and are willing to share information with the company.

The efficiency of employee ownership arrangements is also questioned by Hansmann (1996). He argues that collective action problems arise in any enterprise that is jointly owned by multiple individuals, and governance arrangements will be more efficient if control rights are limited to a single class of individuals with fairly homogeneous interests. This generally favours ownership by financial investors, since they have a common interest in the highest profits, but he notes that 'in practice it appears that, when the employees involved are highly homogeneous, employee ownership is more efficient than investor ownership'. With a heterogeneous workforce, however, 'direct employee control of the firm brings substantial costs – costs that are generally large enough to outweigh the benefits that employee ownership otherwise offers' (ibid.: 119).

One of the often-cited drawbacks of group incentive schemes is that the connection between individual performance and reward grows weaker as the number of employees involved grows larger. This is commonly referred to as the '$1/N$ problem': with N employees in a company, on average each employee will receive only $1/N$ of any extra surplus generated by his or her improved performance. This problem may be theoretically solved by establishing and enforcing a cooperative solution, in which each employee agrees to higher work norms (rather than 'free riding' on the efforts of others) and all benefit as a result of better performance. What it would take in practice, however, to establish such a solution and convince employees to participate is not specified by the theory. To encourage better performance through group incentive schemes, 'something more may be needed – something akin to developing a corporate culture that emphasizes company spirit, promotes group co-operation, encourages social enforcement mechanisms, and so forth' (Weitzman and Kruse, 1990: 100).

The firm's decision-making structure, other human resource policies and managerial approach to workers may be large elements of the 'something more' that is needed. In particular, it is often suggested that group incentive schemes need to be structured so as to draw upon additional worker *skills* and *information* about the work process (Applebaum and Berg, 2000). Such skills and information may become available if there are programmes to encourage employee involvement in workplace decisions, open new channels to furnish employees with more information and solicit ideas from them, and assure workers that any productivity improvements will not result in redundancies or reduced job security. Such changes in the workplace combined with employee-owned stock may help to foster a sense of partnership/ownership, resulting in greater employee commitment and motivation. There is some speculation that transferring property rights in the form of residual return rights (Applebaum and Berg, 2000) and control rights may go some way towards the establishment of a cooperative solution.

Incentive contract theory and transferring property rights to non-owner employees

The question asked by incentive contract theory is why do employees work hard when their work cannot be perfectly monitored, and how can they be motivated to provide productivity-enhancing ideas when they have knowledge of the production process that management does not have (Lazear, 1986)? There are an infinite number of types of incentive contract that employers can choose from, but some have more efficient outcomes than others. One of the primary reasons why incentive contracts are necessary is that employees have access to productivity-enhancing information. The question of how to monitor and motivate employees most effectively is especially pertinent now because of the greater amount of private information that resides with employees (Levine and Tyson, 1990). It has long been recognized that information asymmetries exist in organisations and employees have private information from which management could benefit. Given the increase in educational attainment and company training, as well as developments in information technology, monitoring may become increasingly difficult, which highlights the need for efficacious goal-aligning incentive systems.

Milgrom and Roberts (1992) suggest that ownership, including statutory property rights, is the fundamental means of providing an incentive to create and develop an asset. The two fundamental aspects of ownership are (1) 'residual rights of control', or the right to make decisions about the use of an asset, and (2) the right to 'residual returns', or the right to revenues left over after all obligations have been met. According to Milgrom and Roberts, it is the combination of these two rights that provides the individual incentive effects of ownership because the people who make the decisions bear the financial consequences of their decisions. Milgrom and Roberts also state that these effects are most efficient when property rights are transferable, or can be assigned to the person who is best suited to be in charge. Further developing the notion of shared rights of ownership, Ben-Ner and Jones (1995) present a theoretical framework that combines two aspects of ownership – control and return – and suggest possible firm performance outcomes when these rights are shared with employees.[3] They contend that the greatest efficiency outcomes exist when both these rights are held by employees.

As discussed earlier however, there are arguments against productivity effects being associated with group incentive schemes. One of the strongest charges against the efficacy of such schemes concerns the free-rider or 1/*N* problem. There is also the fact that many employees may be averse to increasing the amount of compensation they put at risk. The firm may be in a better position to absorb any consequences associated with outside factors that affect remuneration. The free-rider problem has been addressed largely with an argument taken from game theory (Weitzman and Kruse, 1990). This argument states that there is a cooperative and a non-cooperative solution to group interactions. As people engage in a repeated game they can choose either to free ride on the efforts of others or to work together. In the case of group-based incentives, when everyone works together everyone will be better off. Consequently as the game is repeated those involved may eventually move towards a cooperative solution.

In their theoretical work Drago and Turnbull (1988) propose that group incentives are more efficient than individual incentives in team production settings, provided a climate of trust and cooperation is developed. It may be that broadly granting equity compensation, for example in the form of broad-based stock options, may signal that 'we are all in this together', which may in turn help the development of a culture of cooperation.

There have been a number of fundamental changes in the workplace that may be making it increasingly advantageous for firms to use equity compensation. There is also speculation that in settings where monitoring costs are especially high it may be more cost effective to find substitutes for formal monitors. This may be especially true in high technology firms, where inputs from human capital are especially important for new product innovations (Core and Guay, 2000). Moreover, according to Applebaum and Berg (2000) new manufacturing practices are making it increasingly advantageous to introduce equity compensation.

Incidence, company characteristics and determinants of share ownership

Share ownership: incidence

There are a variety of forms of employee ownership. Employee ownership is not a simple, one-dimensional concept that permits easy classification of a firm as 'employee-owned', or of an employee as an 'employee-owner'.[4] A company may be, for example, 100 per cent owned by only 25 per cent of employees, or only 25 per cent owned by all employees (with the rest being held outside the firm), or 100 per cent owned by all employees but with one person holding a majority of the stock. Four important dimensions of employee ownership are:

1. The percentage of employees who participate in ownership.
2. The percentage of ownership held within the company by employees.
3. The inequality of ownership stakes among employee-owners.
4. The prerogatives and rights that ownership confers upon employees.

The prerogatives and rights conferred by employee ownership are partly determined by whether ownership is direct (where employees can freely buy and sell company stock) or indirect (where stock is held by an employee trust or cooperative), and partly by the voting rights and other forms of participation that accompany the ownership. In the United States the main vehicle for employee ownership is ESOP, which was first given recognition and special tax treatment as a form of pension plan in the 1974 ERISA law. There are currently about 8.2 million participants (representing 7.7 per cent of the private-sector workforce) in almost 9000 ESOPs with combined assets of US$411 billion (Kruse, 2002; US DOL, 2002).

In recent years the United States, like many European countries, has established pension savings schemes in which employees are given tax incentives to invest their money in a basket of mutual funds to draw on in their retirement. Oddly enough these plans, which do not even bear the employee ownership label are the fastest growing form of direct employee ownership in the United States today. In addition to ESOPs there are just over 12.4 million participants in large non-ESOP contribution pension plans that hold a total of US$147 billion of employer stock (Kruse, 2002). The majority of participants and assets are in plans maintained by publicly held firms. A large amount of employee ownership is held in 401(k) plans, which may or may not be integrated with ESOPs. Over half of ESOP participants and assets are in plans that are also 401(k)s, commonly called KSOPs. Federal tax laws allow workers to contribute pretax salary dollars to a maximum of about US$10 000 per year, adjusted upwards for inflation.

It is important to realize that unlike ESOPs, 401(k) plans are mostly made up of voluntary contributions by workers, although some employers match their contributions in order to give them an incentive to contribute. The 401(k) plans are established by employers but are usually managed by the workers themselves on the Internet, through major on-line brokerages such as Fidelity, Charles Schwab, Solomon Smith Barney and Merrill Lynch. Employers typically provide a choice of investment options. These are usually stock, bond, money market and real estate trust mutual funds offered by the financial services firm that manages the Internet site and the benefit plan. The workers can choose between the various kinds of investment and may switch funds back and forth among the investment options. Employee ownership is part of both ESOP and non-ESOP 401(k) plans because one of the investment options available to employees is typically an employer stock fund. Moreover the matching contributions by employers are often in company stock. In 2001 about 2000 of the plans in mainly large publicly traded companies involved employee ownership of company stock. A recent study at Rutgers University found that 40 per cent of 401(k) plans with more than 5000 workers featured employee ownership, with 15 per cent of the savings plans' assets being invested in employer stock. With regard to smaller public companies, 20 per cent of 401(k) plans with 1000–5000 workers had the feature of employee ownership, with about 6 per cent of the plans' assets being invested in company stock. About a third of all employees in the United States who participated in such plans were in plans with the feature of employee ownership.

Employees may own stock directly in their companies through stock purchase programmes or by exercising stock options, which was done by 8.9 per cent of employees in 1983 (Brickley and Hevert, 1991), or they may own their companies as members of worker cooperatives (Jones, 1979; Bonin *et al.*, 1993). Combining the various means of owning employer stock, and roughly adjusting for the fact that in the United States many employees and companies offer multiple plans, about one fifth of American adults have reported holding stock in the company in which they work.[5] While a large number of US employees own employer stock, almost all of this stock is in firms that are only minority employee-owned. Among the US companies with more than 10 employees, in approximately 2000 the majority of stock is owned by employees.[6] Only a few of the large public companies are majority employee-owned (United Airlines being the most prominent one until its recent bankruptcy), but among public companies in general (where the SEC defines a 5 per cent stockholder as a major stakeholder), in almost 1000 more than 4 per cent of stock is held by employees, with an average employee holding of 12 per cent (Blasi and Kruse, 1991). There has been substantial growth of public firms with more than 20 per cent of broad employee ownership (Blair *et al.*, 1998).

Employee ownership has been a growing feature in a number of former socialist countries in transition to greater private ownership, including China (Tseo, 1996), Russia (Blasi *et al.*,

1997) and the countries of Central and Eastern Europe (Uvalic and Vaughan-Whitehead, 1997; Smith *et al.*, 1997). A further 12 countries have some form of constitutional or statutory mandate for profit sharing, although enforcement is unclear and there are no data on how many workers are covered (Florkowski, 1990).[7] The National Center for Employee Ownership has prepared an extensive report on employee ownership legislation around the world. The report includes an explanation and overview of the legislation, and takes a close look at the situation in each country.[8]

Share ownership: company characteristics

What types of firm adopt employee ownership when it is not mandatory? At least 16 studies have been conducted on this question, most of them using cross-sectional data to predict plan presence and a few using panel data to predict plan adoption (summarized in Kruse, 1993, 1996; also see Kruse and Blasi, 1997; Blasi and Kruse, 1991; Blair *et al.*, 2000; Patibandla and Chandra, 1998; del Boca and Cupaiuolo, 1998). Overall the studies do not support any one dominant explanation for the adoption of plans, but they do come to one very clear-cut conclusion: the dominant impression among many scholars and members of the press that it is mainly failing firms that introduce employee ownership has no solid evidence to support it. The source of this false impression, apparently, was the substantial media coverage given to the high-profile rescue of a handful of weak steel, airline, haulage and other firms in the United States in the 1980s and early 1990s. That employee ownership may be used as a substitute for supervision is supported by the findings of Patibandla and Chandra (1998), however the various studies are divided on whether they are more or less common in capital-intensive firms where employee malfeasance can be more costly. Two studies of ESOPs in public companies in the United States (Blasi and Kruse, 1991; Blair *et al.*, 2000) found wide dispersion among various industries, contrary to the assertions of Hansmann (1996). Both types of plan are more likely to be adopted by large companies, going against the idea that collective incentives are more attractive where there is less of a free-rider problem, and suggesting the existence of fixed costs in establishing these plans.

With regard to motivation for greater compensation flexibility, two studies have found that the adoption of employee ownership is positively linked to higher variability in company profits. The reluctance of risk-averse employees to own stock when profits are variable appears to be outweighed by firms' desire to share some of the market risk with their employees (although risk-averse employees may benefit from greater employment stability and firm survival rates, as will be discussed). A desire for flexibility may also be at the root of firms' adoption of profit sharing or employee ownership following changes in performance, since these plans may help them to raise or lower compensation without changing the fixed wage levels. Four studies have found that worse firm performance predicts the adoption of these plans, but two have found the opposite. Some employers may adopt employee ownership plans to discourage unionization, hoping that such plans will encourage employees to focus on company performance and identify with the firm (accounting in part for unionists' long-standing uneasy relationship with employee ownership and profit sharing). The findings, however, are split on whether unionization is higher or lower in firms with employee ownership. Finally, tax, legal or other financial concerns may motivate the adoption of employee ownership. Two advantages of employee ownership plans in the United States is that they can provide a ready source of accessible capital for firms and help ward off hostile takeovers, although it is not apparent that these are major factors in their adoption (Kruse, 1996).

In sum, a substantial minority of workers are covered by employee ownership arrangements in industrialized countries, but the disparate findings of numerous studies have not provided clear answers on which factors predict the use of profit sharing and employee ownership. There have been contradictory findings on even basic variables such as unionization and capital intensity. One interpretation is that the decision to implement a plan is largely idiosyncratic, reflecting the large role played by employer discretion and/or specific workplace cultures and characteristics that are not easily measured. Hence a case can clearly be made for further research with better measures of factors that likely to influence adoption. In particular there is a need for more studies using panel data to predict the adoption decision, which could help sort out heterogeneity and causality issues. One conclusion is clear, however: the facile assumption of many economists and members of the public that it is mainly failing firms that introduce employee share schemes is grossly overstated and is mainly a reaction to popular press and TV coverage, not research.

Broad-based stock options plans: incidence

The introduction of broad-based stock option plans has been on the rise over the last decade. However only a few researchers have conducted detailed case studies and econometric research of the impact of these plans on company performance (these studies are reviewed in Weeden *et al.*, 1998, 2000). Because these studies do not always differentiate between employees who are eligible for stock options and those who actually receive them, and because many focus on large companies or opportunity samples of consultant clients, they may significantly over-state the incidence of stock options in the economy. Nevertheless four of the studies sampled important populations of companies and found an increasing use of such plans. First, the William M. Mercer studies of the proxies of the 350 largest public companies found an increase in the percentage of companies granting stock options to all employees, with a rise from 5.7 per cent in 1993 to 10.3 per cent in 1997 (Weeden *et al.*, 1998: 199). Second, the Center for Effective Organizations at the University of Southern California studied 279 Fortune 1000 firms in 1993 and 212 firms in 1996 and found that the percentage offering such plans to all employees had stabilized at 10 per cent, but the percentage offering broad plans to more than 20 per cent of employees had risen from 30 per cent to 51 per cent (Lawler *et al.*, 1998: 34). Third, the Arthur Anderson survey of the largest 1250 global corporations found that 33 per cent offered such programmes to all employees and 11 per cent planned to add them in the future. Finally, in 1998 US Federal Reserve Board economists in 12 regions surveyed 415 companies in vari-ous industries and found that about a third had broad-based pro-grammes and 37 per cent had broadened the participation in the past two years. Also, 6.7 per cent of companies offered stock options to employees of lower occupational levels, such as managers and profes-sional workers. Unlike samples of high-tech firms, where smaller firms are more likely to offer stock options to all employees, this broader sam-ple showed that larger companies were more likely to do so.

While the above studies indicate that a significant and growing share of US employees are entitled to stock options, a much lower figure is provided by a Bureau of Labor Statistics survey, which found that only 1.7 per cent of all private industry employees received stock options in 1999 (BLS, 2000).

While it is tempting to ascribe the rising incidence of stock option plans to their good economic performance, a recent US Federal Reserve Board study underlines the widely held view that such plans may be popular because the generally accepted accounting principles allow firms to record the expense for these options as zero. This is because they measure the value of an option by its intrinsic value – that is, the difference between the market price on the grant data and the exercise price. When firms grant options with a fixed exercise price that is equal to or greater than the market price of the grant date (so-called fixed-plan options), the intrinsic value of the option, and thus the recorded expense, is zero (see Lebow *et al.*, 1999: 4–5). While this extremely favourable method of accounting has been controversial with the Financial Accounting Standards Board (FASB), institutional investors and some shareholders, corporations successfully engaged in repeated struggles with these groups in the 1990s to retain the favourable practice. As a compromise, from 1997 the FASB's Statement Number 123 required companies to report, in a footnote to the financial statements in their annual reports, the *pro forma* effect on net income and earnings per share had they been required to take an accounting charge for the fair market value of all stock options on the date of grant. By the winter of 2003 both the US FASB and the International Accounting Standards Board were considering requiring expensing for stock options. A 1998 survey of the largest 200 industrial and service corporations found that the *pro forma* negative mean impact on net income was 3.8 per cent for 181 of the companies, but the figure was greater than 6 per cent for 13 per cent of the companies and greater than 10 per cent for 8 per cent of the companies (Pearl Meyer, 1998). It should be pointed out that this is clearly not a study of broad-based plans and probably focuses mainly on executive and management plans, but it does provide some insight into how *pro forma* adjustment affects large corporations with stock option plans for any category of participant employee.

Broad-based stock option organizations: company characteristics

In recent research we found a number of company characteristics that differ from those of similar non-stock option firms (Sesil *et al.*, 2000). Stock option companies tend to have higher sales and employment levels and greater capital intensity than otherwise similar firms. In addition they are more likely to be found in the manufacturing (including high technology) and service sectors. In a second study (Sesil *et al.*, 2002) we compared high technology firms that offered broad-based stock options with high technology firms that did not in order to evaluate the performance effects. We found essentially the same company characteristics, including the fact that there was significantly greater R&D expenditure per employee. Among high-tech firms, broad-based stock options were more common in semiconductor and software companies then in pharmaceutical or high-tech manufacturing. We also compared the usage of these stock options in union and non-union firms (Kroumova *et al.*, 2002) and found that unionized firms were 9.4 per cent less likely to have a stock option plan in 1997. However it should be noted that broad-based stock option plans were not uncommon among unionized firms in the United States and had been adopted by a modest number of them. Again, unionized stock option firms were larger in terms of both sales and employment levels in 1997.

Performance effects

Share ownership: impact on performance

Over the past 20 years at least 32 studies have tackled the question of whether and how employee ownership affects firm performance. This section briefly summarizes the main conclusions from a review of 29 of these studies in Kruse and Blasi (1997), plus the findings of three other studies (Smith *et al.*, 1997; Ohkusa and Ohtake, 1997; McNabb and Whitfield, 1998).[9] Some of these studies are of US ESOPs only (comparing ESOP and non-ESOP firms either cross-sectionally or before and after the adoption of an ESOP), others look at worker cooperatives and attempt to measure the effects of different cooperative features, and the remainder are of other forms or combinations of employee ownership, using comparisons with non-employee-owned firms and/or comparisons based on employee ownership features within firms. As with the evidence on employee attitudes and behaviour under employee ownership, the studies on firm performance are split between neutral and favourable findings. While the majority of the studies could not reject the null hypothesis of no significant relationship between employee ownership and performance, our meta-analysis of the ESOP studies has shown that we can reject this null hypothesis, based on the disproportionate number of positive and significant estimates (79 per cent of the 333 reported coefficients were positive and 17 per cent had T-statistics greater than 2). The average estimated productivity difference between ESOP and non-ESOP firms is 6.2 per cent, and the average estimated increase in productivity following adoption is 4.4 per cent (averaging both statistically significant and non-significant representative coefficients across the studies). These studies use data from 1975 onwards, so the results reflect both bull and bear markets. While one might expect greater effects when employees own a larger percentage of the company, the studies have mixed findings on whether the percentage owned by employees predicts higher performance. This suggests that the status of being an employee owner and the perceived influence on the company, rather than the size of the ownership stake, may be the crucial variable – a finding echoed in the attitude studies.

With regard to worker cooperatives, an analysis of Pacific Northwest plywood cooperatives indicated that they had higher productivity (Craig, 1995), while the studies analyzing cooperative features found that three – membership, individual capital stakes, and bonus per worker – were linked to better firm performance. While most of the studies are of firms in Western industrialized countries, it is worth noting that two on employee ownership in transitional economies (Poland and Slovenia) found that firms with employee ownership had higher productivity (Jones, 1993; Smith *et al.*, 1997).

An important research issue in performance studies is selection bias in the types of firm and worker that choose employee ownership. Good performance may be a cause rather than an effect of employee ownership, or both may be dependent on other factors within the firm. The panel studies address the most basic form of selection bias by controlling for preadoption performance levels. A number of studies have attempted to adjust for the potential endogeneity of employee ownership, with little substantive difference in the results. There are few data on the types of worker who choose to work in employee ownership companies, but an analysis of workers who had enrolled in a group incentive scheme found that initially high and low performers were most likely to drop out, and that average worker quality did not change (Weiss, 1987). Therefore the estimates are unlikely to be biased by firm or worker selection issues.

Other important aspects of firm performance are firm survival, growth and stability. The theoretical literature on labour management gives no reason to expect that employee ownership will have positive effects on employment behaviour, and in fact tends to predict perverse responses to positive demand shocks. It should be noted that the institutional and decision-making structure of most firms with employee ownership is far from that assumed in the literature on labour-managed firms – it is extremely rare for all employees to participate both in ownership and in company decisions on a one person one vote basis. Nonetheless it is possible that employee-owners will exert formal or informal pressure on managers to make employment decisions, as predicted in the literature. Several studies have looked at employment behaviour in and the survival of employee ownership firms. The one study to focus on the predictions of the labour-managed-firm literature examined US plywood cooperatives and compared their employment behaviour with that of conventional plywood firms (Craig and Pencavel, 1992; Pencavel, 2001). There was no perverse employment response to demand shocks among the cooperatives; rather they appeared to be inclined to put a large weight on employment, adjusting pay rather than employment as demand changed.[10]

Another study analyzed US public companies with broad-based employee ownership plans that included more than 17 per cent of company stock as of 1983 (Blair *et al.*, 2000). These companies also appeared to put greater weight on employment than conventional companies, given that they were more likely than comparable public companies to survive until 1995 and had a significantly lower variability of employment (among both survivors and non-survivors). Employment stability did not, however, appear to be at the expense of firm efficiency, given that the stock market performance of the employee ownership firms was slightly better than that of other firms. A more recent analysis of private companies with ESOPs also found that they had a higher survival rate than non-ESOP firms in the same industries (NCEO, 2002).

The employee ownership companies in the study of public companies did not have faster employment growth than other public companies, in contrast to the findings of three studies, that compared employment growth before and after the adoption of ESOPs (Quarrey and Rosen, 1993; Winther and Marens, 1997; NCEO, 2002). These studies found that employment growth was faster after ESOP adoption, particularly among firms that had greater levels of employee participation in decision making. Finally, the survival of French worker cooperatives was examined by Estrin and Jones (1992). Contrary to predictions that the cooperatives would either fail or degenerate into capitalist firms as workers were hired, they found a high rate of survival and no evidence of degeneration, although the financial structures may have become increasingly inefficient over time.

Broad-based stock options: impact on performance

The financial impact of broad-based stock option plans has been mainly evaluated in terms of their impact on outside shareholders. Four studies have estimated the percentage of market value represented by all outstanding options. In the late 1990s the percentage of dilution ranged from 5.5 per cent at the median to 17.4 per cent, with the higher estimates consistently coming from high technology company surveys, although a study conducted by the National Center for Employee Ownership in 1998 found the average dilution to be 12.6 per cent, with a third of the companies above 15 per cent. A study of the 200 largest industrial and service corporations put the average at about 13.2 per cent for all options outstanding for all equity programmes other than stock purchase plans and ESOPs, although it is unclear whether the study included only broad-based stock option plans (Pearl Meyer, 1998). The largest study dealt with the top 1500 Standard & Poor's corporations and considered both stock option and other stock plans. An analysis of the data found that overhang (that is, the potential dilution from all options outstanding) dramatically increased from 5 per cent to 13 per cent between 1988 and 1997. The researchers concluded that companies with an overhang of 10.6 per cent (close to the ceiling of 10 per cent publicly announced by many institutional investors) had a median total shareholder return that was significantly greater than the highest third of companies with an overhang of 18.7 per cent. High technology companies had a higher overhang than other industries, but their five-year sales growth was also higher, and they could tolerate a 16 per cent overhang without damaging total shareholder return (Watson Wyatt Worldwide, 1998). Given that most institutional investors object to dilution potential above 10 per cent, it is clear that broad-based stock options could cause a significant drain on total shareholder return. Indeed a conflict appears to be brewing with outside shareholders over options in general. According to Watson Wyatt Worldwide (1998), the average overhang among major companies hit 13 per cent in 1997, up from 5 per cent in 1988.

Other studies have examined the repricing of options when corporations change the option strike price after it becomes clear that their employees will not reap any financial benefit because the share price is not increasing as rapidly as had been hoped. These studies found that 15–36 per cent of companies had repriced their options, with 36 per cent engaging in repricing. Repricing is yet another area where government regulators are changing their views on equity compensation trends. The US Securities and Exchange Commission (SEC) changed its long-standing position in 1998 and required General DataComm Industries to include a resolution by an institutional investor (the State of Wisconsin Investment Board) for a binding shareholder vote for prior shareholder approval of repricing. In the past the SEC had viewed such practices as ordinary business operations to be governed by boards, and not made subject to shareholder decision making (Pearl Meyer, 1998: 15). Among 20 very large companies with broad-based plans, the average commitment of common shares outstanding was 3.4 per cent. Three of these companies had adopted an evergreen provision for stock option share authorization whereby 1 per cent of their shares were automatically added to the stock option pool each year (Hewitt Associates, 1997: 24). The key question about the dilution issue is whether the dilution effect of broad-based stock option plans is greater or less than their incentive effect on total shareholder return.

In the research mentioned earlier we evaluated the impact of broad-based stock options on the performance of firms. This broad analysis, included high technology firms and unionized and non-unionized firms. In general firms that offered broad-based stock options to their employees had better performance outcomes then otherwise similar firms that did not. We also found that firms that granted stock options to all employees performed better in any given year. In 1997 we found that over the full sample the broad-based stock option firms had higher levels of labour productivity, return on assets, Tobin's q and total shareholder returns (Sesil *et al.*, 2000).

In the more restricted samples of high-technology (Sesil *et al.*, 2002) and union broad-based stock option firms (Kroumova *et al.*, 2002), all firms exhibited a better performance in 1997, and during the period 1992–97 these firms were faster-growing in terms of employment, sales and many performance indicators. We also found that the total shareholder returns of firms that broadly granted stock options were considerably better than for the market as a whole.[11] When we evaluated a number of market, accounting and output based measures we consistently found that productivity was higher in firms that offered broad-based stock options. We also found that after the introduction of broad-based stock options the market responded by significantly increasing the perceived value of the firm's intangible assets. These results continued to hold up in before-and-after within-company comparisons when looking at labour productivity.

We found essentially the same performance outcomes when we looked at high technology firms. In addition to better labour productivity we found some evidence of a greater degree of new idea generation, as measured by patent applications. While there is evidence that firms classified as not offering broad-based stock options also had a high degree of new product innovation, we cannot be entirely sure that these firms did not offer such options. Broad-based stock option plans have become the norm in so many high technology firms that some measurement error is likely to be associated with our non stock option pair. Consequently there may be a downward bias in our coefficients. With regard to unionized firms, there was considerably higher labour productivity and performance in firms with broadly dispersed stock options. In unionized stock option firms labour productivity was approximately 30 per cent higher than in non union, non stock option companies. A before-and-after analysis revealed significantly higher labour productivity and market value over replacement costs in unionized stock option firms.

It should be noted that these studies mostly covered plans that were adopted in the 1990s, during a stock market boom when stock options seemed likely to pay off. It is very possible that the results would be different for plans adopted in a bear market, so further research on broad-based plans after the stock market peak in 2000 would be valuable.

Impact on employees' attitudes and wages

How does employee ownership affect employees' attitudes and behaviour? Surveys conducted in the United States leave little doubt that employees feel quite positively about employee ownership, and a review of over two decades of public opinion polls and surveys on employee ownership and profit sharing indicate strong public support for the ideas and the practices (Kruse and Blasi, 1999). Employee ownership may have positive effects if employees value ownership *per se* or perceive that it brings greater income, job security or control over jobs and the workplace. On the other hand it may have negligible or even negative effects if employees perceive that it makes no difference to their working lives, dislike the extra risk to their income or wealth or have raised expectations that are not met.

In the past two decades over two dozen studies have been published on employees' attitudes and behaviour under employee ownership. This section summarizes the key conclusions from a review of 26 of these studies (Kruse and Blasi, 1997), along with the findings of three other studies (Grunberg *et al.*, 1996; Keef, 1998; Pendleton *et al.*, 1998).[12] Most of the studies made cross-sectional comparisons between employee-owners and non-owners (who may be in the same firm or in different firms), a few made longitudinal comparisons before and after the adoption or termination of employee ownership, and others looked at groups of employee-owners to see how attitudes were related to different plan features or employee characteristics.

The studies surveyed here each addressed a number of topics, including employee satisfaction (analyzed in 10 studies), organizational commitment/identification (12 studies), employee motivation (six studies), attitudes towards unions (three studies), perceived and desired employee participation in/influence over decision making (11 studies), satisfaction with an ESOP (two studies) and behavioural measures such as turnover, absenteeism, grievances, tardiness and injuries (six studies).

The first conclusion from reviewing these studies is that no automatic improvement of attitudes and behaviour is associated with being simply an employee-owner. Some studies found greater satisfaction, commitment and motivation among employee-owners, but others could find no significant differences between owners and non-owners, or before and after an employee buyout. When significant differences were associated with employee ownership, these almost always related to better attitudes and behaviour. Second, most of the studies of organizational commitment and identification found that these factors were stronger under employee ownership, but there were mixed findings – ranging from favourable to neutral – on job satisfaction, motivation and behavioural measures.[13] A worsening of attitudes and behaviour was rare under employee ownership – only one study found lower satisfaction among employee-owners compared with a nationwide sample, but this was in an ESOP company where the union had lost a bitter strike the year before.[14] Third, while several studies found that attitudes had improved under employee ownership, this was usually due to the status of being an employee-owner, rather than to the size of the ownership stake. Fourth, a number of studies found that attitudes and behaviour were positively linked to greater perceived or actual participation in/influence over decision making. Increased employee participation and influence made greater use of employees' skills and knowledge and may have been an important complement to employee ownership in respect of improved attitudes and performance. It should be noted, however, that these studies could not definitely establish causality: better attitudes and behaviour might have led to greater perceived or actual participation, or they may have reflected similar orientations towards the company. The importance of participation is indicated by the finding by Pendleton *et al.* (1998) that the opportunity to participate in decision making was more important than ownership *per se* in generating a feeling of ownership. Fifth, despite the possible benefits to be had from increased participation in decision making there was no automatic connection between employee ownership and perceived or desired employee participation. Decision making in a large number of the employee ownership firms surveyed was no different from in conventional firms. This suggests that many firms with employee ownership were not doing enough to develop a corporate culture and employee empowerment mechanisms to complement employee ownership.

One particularly interesting study used data from a representative survey of US workers to assess workers' views of company and coworker performance. Freeman and Rogers (1999) analyzed the 'participation gap' experienced by US workers, who generally wanted greater participation in workplace decision making. This survey was used in a later study by Freeman and Dube (2000), who found that employees in employee ownership and profit-sharing firms reported higher levels of company and coworker productivity, and were more satisfied with their jobs and more loyal to their employers. The highest scores, however, came from workers in companies that combined profit sharing, employee ownership and employee involvement in decision making, suggesting that these practices are important complements to each other.

A final noteworthy finding on employees' attitudes concerns the effect of employee ownership on attitudes towards unions. While some unions had resisted employee ownership because it might have divided workers' loyalties or made the union seem obsolete, there was no evidence of a reduced need or desire for union representation in employee ownership firms (shown in part by the strikes that had occurred at employee-owned firms).

Do employees sacrifice other pay and benefits for a share in ownership, or does this simply add to workers' income and wealth? In contrast to the numerous works on employees' attitudes and firm performances, there have been few studies on this topic. There were a number of cases in the early 1980s in which unionized employees accepted employee ownership or profit sharing in exchange for reduced pay or benefits (Bell and Neumark, 1993). In addition some employees have taken lower wages as part of employee buyouts, such as occurred at United Airlines. In general, however, workers in employee ownership firms do not appear to have lower average wages or compensation. Blasi *et al.* (1996) examined public companies whose broad-based employee ownership plans included at least 5 per cent of company stock as of 1990, making employees major stakeholders according to SEC definitions. Companies with such an employee ownership stake had 8 per cent higher average compensation levels than other comparable public companies, and compensation increased with the percentage of stock held by employees. Compensation growth from 1980 to 1990, however, was no different between the two types of company. A closer examination of pay and benefits in ESOP and non-ESOP firms has been conducted by Kardas *et al.* (1998) and Scharf and Mackin (2000), who conclude that ESOPs appear to add to workers' pay as they come on top of, rather than at the expense of, regular pay and other benefits. ESOPs also appear to add to pension wealth, coming on top of other pension assets, but do not seem to affect the distribution of pay within firms.

In sum, while some employees have accepted lower compensation in exchange for employee ownership and/or profit sharing in some situations (such as in concessionary situations), the overall average pay of workers in firms with ESOPs appears to be at least as high as – and is probably higher than – that of other workers. However we again stress that trading existing pay and benefits for stock is not the main explanation of the receipt of employee ownership or broad based options in the United States today or over the past two decades. The higher overall average pay of workers involved in such plans may partly reflect higher average productivity levels in employee-ownership and profit-sharing companies (representing a compensating differential for greater expected effort) or the use of efficiency wages in combination with employee ownership and profit sharing to motivate workers. While there is some evidence that ESOPs add to pension wealth, there has been no research on how employee ownership and profit sharing relate to the overall wealth of individuals.

In one of our studies we evaluated compensation levels at and the growth of broad-based stock option companies and found that these firms offered higher pay than other firms prior to the introduction of stock options and continued to pay better after their introduction (Sesil *et al.*, 2000). This finding counters the notion that some firms use stock options as a substitute for fixed wages. This is similar to the finding of a study of profit-sharing firms, which also paid higher wages prior to the introduction of profit-sharing plans and continued to do so after their introduction (Kruse, 1993).

Conclusions

Several broad conclusions can be drawn from the foregoing review:

1. Employee equity stakes do not magically and automatically improve employees' attitudes and behaviour, or firm performance wherever they are introduced.
2. While there is evidence that employees' attitudes and behaviour and firm performance are either improved or unaffected by employee ownership, it is rare to find a worsening of attitudes or performance under employee ownership.
3. Employee ownership is linked to 4–5 per cent higher productivity on average, although the dispersion of performance outcomes is just as great as in other firms.
4. Employment stability and firm survival may be enhanced by employee ownership.
5. Pay is higher among employee-owners.

These conclusions fly in the face of both the very rosy views and the very unfavourable views of employee ownership. While numerous studies have yielded important insights, they have not answered the question of whether employee ownership and broad-based stock option plans are fundamentally good or bad for workers and firms. Based on the accumulated evidence, it is very likely that employee ownership has improved the working environment in and performance of many firms, and many workers have benefited from increased pay, firm survival and employment stability. However it is clear that employee ownership has made little difference in many workplaces, and in a few cases has undoubtedly exposed workers to significant financial risks.

Why does employee ownership appear sometimes to have a good effect but often to have no effect? Some studies have tried to identify the organizational mechanisms that lead to better outcomes under employee ownership, for example by examining whether employee participation in decision making can create a greater sense of partnership and ownership. A few studies have found that employee participation in decision making is associated with improved attitudes and employment growth, although others could find no such connection. At the minimum, the results indicate that substantial expansion of employee ownership and broad-based stock options is very unlikely to hurt, and may well enhance, the economic outcomes for workers, firms and economies.

Given that the existing studies show that employee ownership may have the potential to improve economic well-being, what new research should be done? The few studies on employment stability, growth and firm survival have provided a tantalizing indication that employee ownership may add to job security without sacrificing firm performance. There clearly should be more research on this topic, given the growing concern about economic insecurity due to international trade, technological change and capital mobility.

Valuable complements to the above research would be to study pay levels and trends among workers in employee ownership and broad-based stock option companies, to examine why pay levels appear to be higher in such companies, and to ascertain the extent to which workers' pay and wealth may trade off against employment security and other outcomes.

With regard to employees' attitudes and behaviour and firm performance, there is a need for new data and measures that can make sense of the previous findings by identifying the organizational mechanisms through which employee ownership has an effect. The disparate measures of employee participation that have been used have not produced a clear answer, indicating measurement problems and/or the importance of other workplace policies and characteristics. Intensive case studies may be a valuable prelude to the development of better measures. The era of cross-sectional studies on such topics is basically past, so future studies should be based on panel data from samples that are as representative as possible in order to establish causality, examine trends and be more confident about generalizing. Such research could provide insights into whether employee equity stakes are likely to cover only a minority of firms and workers, or have a significant potential to become more widespread.

Notes

1 *The Economist*, 10 March 2001: 17.
2 Given the variation in the form and function of employee ownership between countries and the quantity of research in each country, our focus will largely be on the United States.
3 For a more complete explanation of the hypothesized productivity effects of control and return rights see Ben-Ner and Jones (1995).
4 There is a rich body of literature on other forms of employee ownership, such as leveraged management buyouts and worker cooperatives, our review and analysis focuses on the broad forms of employee equity ownership associated with shared capitalism.
5 This is based on a December 1993 Gallup survey and a January 1997 Princeton Survey Research Associates survey, summarized in Kruse and Blasi (1999).
6 Estimate by Corey Rosen of the NCEO, Oakland.
7 The countries are Bolivia, Brazil, Chile, Columbia, Ecuador, India, Mexico, Nigeria, Pakistan, Panama, Peru and Venezuela.
8 Available at http://www.nceo.org/library/aroundtheworld.html.
9 As with the employee attitude studies surveyed above, these studies used systematic data collection across a large sample of firms (excluding individual case studies), and statistical techniques to control for other influences on performance and to rule out sampling error.
10 The study did find that product supply curves were more inelastic for cooperatives than for conventional firms, which is consistent with theory on the labour-managed firm.
11 These descriptive statistics do not control for either omitted variable bias or reverse causality. These issues are addressed in the performance effects section of this chapter.
12 These studies were selected because they used systematic data collection from representative samples of employees, and used statistical techniques to rule out sampling error. Many but not all of the studies used multivariate analysis to hold constant the effect of other salient variables on employees' attitudes or behaviour.
13 The behaviours studied included turnover, absenteeism, grievances, tardiness and injuries.
14 Reminders by the management that the strike would hurt the ESOP account values brought the response 'We don't vote; we don't control the company; we don't care' (Kruse, 1984).

References

Alchian, A. A. and H. Demsetz (1972) 'Production, Information Costs, and Economic Organization', *American Economic Review*, 62 (December): 777–95.

Applebaum, E. and P. Berg (2000) 'High-Performance Work Systems: The Historical Context', in M. M. Blair and T. A. Kochan (eds), *The New Relationship: Human Capital in the American Corporation*, Washington, DC: Brookings Institution.

Bell, L. and D. Neumark (1993) 'Lump-Sum Payments and Profit-Sharing Plans in the Union Sector of the United States Economy', *Economic Journal*, 103: 602–19.

Ben-Ner, A. and D. Jones (1995) 'Employee Participation, Ownership, and Productivity: A Theoretical Framework', *Industrial Relations*, 34, 4: 532–53.

Blair, M., D. Kruse and J. Blasi (2000) 'Is Employee Ownership an Unstable Form? Or a Stabilizing Force?', in M. M. Blair and T. A. Kochan (eds), *The New Relationship: Human Capital in the American Corporation*, Washington, DC: Brookings Institution.

Blasi, J. R., M. Conte and D. Kruse (1996) 'Employee Ownership and Corporate Performance Among Public Corporations', *Industrial and Labour Relations Review*, 50, 1: 60–79.

—— M. Kroumova and D. Kruse (1997) *Kremlin Capitalism: Privatizing the Russian Economy*, Ithaca, NY: Cornell University Press.

—— and D. Kruse (1991) *The New Owners: The Mass Emergence of Employee Ownership in Public Companies and What it Means to American Business*, New York: HarperBusiness.

BLS (2000) 'Pilot Survey on the Incidence of Stock Options in Private Industry in 1999', press release, Bureau of Labor Statistics, US Department of Labor, USDL 00–290.

Bonin, J. P., D. Jones and L. Putterman (1993) 'Theoretical and Empirical Studies of Producer Cooperatives: Will the Twain Ever Meet?', *Journal of Economic Literature*, 31: 1290–320.

Brickley, J. A. and K. T. Hevert (1991) 'Direct Employee Stock Ownership: An Empirical Investigation', *Financial Management*, Summer: 70–84.

Core, J. and W. Guay (2000) 'Stock options plans for non-executive employees', University of Pennsylvania.

Craig, B. (1995) 'Participation and Productivity: A Comparison of Worker Cooperatives and Conventional Firms in the Plywood Industry', *Brookings Papers on Economic Activity*, Washington, DC: Brookings Institution: 121–60.

—— and J. Pencavel (1992) 'The Behavior of Worker Cooperatives: The Plywood Companies of the Pacific Northwest', *American Economic Review*, 82: 1083–105.

del Boca, A. and E. Cupaiuolo (1998) 'Why Do Firms Introduce Financial Participation? Evidence from a Sample of Small and Medium Italian Manufacturing Companies', *Economic Analysis: Journal of Enterprise and Participation*, 1, 3: 221–38.

Drago, R. and G. K. Turnbull (1988) 'Individual vs. Group Piece Rates Under Team Technologies', *Journal of Japanese and International Economics*, 2: 1–10.

Estrin, S. and D. C. Jones (1992) 'The Viability of Employee-Owned Firms: Evidence from France', *Industrial and Labor Relations Review*, 45, 2: 323–38.

Fernie, S. and D. Metcalf (1995) 'Participation, Contingent Pay, Representation and Workplace Performance: Evidence from Great Britain', *British Journal of Industrial Relations*, 33, 3: 279–315.

Florkowski, G. (1990) 'Profit Sharing and Public Policy: Insights for the United States', *Industrial Relations*, 30, 1: 96–115.

Freeman, R. and A. Dube (2000) 'Shared Compensation and Decision-making in the U.S. Job Market', draft paper, Cambridge, MA: Harvard University (Department of Economics) and NBER.

—— and J. Rogers (1999) *What Workers Want*, New York and Ithaca: Cornell University Press and Russell Sage Foundation.

Grunberg, L., S. Moore and E. Greenberg (1996) 'The Relationship of Employee Ownership and Participation to Workplace Safety', *Economic and Industrial Democracy*, 17, 2: 221–41.

Hansmann, H. (1996) *The Ownership of Enterprise*, Cambridge, MA: Harvard University Press.

Hewitt Associates (1997) *Non-executive Stock Option Survey Report, 1997: Variable Compensation Measurement Database*, Lincolnshire, IL: Hewitt Associates, VCM Points Programme.

Jones, D. C. (1979) 'US Producer Cooperatives: The Record to Date', *Industrial Relations*, 8: 343–56.

—— (1993) 'The Productivity Effects of Employee Ownership Within Command Economies: Evidence from Poland', *Managerial and Decision Economics*, 14: 475–85.

Kandel, E. and E. Lazear (1992) 'Peer pressure and partnerships', *Journal of Political Economy*, 100, 4: 801–17.

Kardas, P., A. L. Scharf and J. Keogh (1998) 'Wealth and Income Consequences of Employee Ownership: A Comparative Study from Washington State', draft paper, Washington State Department of Community, Trade, and Economic Development.

Keef, S. P. (1998) 'The Causal Association between Employee Share Ownership and Attitudes: A Study Based on the Long Framework', *British Journal of Industrial Relations*, 36, 1: 73–82.

Kroumova, M. K., J. C. Sesil, D. L. Kruse and J. R. Blasi (2002) 'Broad-based Stock Options – A Union Non-Union Comparison', in D. Lewin and B. E. Kaufman (eds), *Advances in Industrial and Labor Relations*, vol. 11, New York: JAI Press: 69–94.

Kruse, D. (1984) *Employee Ownership and Employee Attitudes: Two Case Studies*, Norwood, PA: Norwood Editions.

—— (1993) *Profit Sharing: Does It Make A Difference?*, Kalamazoo: W. E. Upjohn Institute for Employment Research.

—— (1996) 'Why Do Firms Adopt Profit-Sharing and Employee Ownership Plans?', *British Journal of Industrial Relations*, 34, 4: 515–38.

—— (1998) 'Profit Sharing and the Demand for Low-Skill Workers', in R. Freeman and P. Gottschalk (eds), *Generating Jobs: Increasing the Demand for Low-Skill Workers*, New York: Russell Sage Foundation.

—— (2002) 'Research Evidence on the Prevalence and Effects of Employee Ownership', *Journal of Employee Ownership Law and Finance*, 14, 4: 65–90.

—— and J. Blasi (1997) 'Employee Ownership, Employee Attitudes, and Firm Performance: A Review of the Evidence', in D. Lewin, D. J. B. Mitchell and

M. A. Zaidi (eds), *The Human Resources Management Handbook, Part 1*, Greenwich: JAI Press.

—— and —— (1999) 'Public Opinion Polls on Employee Ownership and Profit Sharing', *Journal of Employee Ownership Law and Finance*, 11, 3 (Summer).

Lawler, E. E. with S. A. Mohrman and G. E. Ledford Jr. (1998) *Strategies for High Performance Organizations – The CEO Report*. San Francisco: Jossey-Bass.

Lazear, E. P. (1986) 'Salaries and Piece Rates', *Journal of Business*, 59: 405–31.

—— (1995) *Personnel Economics*, Cambridge, MA: MIT Press.

Lebow, D., L. Sheiner, L. Slifman and M. Starr-McCluer (1998) *Recent Trends in Compensation Practices*, Washington, DC: US Federal Reserve Board, 15 July.

Levine, D. I. and L. D. Tyson (1990) 'Participation, Productivity and the Firm's Environment', in A. S. Blinder (ed.), *Paying for Productivity: A Look at the Evidence*, Washington, DC: Brookings Institution.

McNabb, R. and K. Whitfield (1998) 'The Impact of Financial Participation and Employee Involvement on Financial Performance', *Scottish Journal of Political Economy*, 45, 2: 171–87.

Milgrom, P. and J. Roberts (1992) *Economics, Organization, and Management*, London: Prentice-Hall.

Nalbantian, H. R. (ed.) (1987) *Incentives, Cooperation, and Risk Sharing*, Totowa, NJ: Rowman & Littlefield.

National Center for Employee Ownership [NCEO] (1998) *Current Practices in Stock Option Plan Design*, Oakland, CA: National Center for Employee Ownership. Second edition 2001.

—— (2002) 'Largest Study Yet Shows ESOPs Improve Performance and Employee Benefits', at http://www.nceo.org/library/esop_perf.html.

Ohkusa, Y. and F. Ohtake (1997) 'The Productivity Effects of Information Sharing, Profit Sharing, and ESOPs', *Journal of the Japanese and International Economies*, 11, 3: 385–402.

Patibandla, M. and P. Chandra (1998) 'Organizational Practices and Employee Performance: The Case of the Canadian Primary Textile Industry', *Journal of Economic Behavior and Organization*, 37, 4: 431–42.

Pearl Meyer (1998) *The Equity Stake – 1998: Study of Management Equity Participation in the Top 200 Corporations*, New York: Pearl Meyer & Partners.

Pencavel, J. (2001) *Worker Participation: Lessons from the Worker Co-ops of the Pacific Northwest*, New York: Russell Sage Foundation.

Pendleton, A., N. Wilson and M. Wright (1998) 'The Perception and Effects of Share Ownership: Empirical Evidence from Employee Buy-outs', *British Journal of Industrial Relations*, 36, 1: 99–123.

Putterman, L. and G. Skillman (1988) 'The Incentive Effects of Monitoring Under Alternative Compensation Schemes', *International Journal of Industrial Organization*, 6, 1: 109–19.

Quarrey, M. and C. Rosen (1993) *Employee Ownership and Corporate Performance*. Oakland, CA: National Center for Employee Ownership.

Scharf, A. and C. Mackin (2000) *Census of Massachusetts Companies with Employee Stock Ownership Plans (ESOPs)*, Boston: Commonwealth Corporation.

Sesil, J., M. K. Kroumova, J. R. Blasi and D. L. Kruse (2002) 'Broad-Based Stock Option in U.S. New Economy Firms', *British Journal of Industrial Relations*, 40, 2: 273–94.

—— M. Kroumova, D. Kruse and J. Blasi (2000) 'Broad-Based Employee Stock Options in the U.S.: Company Performance and Characteristics', *Academy of Management Best Papers Proceedings*, CD-ROM, G1-G5, Toronto (August).

—— D. L. Kruse and J. R. Blasi (2001) 'Sharing Ownership via Employee Stock', WIDER Discussion Paper no. 2001/25, Helsinki: UNU/WIDER.

Smith, S., B.-C. Cin and M. Vodopivec (1997) 'Privatization Incidence, Ownership Forms, and Firm Performance: Evidence from Slovenia', *Journal of Comparative Economics*, 25, 2: 158–79.

Tseo, G. (1996) 'Chinese Economic Restructuring: Enterprise Development through Employee Ownership', *Economic and Industrial Democracy*, 17, 2: 243–79.

US DOL (2002) 'Abstract of 1998 Form 5500 Annual Reports', *Private Pension Plan Bulletin*, 11 (Winter), Pension and Welfare Benefits Administration, US Department of Labor.

Uvalic, M. and D. Vaughan-Whitehead (eds) (1997) *Privatisation Surprises in Transition Economies: Employee Ownership in Central and Eastern Europe*, Cheltenham: Edward Elgar.

Wagner, J. A. (1994) 'Participation's Effects on Performance and Satisfaction: A Reconsideration of Research Evidence', *Academy of Management Review*, 19, 2: 312–30.

Watson Wyatt Worldwide (1998) *Stock Option Overhang: Shareholder Boon or Shareholder Burden?*, Bethesda, MD: Watson Wyatt Worldwide.

Weeden, R. and E. Carberry (2000) *Current Practices in Stock Option Plan Design*, Oakland, CA: NCEO.

—— —— and S. Rodrick (1998) *Current Practices in Stock Option Plan Design*, Oakland, CA: NCEO.

Weiss, A. (1987) 'Incentives and Worker Behavior', in H. Nalbantian (ed.), *Incentives, Cooperation, and Risk Sharing*, Totowa, NJ: Rowman & Littlefield, 137–150.

Winther, G. and R. Marens (1997) 'Participatory Democracy May Go A Long Way: Comparative Growth Performance of Employee Ownership Firms in New York and Washington States', *Economic and Industrial Democracy*, 18, 3: 393–422.

Weitzman, M. L. and D. L. Kruse (1990) 'Profit Sharing and Productivity', in A. S. Blinder (ed.), *Paying for Productivity: A Look at the Evidence*, Washington, DC: Brookings Institution.

5
Hardening a Soft Budget Constraint through 'Upward Devolution' to a Supranational Institution: The Case of the European Union and Italian State-Owned Firms

Elisabetta Bertero and Laura Rondi

Introduction

A firm's budget constraint is soft when financial discipline is relaxed, refinancing is easily obtainable when needed and bankruptcy is an unlikely threat. The soft budget constraint syndrome (SBCS) was identified by Kornai (1998) as a characteristic of state-owned enterprises (SOEs) in planned economies. Recent studies have formalized its theoretical underpinnings and explored its implications for firms in transitional economies.[1]

SBCS has two complementary features. One is the inability of the *provider* of funds to stick to its *ex ante* financial commitments when firms run into trouble. If this happens regularly, credibility and reputation are weakened. In the macroeconomic literature, this has been called 'time inconsistency' (Kydland and Prescott, 1977). The other is an agency problem (Bardhan and Roemer, 1992). When the *recipients* of funding – the managers – learn about the behaviour of funding institutions, they have an incentive to treat financial constraints as not binding. The resulting moral hazard leads to excessive managerial discretion and suboptimal investment (Bertero and Rondi, 2002).

Although the term SBCS is typically applied to transitional economies and SOEs, it is also relevant to private firms and financial institutions in market economies. The 'free cash flow' hypothesis and the related disciplining role of debt (Jensen, 1986; Hart and Moore, 1995) are essentially soft budget constraint issues. 'Too large to fail' and 'too many to fail' (Goodhart and Schoenmaker, 1995; Mitchell, 1998) are also soft budget constraint issues in which banks are rescued to avoid systemic risk.

How can SBCS be cured? Changing the capital structure of firms (Jensen, 1986) and the random rescue of failing banks (Maskin and Xu, 2001) have been suggested as ways of hardening the budget constraint of private companies and avoiding the associated moral hazard. For SOEs, insofar as state ownership is a cause of SBCS, privatization is one answer. At the beginning of the post-socialist transition it was widely believed that 'the "Holy Trinity" of liberalization, privatization and stabilization would suffice to produce an efficient market economy' (Kornai, 2001: 1591). But the debate on the Russian and Chinese models of transition has shown that ownership is only part of the problem and therefore privatization is only part of the answer.[2] Another possibility, described by Kornai (2001) as 'a task of equal rank' with privatization, is to harden the budget constraint. This chapter concentrates on the latter cure.

For transitional economies, Maskin and Xu (2001) show that decentralizing the financial system hardens SOEs' budget constraint by making *ex post* renegotiations more difficult. Berglof and Roland (1998) argue that decentralization works because it creates competition. Qian and Roland (1998) interpret decentralization as a form of federalism, that is, the organization of government in hierarchical levels with different monetary and fiscal responsibilities. Their model shows that keeping monetary authority at the federal level while devolving taxing and spending authority to competing local governments hardens the soft budget constraint of locally owned SOEs (which are at the bottom of this three-level hierarchy). They illustrate their model using the Chinese experience.

This chapter identifies a mechanism that involves decentralization and federalism to harden SOEs' budget constraint, but in a context that is very different from the Chinese one. It shows that when a supranational institution, which maximizes the welfare function of an international constituency, is able to impose monetary and fiscal policies on national governments, this financially constrains domestic SOEs. The process mitigates the time inconsistency problem of national governments because it requires them to abide by their *ex ante* commitments. In this chapter, therefore, federalism is the result of the 'upward devolution' of economic policies to a supranational authority.[3] The outcome is again a three-level hierarchy in which the monetary authority at the top level (in our case the supranational institution) keeps in check the fiscal policy of the next level (in our case the national governments) and this constrains SOEs' funding. The chapter also contributes to the literature on the organization of government and the role of multiprincipals – in our case the first principal is above the jurisdiction of domestic governments – as a disciplinary device (Tirole, 1994; Martimort, 1996; Persson *et al.*, 1997).

The methodology we use is a case study. We analyse the hardening of the budget constraint of Italian SOEs[4] in the late 1980s and find that a determining factor was the financial discipline imposed by the European Community (EC) and then the European Union (EU) on the Italian government.[5] In the case of China it was the downward devolution to local governments that created the federal structure. Because the federal government's monetary policy includes the distribution of grants to local governments, it is the competition for financial resources among local governments that creates discipline (Qian and Roland, 1998; see also Sun *et al.*, 1999). As stated above, in our study it is the upward devolution to the European level that creates the federal structure. Because the mechanism operates in a market economy, it is monetary, fiscal and competition policies that create discipline. In contrast to most of the literature on SBCS, this study examines the behaviour of SOEs in a market economy. Because firms' boundaries are clearly drawn by the markets (Maskin and Xu, 2001), and because the effects of transition do not need to be taken into account, this provides a different, arguably clearer, perspective on the phenomenon. The mechanism we identify in the case study works in several other contexts. Indeed the power of supranational institutions to tighten SOEs' budget constraints applies to a number of supranational institutions and their policies (for example the IMF, the World Bank and the WTO) and to firms other than state-owned ones in transitional, developing and market economies.

Soft budget constraint and state ownership

For private firms it is their relative size and the sector in which they operate or its maturity (Jensen, 1986) that make them more prone to SBCS; for firms owned by the state it is the discretionary nature of their budget constraint that makes them vulnerable to SBCS.

The economic rationale for government ownership is rooted in the theory of market failure and in welfare economics. Market failures are a result of market imperfections, such as externalities, public goods, natural monopolies due to increasing returns to scale, imperfect information, imperfect mobility of factors and incomplete markets. State-owned firms are meant to counterbalance these market imperfections, but this implies that the simple maximization of shareholders' wealth under a hard budget constraint is inappropriate for them. By definition, public firms have multiple objectives and multiple principals, and operate under a number of variable constraints (Tirole, 1994). This makes their behaviour rather complex and their performance more difficult to assess (Lawson, 1994). For example, among the multiple objectives of public enterprises are regional growth and industrial development, particularly in certain industries, which justifies the presence of state ownership even in competitive sectors.[6] It is recognized that state ownership was successful with respect to these objectives in several Western European countries after the Second World War because it allowed industrialization to be driven by criteria other than profits (Shonfield, 1977).

The economic rationale of state ownership implies that SOEs' objectives are unlikely to be purely financial and that their budget constraint is unlikely to be hard and inflexible at all times. However the current perception is not that SOEs successfully maximize a number of objectives and therefore need some flexibility in their budget constraint. Rather the perception is that their budget constraint is so soft that it ends up being a vehicle for serious allocational inefficiencies and corruption (Shleifer and Vishny, 1994). What distinguishes their soft budget constraint and produces these unwanted effects? Financial support for SOEs can be delivered with non-discretionary instruments (for example subsidised loans) or with discretionary instruments (for example injections of endowment funds in times of distress). The first affects the *ex ante* allocation of resources and incentives (Hart *et al.*, 1997); the second affects *ex post* allocational efficiency. It is with the second tool that SBCS arises. In other words, if public enterprises were only supported with non-discretionary subsidies allocated on the basis of fixed financial rules, the government would be able to commit itself *ex ante* and managers would not expect to be bailed out.

What distinguishes the soft budget constraint of public enterprises lies in the nature of its discretionality. In the introduction we distinguished between what we consider to be two complementary aspects of SBCS: the time inconsistency aspect and the agency problem. Most of the literature emphasizes the latter, which includes Kornai's original 'paternalistic' argument. However the former has received increasing attention in the transition literature, where it is called the dynamic commitment problem (Berglof and Roland, 1998), in line with the 'old' time inconsistency problem in the macroeconomic literature (Barro and

Gordon, 1983; Kydland and Prescott, 1977). Time inconsistency arises from the discretionality of optimal policies, which policy makers are free to reoptimize in each period, selecting the best action given the current situation. If it is assumed that agents are rational and have some knowledge of the maximizing function, the policies chosen become paradoxically suboptimal. In other words, with respect to soft budget constraint, independently of the agency relationship between politicians and managers, government financing of SOEs has to take into account the rationality of taxpayers, trade unions, workers and other stakeholders in the SOEs, including creditors and government departments other than the Treasury. Once these players get to know the basic principles of government funding and the objectives maximized by the government through SOEs, they will expect discretionary policies to lead to a soft budget constraint, and accordingly modify their current behaviour in order to make soft refinancing inevitable.[7] Time inconsistency is particularly severe for SOEs because they face what Dewatripont and Maskin (1995) call a centralized credit market, that is, a credit market in which firms can only obtain refinancing from the original creditor. For SOEs the financial constraint and its subsequent relaxation both come from the shareholder/government or its banks, with which the firm has close administrative links. Furthermore their financing is also centralized by the fact that both debt and equity come from state-owned banks and the Treasury. The argument in Berglof and Roland (1998) is that a soft budget constraint is due to the endogenous lack of credibility for liquidating a project instead of refinancing it due to the known sunk costs incurred.

The other aspect of SBCS is a principal–agent problem between the provider of funds and SOE managers, and the consequent moral hazard. When managers learn that the budget constraint is not binding because the provider of funds is unable to stick to *ex ante* commitments, they have an incentive, as in widely held quoted firms with little monitoring, to maximize personal gains or take excessive risks. This mechanism is complex for SOEs for two reasons. First, SOEs face a rather complicated nexus of agency problems due to their multiple principals – taxpayers, the government and several ministries (Laffont and Tirole, 1993; Tirole, 1994; Shleifer and Vishny, 1994; Prendergast, 2000). Second, the principal that provides refinancing is not only the principal that provided the original funding, but also the principal that requires SOEs to maximize a range of objectives and with which SOEs have a subordinate relationship (Kornai, 1998) and close administrative links. This administrative proximity and interdependence with the provider of funds and ultimately politicians can lead to collusion in maximizing party-political and vote-seeking objectives (Bertero and Rondi, 2002). In sum, the problem with SOEs' soft budget constraint is its high degree of discretionality, which lends itself to abuse for political and vote-seeking objectives. The absence of credible financial discipline and the easy access to government funds for objectives beyond the economic ones have led to serious allocational inefficiencies and given SOEs a reputation for inefficiency and corruption in transitional, developing and market economies.[8]

The upward devolution of economic policies to the European level

The remedy to cure both aspects of SBCS is the devolution of some domestic economic policies to a supranational institution. In the first part of our case study we analyse the policies devolved by member governments to the EC/EU and identify the macroeconomic and microeconomic channels through which this upward devolution occurred. The macroeconomic policies included the exchange rate policies of the European Monetary System (EMS) and the monetary and fiscal policies adopted in preparation for European Monetary Union (EMU). The microeconomic policies included competition policy and the regulation of state aid.

Macroeconomic policies

In the 1970s the average gross public debt to GDP ratio in the OECD countries increased by 10 per cent, productivity growth declined and inflation accelerated. In the late 1970s attention was narrowly focused on the fiscal and monetary policies that would reduce budget deficits:

> Rationales for reform developed to a large extent from [these] experiences,...when the coincidence of slowing economic growth, rising structural unemployment and accelerating inflation began to persuade governments that the usual goals of economic policy were no longer being served by a continuing expansion of the public sector. Governments turned towards greater self-restraint as evidence accumulated that higher taxes and budget deficits could contribute to allocative distortions which reduced long-run growth potential (OECD, 1989: 156).

On 1 January 1979 the EMS became operational in this international policy climate. External and internal monetary stability were its main goals. External stability would be achieved through a multilateral mechanism to keep exchange rates within bands. Internal stability would be obtained indirectly, because maintaining the exchange rate within those bands would keep inflation under control. In turn this meant that fiscal policy had to be restrained (Gross and Thygesen, 1992). The EMS put pressure on domestic monetary, fiscal and structural policies in various ways. One was through the negotiations for the EMS realignments. Each negotiation implied a reassessment of the effect of inflation on exchange rates and therefore of the success of governments in curbing inflation and reducing deficits. Further pressure was created by the fact that it was impossibile for members of the EMS to rely on competitive devaluation to boost competitiveness. This highlighted the need for structural reforms to reduce production costs, such as reforms of the labour market and the pension system.

In 1989 this pressure became an ultimatum under the Delors Report. Precise figures were released for the fiscal ratios required for entry to EMU: less than 3 per cent for deficit to GDP and less than 60 per cent for debt to GDP. With the signing of the Maastricht Treaty in December 1991 governments committed themselves to meet these targets by 1997. Under the terms of the Stability and Growth Pact (1997) they committed themselves to keeping their budget deficit within 3 per cent at first and then to balance it once in EMU.[9] Devolving the exchange rate policy through the EMS and devolving monetary policy in preparation for EMU severely constrained the fiscal policy of member states. This forced a reduction of budget deficits, and consequently greatly reduced the financial resources available to SOEs. 'Wasting' resources by sustaining their soft budgets was no longer politically acceptable.

Microeconomic policies

The devolution of microeconomic policies – competition policy and state aid regulation – to the European level affected SOEs in a more direct way. The European Commission's concern about the anticompetitive effects of state intervention dated back to the Treaty of Rome (1957). A fundamental principle in the Treaty prohibited the EC governments to provide financial aid to domestic firms because of its negative impact on competition. However in the 1960s and 1970s competition policy was not a priority and state aid was not restricted (CER-IRS, 1992). Exceptions to the principle were spelled out in Article 92[10] and permission was granted by a system of applications for special status (Article 93) to the European Commission (Cafferata, 1995; Besley and Seabright, 1999). Although it is common to associate state aid with SOEs, the regulation of state aid in the Treaty of Rome was neutral with respect to the organization and ownership of firms so as to avoid discrimination among member states with an uneven distribution of state ownership (Ehlermann, 1992). In the early 1980s competition policy acquired greater importance and attention was focused specifically on flows to SOEs. Whereas state aid to private firms was easily detectable, the aid component of endowment funds to SOEs was difficult to ascertain. Hence aid to SOEs was treated as a special case. A directive required member states to ensure transparency in the size and objectives of financial flows to SOEs (Ehlermann, 1992; European Commission, 1999).[11] The application of this directive was extended in 1985 to include public enterprises operating in water supply, energy, transportation and telecommunication.[12]

In June 1984 negotiations started for the Single European Act, which was aimed at creating a single market, that is, 'an area without internal barriers in which the free movement of goods, persons, services and capital is ensured' (Article 8a). In March 1985 a white paper, *The Completion of the Internal Market* (the Cecchini Report) was published and the Act was signed in February 1986. A few months later the European Council agreed a timetable – to be implemented by December 1992 – for 279 detailed measures aimed at abolishing tariff and non-tariff barriers.[13] Although the main reason for the single market was the macroeconomic benefits it would bring – higher growth, lower unemployment and inflation – the transmission mechanism would be microeconomic. The single market was expected to stimulate cost savings by eliminating non-tariff barriers and to increase competitive pressure by enlarging and integrating the European market. In this context competition policy was of paramount importance and state aid came to be viewed as an impediment to the success of this far-reaching programme. State aid to all firms, public or private, came to be viewed as an implicit threat for the economic and social cohesion of the EC. The richer countries could afford generous transfers within their economies and this could distort the regional structural fund policies (CER-IRS, 1992). At first monitoring the allocation of state aid to any firm was a precondition for the completion of the single market, but then it became a permanent feature of the programme. The first survey on state aid was published in 1988 and has been regularly published since.[14] Soon after attention again turned to aid to SOEs. In 1988 the Commission required member states to agree a set of accounting standards to identify the proportion of aid in public transfers to SOEs (CER-IRS, 1992). In 1991 an EC communication addressed the issue of the size, quantity and definition of state aid to these enterprises.[15] It required SOEs whose annual sales were greater than ECU 250 million to forward to the Commission an annual report on the amount of public transfer from state agencies. Most importantly it established the 'market economy investor principle' (MEIP), which compares the terms in which the government provides funds to SOEs with the terms under which a private financial investor would provide the same funds in market conditions. The difference is classified as aid and subject to the approval of the Commission (Harbord and Yarrow, 1999).

Finally, state ownership itself came under scrutiny. Once priority was given to the reduction of budget deficits, increased competition and the reduction of state aid, as defined by the MEIP, public ownership became questionable. At the EU level, privatization became a prerequisite for improved competition. It began with a debate on whether aid supplied for the rescue and restructuring of SOEs should be conditional on privatization (Ehlermann, 1995). From the early 1990s EU pressure to reduce aid became explicit pressure to reduce state ownership.[16]

Italian SOEs: the early years and the softening of their budget constraint

Before turning to the second part of our case study – the effects of European policies on Italian SOEs – it is necessary to understand how the budget constraint of Italian SOEs became soft in the first place. In this section we explore their early years, which were characterized by a healthy distance between public managers and politicians and a reasonably hard budget constraint, and the developments in the 1970s to mid 1980s, which were characterized by political interference and a soft budget constraint.

The early 'healthy' years (the 1930s to the 1960s)

The historical roots of Italian public ownership date back to the nineteenth century, when the need for investment in financially demanding, capital-intensive technologies was not being met by private investors.[17] The official birth date of state ownership was 1933, when the Institute for Industrial Reconstruction (IRI) was created to bail out major Italian banks and the many industrial companies in their portfolios.[18] State ownership in Italy was neither part of the fascist regimes' economic programme nor, as in the case of France and the UK, part of a planned nationalization policy. Most of the companies belonging to the IRI operated under market conditions in competitive sectors, were incorporated as joint stock companies and participated in the Confederation of Italian Industry (Confindustria). The IRI itself was incorporated as a holding company under private law. Although the Ministry of Finance had overall oversight of the holding the IRI was run by a team of professional managers who succeeded in remaining independent from political influence. The IRI's objective, in the interest both of private firms and of public policy, was to restructure firms and return them to the private sector.

However after the Second World War the IRI's companies and banks were not privatized, for two reasons: lack of private domestic capital for a massive privatization programme and their usefulness in speeding up reconstruction, a view shared by politicians and public managers (Bottiglieri, 1984). On the contrary, direct intervention by the state in the economy increased under the postwar democratic regime. In 1953 a new public holding in the oil and gas industry, the ENI, was created on the ground that economic recovery and growth required strong foundations in the energy sector. Like their counterparts in the IRI, the managers of the ENI were successful in safeguarding their independence from the political system and concerned themselves primarily with profitability, efficiency and the development of a modern industrial system. Managers were selected for their technical skills by top executives and there was no interference from politicians (Scognamiglio, 2001). Investment projects were financed through cash flow, bank loans and, in limited amounts, equity (through endowment funds, *fondi di dotazione*). The residual control rights were in the hands of management (Barca and Trento, 1997).

Our assessment of these facts is that, in this postwar period, Italian SOEs operated under a rather hard budget constraint. The lack of financial capital, the healthy distance between managers and politicians, the poor state of the Italian economy, the reconstruction effort, the backwardness of industrial equipment, US intervention through the European Recovery Plan and the high growth rate all contributed to a hard budget constraint environment. Moreover the interests of politicians, eager to be re-elected on the basis of a successful economic performance, were aligned with those of the efficiency-pursuing public managers. Later assessments of the performance of Italian SOEs in this period praise SOE managers for their contribution to the recovery of the Italian economy, and even for reinforcing competition (Posner and Wolf, 1967; Shonfield, 1977; Martinelli, 1981; Borghini and Podestà, 1987; Barca and Trento, 1997). SOEs helped to pave the way for the extraordinary 1958–63 economic boom (the so-called *miracolo economico*).

Slipping into a soft budget constraint regime (the 1970s to the mid 1980s)

The establishment of two new institutions marked the beginning of a change in the relationship between public managers and politicians, and of a period in which SOEs were required to implement incompatible objectives that encouraged moral hazard. First, in 1956 the Ministry for State Holdings was established and given the mandate of translating policy guidelines into operational objectives for SOEs. The Christian Democratic Party and its associated trade union, the CISL, promoted the new ministry, arguing that SOEs should take special interest in the development of Southern Italy and the improvement of workers' conditions.[19] In the same period the obligation for SOEs to pursue profitability was reaffirmed (Saraceno, 1977). Second, in 1967 the Interministerial Committee for Economic Planning (CIPE) was established. Its mandate was to implement the 1966–70 Economic Plan for Development, which included formulating economic and social policy guidelines for SOEs that the Ministry for State Holdings would make operational.[20] The CIPE reconfirmed that SOEs should pursue 'economic efficiency'. Until then it had been SOE managers who had submitted projects for approval to the Ministry of Finance, but from then on the CIPE set investment plans and the managers had to carry them out. This inversion of roles constituted a major change because it transferred the residual control right from managers to politicians.[21] Figure 5.1 shows the multilayered structure of the SOE's corporate governance.

Moreover the deteriorating economic conditions in the early 1970s undermined the financial independence of the public holdings.[22] The low level of endowment funds became insufficient for investment and the rescue of troubled firms. As public holdings became financially dependent on the government and parliament, public managers became more dependent on politicians for recruitment, job security and top appointments. In 1978 a new law gave a parliamentary committee the mandate to appoint SOE chairpersons and vice-chairpersons.[23] This implicitly made it acceptable for the nomination of top positions to be split among the political parties in the coalition government and to use these posts for political bargaining. Competence and experience were no longer necessary requirements for top SOE executives (Grassini, 1981)[24], and a 'party-political hidden shareholder' emerged (Scognamiglio, 1981). The complicated governance structure, ambiguous and inconsistent objectives,[25] financial difficulties and the lack of transparency of accounts made political pressure by vote-seeking politicians more difficult to resist.

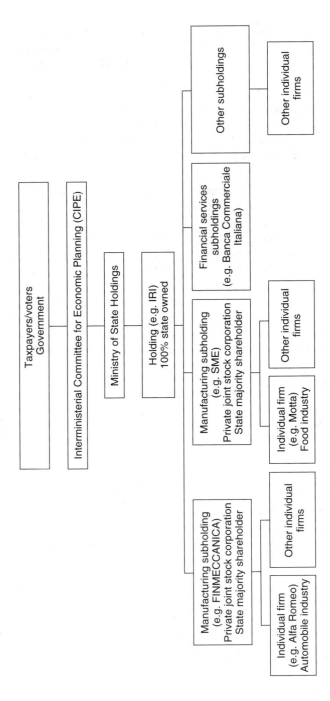

Figure 5.1 Corporate governance of Italian public enterprises

Data on public transfers to state holdings from the 1950s to the late 1980s show the increased dependence of SOEs on state help. Lo Passo and Macchiati (1998) report that transfer of endowment funds to the IRI and ENI were of modest size until the late 1950s, when the budget constraint was reasonably tight, slowly increased in the 1960s and early 1970s and increased rapidly in the late 1970s. Estimates by the OECD (1985) show that between 1965 and 1972 transfers to SOEs equalled those to private firms as a percentage of GDP and amounted to 1.4 per cent. By 1978 transfers to state firms had risen to 3.3 per cent of GDP whereas subsidies to private firms had fallen to 0.7 per cent. Data estimated by Brosio and Silvestri (1983) show that the share of the state transfers to the industrial sector that went to public holdings rose from 6 per cent to 46 per cent over the decade 1970–79. Figure 5.2 shows the SOEs' poor results in the 1970s and 1980s. By the end of the 1970s the SOEs' performance was characterized by huge losses, low productivity and high debt. In the early 1980s a deep recession made things worse. As the profitability of the IRI and ENI further deteriorated (the IRI's deficit in 1981 was Lit3134 billion, on approximately 0.8 per cent of GDP), endowment funds soared. Between 1976 and 1983 total endowment funds to the IRI and ENI rose from 1.8 per cent to 3.7 per cent of GDP. Accommodating endowment funds, high levels of

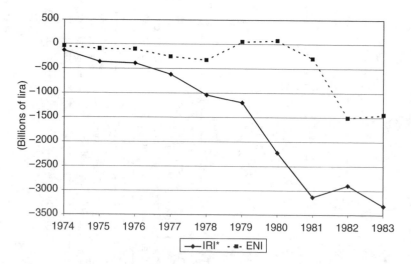

Figure 5.2 Net income of public holdings, Italy, 1974–83
Note: *Banks excluded.
Source: Consolidated reports, as reported in Coltorti (1990).

state-guaranteed debt, political interference and collusion between managers and politicians combined to create a soft budget constraint regime for Italian SOEs.

Italian SOEs and the effect of European policies

The above circumstances changed during the late 1980s and early 1990s, at first slowly and then at great speed. The second part of our case study analyses the effect of European macroeconomic and microeconomic policies on Italian SOEs and on their budget constraint.

The switch of the budget constraint regime

The macroeconomic channel

Italy became a member of the EMS from its inception in 1979. At the time Italy had one of the largest deficits of the member countries – 10.6 per cent of GDP. During the negotiations for the EMS realignments pressure was put on the Italian government to reduce its deficit. Between 1979 and 1987 the government participated in eight such negotiations, during each of which there were discussions and assessments by the other EMS partners of the effect of Italy's high inflation on exchange rates and of the appropriateness of its policies to curb that inflation and reduce the deficit, both of which were preconditions for remaining in the EMS. The forced exit of the Italian lira (and of the British pound) from the EMS years later (in 1992) shows that the threat was credible. The other effect of the EMS was the loss, in the export-led Italian economy, of the much used and popular policy of 'competitive devaluation', which had enabled the government to improve the external trade balance and sustain the industrial sector. Without regular devaluations, exporting firms – a large and influential group that included several SOEs – were forced to restructure and reduce their production costs (Barca and Magnani, 1989), particularly their labour and pension costs. The relative inflexibility of the Italian labour market compared with those in the other European countries began to be questioned (Emerson, 1988).

There were four measures – considered, revolutionary for Italy at the time – that provide indicative examples of the effects of these pressures in the 1980s. First, in 1981 the so-called 'divorce' agreement between the Bank of Italy and the Treasury was approved. This released the bank from the obligation to buy residual government bonds at issue. Second, in 1984 the automatic wage indexation mechanism was abolished and other measures were introduced to reduce employment-related costs for firms. Third, in July 1985 a formal promise was made by the Italian government to reduce the budget deficit within the negotiations of the eighth realignment, when the lira was devalued by 8 per cent against all other currencies. A number of measures were discussed to achieve this goal, for example reforming the pension system and increasing the tax burden. A reduction of subsidies to public enterprises was also discussed. Fourth, in 1986, for the first time, two large state-owned enterprises – Alfa Romeo and Lanerossi – were privatized. The effect of the macroeconomic pressure in the second half of the 1980s is evident in the fiscal data. Table 5.1 reports data on government balances and the decline of the deficit from 1985 onwards. Figure 5.3 shows that the rapid growth of public debt in the early 1980s started to slow from around 1986. Inflation, which averaged 14.1 per cent in the 1981–85 period, fell to 5.9 per cent in 1986–90.

The microeconomic channel

On the microeconomic side, the devolution of competition policy to the European level, particularly with the single market programme, forced the Italian government to adopt a more efficient approach to the allocation of resources to SOEs. Reduced resources and greater allocational efficiency severely tightened the budget constraint of these firms in the late 1980s. We shall first look at how EC/EU policies and interventions directly affected Italian SOEs and then consider their effects on the resources available to these firms. The change of attitude at the EC level towards state aid to SOEs that came with the directives on transparency was particularly needed in Italy at the beginning of the 1980s. The annual reports on state

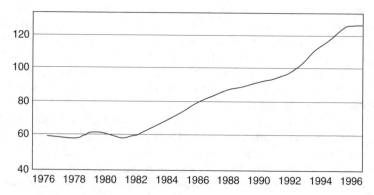

Figure 5.3   Italian public debt, 1976–96 (percentage of GDP)
Source: Bank of Italy, *Annual Report 1996*.

Table 5.1 Italian government balances, 1980–99 (percentage of GDP)

	1980	1981	1982	1983	1984	1985	1986	1987	1988	1989	1990	1991	1992	1993	1994	1995	1995[2]	1996	1997	1998	1999
Revenues[1]	30.6	31.7	34.2	36.0	35.0	34.8	35.2	36.0	36.6	38.2	38.8	39.7	42.0	43.4	40.6	40.6	45.6	45.8	48.2	46.6	46.9
Public expenditure,	42.5	46.7	49.0	50.5	50.2	51.1	49.7	49.2	49.4	50.5	51.9	52.5	54.3	55.6	52.5	50.9	53.2	52.9	50.9	49.4	48.8
of which: Interest	5.3	6.2	7.2	7.6	8.2	8.2	8.5	8.0	8.2	8.9	9.6	10.2	11.4	12.1	10.7	11.2	11.5	11.5	9.4	8.1	6.8
Primary deficit (surplus:−)	3.6	5.4	4.5	3.5	3.6	4.1	3.2	3.0	2.5	1.0	1.1	–	−1.9	−3.0	−1.9	−4.1	−3.9	−4.4	−6.7	−5.3	−4.9
Total deficit	8.9	11.6	11.7	11.1	11.8	12.3	11.7	11.0	10.7	9.9	10.7	10.2	9.5	9.1	8.8	7.1	7.6	7.1	2.7	2.8	1.9

Notes:
1. Tax burden and social security contributions.
2. The series from 1995 to 1999 apply the new version of the European Accounting System (SEC 95 – Sistema Europeo dei Conti).
Source: Bank of Italy annual reports (various years).

holdings were uninformative and lack of transparency was a recognized problem.[26] Without EC intervention, action in this area would have been difficult, given the complex financial and political links between the CIPE, the Treasury, the Public Holdings Ministry and political parties.

Evidence of direct EC pressure is provided by the frequent litigation against the Italian government by the European Commission over specific norms. For example the European Commission regarded as anticompetitive – and therefore illegal – the following norms on the definition of state aid: Law 46/1982 on the Fund of Innovation and Applied Research; Law 64/1986 on some broadly defined aid to southern regions, including transfers for private and state firms investing in the south; Law 4239/1989 on the provision of tax relief to firms involved in mergers and acquisitions, and especially benefiting the merger between the chemical division of ENI, ENICHEM and Montedison; and Law 317/1991 on financial support to small and medium firms. Perhaps the strongest evidence of the EC's influence over the rationalization of SOE funding was its direct involvement in the running of specific SOEs and in litigation on aid to individual enterprises. These hands-on interventions demonstrate the determination of the European Commission to strengthen competition and, from the mid 1980s, prioritize the objectives of the single market. They also show an increased tendency to consider suspicious any capital injection by member states into SOEs and, occasionally, some confusion about the exact rules that should be used to screen applications for state aid (Besley and Seabright, 1999).[27]

Six examples of the EC interventions were in the restructuring of Finsider (the IRI subholding that ran the steel industry), the allocation of aid to Lanerossi (a large textile company within the ENI holding) and Alfa Romeo (a large car manufacturing firm and part of the IRI), the liquidation of EFIM (the holding for the mining and rail engineering sectors), the aid to ENICHEM, and the restructuring of Alitalia (the national airline and part of the IRI). Approval of the major restructuring plan for Finsider in 1987 had to come from the EC's Directorate for Competition Policy (DG IV). One of the conditions imposed was quarterly monitoring by an external consulting firm of the achievement of financial targets (Kumar, 1993). The restructuring brought about the closure of several plants (twelve in three years) and a reduction of employment from 122 000 in 1980 to 76 000 in 1987. It also led to the replacement of Finsider with Ilva.[28] Finsider's liabilities were transferred to the IRI, but this was done only after EC approval. The financial aid that the government had provided to Lanerossi between 1983 and 1987 was declared illegal by the European Commission in 1988 and had to be returned. Similarly, in 1989 the funds granted to Alfa Romeo before it was sold to Fiat in 1986 were judged incompatible with EC competition policy and had to be paid back. The litigation continued until 1991 and was resolved with a final sentence in favour of the European Commission by the European Court of Justice for both Lanerossi and Alfa Romeo (CER-IRS, 1992).

The liquidation of EFIM in 1997 was only completed after several direct interventions by the EU. For example in 1995–96 the Commission blocked the injection of funds into an ex-EFIM firm, Breda Fucine Meridionali, and the firm had to repay the Lit125 billion of aid it had received since 1985. The Commission also required the Italian government to absorb Efim's debt of Lit8500 billion. In 1994 the Commission launched an investigation of the state aid given to ENICHEM in 1992 and 1993 and subsequently rejected the package. This was the direct consequence of an agreement between the Commission and the Italian government (the Van Miert–Andreatta agreement of 1993) that committed the government not only to restructure but also to privatize a number of IRI and ENI firms in order to reduce their indebtedness (see below). In 1996 the Commission investigated the allocation in the Italian budget of state aid to the IRI for the restructuring of Alitalia. The restructuring was rejected in 1997 on the basis of a report by a private consulting firm. Negotiations led to a number of strict constraints on the running of the company, for example limits on investment, the prohibition of fleet increases and a freeze on fares. The involvement of the Commission in the running of SOEs eventually led to a reduction of their financial flows from the state. No ready-made aggregate data is available on these flows, so we chart the decline using a number of sources. Table 5.2, which reports data from EC/EU surveys on state aid, shows the decline in total state aid to all Italian firms between 1981 and

Table 5.2 State aid to Italian firms, 1981–96
(total aid as a percentage of GDP)

1981–86	5.7
1986–88	3.1
1988–90	2.9
1990–92	2.4
1992–94	2.2
1994–96	2.0

Sources: Surveys on state aid in the European Union, various years.

1996. As can be seen, state aid fell from 5.7 per cent of GDP in 1981–86 to 3.1 per cent in 1986–88. Unfortunately the surveys do not report separate figures for SOEs.

Figure 5.4 shows separate figures for private and state firms, but only from 1987, when data became available from the Italian government's own surveys. Although an overall decline is evident for both the private and the public sector, the reduction in aid to public firms was larger and consistent over the entire period. However these data include both horizontal and sectoral interventions and also aid to public utilities (including the railways and other public transport).[29]

In order to obtain a better picture of the overall state funding provided to SOEs and of their budget constraint, we constructed a time series of transfers to the industrial sector. Figure 5.5 is based on data from a number of sources, including Brosio and Silvestri (1983), Artoni and Ravazzi (1986) and CER-IRS annual reports (1989, 1992, 1993, 1997). Figure 5.5 provides a comprehensive picture of state transfers to SOEs because it includes endowment funds and transfers due to the amortization of government guaranteed bonds and loans from the EIB and other international financial institutions. In 1980 transfers to SOEs accounted for 43.7 per cent of total public transfers to the industrial sector. By 1987 their share had fallen to 4.9 per cent, and it averaged 6.1 per cent in the following eight years.[30] Total transfers to the industrial sector as a

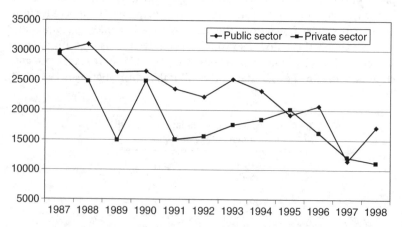

Figure 5.4　State aid to enterprises, 1987–98 (billion lira at 1987 prices)
Note: The public sector data include aid to public utilities, plus horizontal and sectoral interventions; the private sector data include horizontal and sectoral interventions.
Source: Senato della Repubblica (2000).

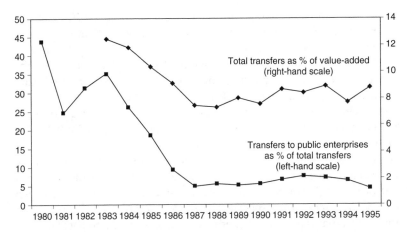

Figure 5.5 Public transfers to the industrial sector and transfers to public enterprises, 1980–95
Source: Artoni and Ravazzi (1986); CER-IRS (1989, 1992, 1993, 1997).

percentage of the value added of industrial transformation decreased from 12.45 per cent to 7.45 per cent over the period 1983–87 but remained fairly stable thereafter. Total public transfers declined as a percentage of GDP and the share to SOEs decreased more than proportionally.

What emerges from these figures is that public transfers rapidly declined between 1980 and 1987. Given that the Italian government was driven in that period by party-political and vote-seeking objectives and found it difficult to stick to its commitments, this decline would have been unlikely without European pressure. In the late 1980s Italian public enterprises found their resources curtailed and their previously accommodating principal frequently pressured by the European Commission to adhere to its rulings. When in distress these firms could no longer count on injections of funds. Moreover they had to adjust to the new single market regulations, including the public procurement rules. The greatly reduced endowment funds, lack of certainty about rescue interventions and the need to abide to European competition policy rules all served to create an environment that fitted the characteristics of a hard budget constraint regime.

Beyond the hard budget constraint and into privatization

There came a point when the devolution of competition policy and the total devolution of monetary policy required by EMU forced the Italian government to abandon state ownership.[31] As Kumar (1993) points out, 'the recent dramatic change in the government's basic position and its intentions to privatize the surviving holding groups themselves, have clearly been selected as result of budgetary, rather than efficiency or ideology, requirements'. The 1989 Delors Report put EMU clearly on the agenda of the Italian government. But the 1991 Maastricht Treaty required, for entry in 1999, a deficit to GDP ratio of less than 3 per cent and a debt to GDP ratio of less than 60 per cent. The Italian ratios were, respectively, 10 per cent and 90 per cent (Figure 5.3 and Table 5.1). It became clear that further restrictive fiscal measures would be needed to achieve these objectives within the required time frame. The catching up took off after the 1992 speculative attack on the lira, which forced it out of the EMS. The fiscal adjustment between 1992 and 1997, which has been described as 'spectacular' (Padoa Schioppa Kostoris, 1998), included a major privatization programme. Monetary and fiscal policies became highly restrictive and turned the primary deficit into a surplus and reduced the government's total deficit and inflation to levels compatible with participation in EMU (Table 5.1). In May 1998 it was announced that Italy could join EMU from its inception in January 1999. The preparations for a radical privatization programme, covering not only the manufacturing sector but also the banking sector, started with a number of laws. The Amato Law[32] provided the structure for the privatization of the banking system and the pre-existing Antitrust Law of 1990 challenged the competitive behaviour of some large public enterprises. Other laws were aimed at modernizing Italy's economic and financial institutions. In 1993 a new banking law brought together all the recent legislation on the liberalization of financial markets.[33]

The privatization of state holdings started with two important laws. Law No. 35, passed on 29 January 1992, turned major state-controlled holdings into joint stock companies. This stopped the granting of endowment funds and forced the government to redefine the economic role of state-owned industries and to draw up a full reorganization plan (Cafferata, 1995; Padoa Schioppa Kostoris, 1998). A law passed in 1993 abolished the Ministry for State Holding (The Partecipazioni Statali) and transferred the ownership of state holdings to the Treasury. This was the clearest signal that they would soon be privatized and that the Treasury was ready to cash in. Also, the party-driven system of top management appointments for state holdings was returned to the government (Amato, 1994).

Meanwhile EU pressure continued. Following a judgement on 29 July 1993 the Italian government was forced to agree to accelerate its privatization programme (Cafferata, 1995). Most importantly, in July 1993 the Italian treasury minister signed an agreement with the European commissioner for competition policy, Van Miert, on a plan for the IRI to reduce its indebtedness and a plan for its privatization. The acceleration of the privatization programme is shown by the revenue pattern. Between 1986 and 1995 the total revenue from privatization was approximately Lit50 trillion, and this was approximately the amount raised in the following two years (Padoa Schioppa Kostoris, 1998). In conclusion, in the 1990s supranational pressure took on a new dimension when privatization became a *de facto* requirement for EU and EMU membership.

The effects of the change of budget regimes: empirical evidence

How did the change of budget regime affect the behaviour of Italian public enterprises? Is there any empirical evidence on the effects on their performance of the hardening of the budget constraint in those years? Two studies on the financial discipline of SOEs and a number of other works have concentrated on the restructuring process that followed this change of environment. Bertero and Rondi (2000, 2002) studied the effects on a sample of Italian state-owned manufacturing firms of the hardening of the budget constraint over the period 1977–93 by carrying out an experiment that exploited the shift of budget regimes in the late 1980s. Drawing from the theoretical framework developed in financial economics for private firms, Bertero and Rondi (2000) tested for the effect of the financial discipline provided by debt across the two regimes. The empirical findings show that when a budget regime shifts from soft to hard, financial pressure has a positive and significant effect on SOE productivity and a negative and significant effect on employment in state firms. Hence under a hard budget constraint, SOEs respond to financial pressure by increasing total factor productivity and cutting employment.

Bertero and Rondi (2002) then extended the analysis to the effects on investment in fixed capital. Drawing from the theory of capital market imperfections they applied the empirical framework to their sample of SOEs in order to analyze investment–cash flow sensitivity over the period 1977–93. Bertero and Rondi draw a parallel between SOEs and Anglo-Saxon public corporations, which under the separation of ownership and control are afflicted by agency problems, managerial discretion, misallocation of cash flow and overinvestment (Jensen, 1986). They argue that under a soft budget constraint the abuse of managerial discretion and collusion between managers and vote-seeking politicians lead to wasteful investment (or overinvestment), which can be detected econometrically via an excess sensitivity of investment to cash flow. In this framework the cash-flow term tests for capital market imperfections arising from SOE agency problems. A significant cash-flow effect is an indication of the abuse of managerial discretion and of overinvestment because, irrespective of other grants or loans, SOE managers may use all the cash flow for investment, including vote-seeking projects in collusion with politicians, or for bribes to obtain additional external financing for empire building. Consistent with these predictions, Bertero and Rondi find that the correlation between cash flow and investment is strong and positive (and robust to the inclusion of debt terms) under the soft budget constraints and that it disappears under the hard budget constraint.

Lo Passo and Macchiati (1998) used a case study approach to examine the restructuring of the IRI and ENI from late 1980s to the late 1990s. Among the main factors enhancing the restructuring process were the reduction of public transfers, enforcement of a hard budget constraint, increased monitoring by the government and the liberalization of the many industries in which SOEs operated. Their analysis revealed that both the IRI and the ENI responded to a change in the policy regime by modifying their group structure, refocusing on the core business, replacing incompetent managers in operating companies and improving profitability.

Two other studies provide indirect evidence of the effects of a harder budget constraint regime on SOEs. Interestingly, the focus of these studies was the effects of privatization on firms' financial and operating performance, and not the restructuring of SOEs. Using a sample of 10 former public utilities over the period 1983–99, Fraquelli (2001) compared their performance before and after privatization and found that significant improvements in efficiency and profitability were obtained in the years just before privatization. The author interprets this as resulting from a reduction of political interference and from an increase in managers' perceived risk of replacement in the run-up to privatization. Benfratello (2001) obtained similar results when investigating the profitability and financial performance of 15 former public manufacturing firms before and after privatization, over the period 1989–97.

In summary, these studies found evidence of the ability of public enterprises in manufacturing and public utilities to restructure when faced with tighter financial discipline. Even studies that were meant to examine the effects of privatization ended up concluding that much of the improvement occurred before the firms were privatized, when a tighter discipline was imposed. Empirical evidence of substantial improvements in SOE performance independently of privatization is available for firms in a number of countries.[34] However the privatization programme in Italy was mainly spurred by EU pressure and was not the consequence of political change or other factors. Therefore, insofar as the privatizations in the late 1980s and early 1990s were not anticipated, the responsiveness of SOEs to the hardening of the budget constraint is significant evidence of the impact of the supranational mechanisms that enforced the new discipline.

Conclusions and policy implications

Easy access to government funds and the consequent soft budget constraint on SOEs are widely understood to be important reasons for their lack of financial discipline and inefficiency (see for example Shleifer and Vishny, 1994). Although SBCS can equally affect private firms and private financial institutions, SOEs are more prone to suffer from it. The time inconsistency of government commitments and the moral hazard affecting SOE managers are among the causes. There is a substantial body of literature to show that a change of ownership is not a sufficient condition to improve SOEs' performance and SBCS. Indeed privatization has not produced the expected results in countries such as Russia, Ukraine, Romania and the Czech Republic (Kornai, 2001). Conversely economic reforms that include the increased use of incentives, creative governance, tightened budget constraints, toughened product market competition and liberalization have proved effective in many countries (Megginson and Netter, 2001).

Pinto *et al.* (1993) show that the January 1990 reforms in Poland, which included a tightening of fiscal and monetary policies, restrictions on bank lending and the sending of 'no bailout' signals, significantly improved the performance of the Polish state sector and of manufacturing firms. Angelucci *et al.* (2002) find that domestic competitive pressure and increased import penetration are associated with improved firm performance in Poland, irrespective of ownership structure. In Bulgaria and Romania, in contrast, competitive pressure and private ownership are complementary, which the authors attribute to these countries' slow progress in the transition process, including governance restructuring, the development of market institutions and the overall privatization programme.

Majumdar (1996) has found that the performance differential between private and public firms in India decreased when the government introduced reforms in the public sector, such as the implementation of private-sector management practices and performance-related incentives. Sun (2001) shows that Chinese joint-stock cooperatives, in which local governments are involved, are adaptively efficient. Li (1997) has found that, for a sample of 272 Chinese state-owned firms over the period 1980–89, economic reforms based on improved incentives and compensation led to marked improvements in marginal and total factor productivity.

Carlin *et al.* (2001) emphasize the role of competition and of a favourable business environment in a cross-country survey of 25 transitional economies. Their findings also indicate that there is no significant relationship between privatization and company performance; that is, that the effect of ownership is not important *per se*. In contrast the presence of a soft budget constraint appears to have a broadly negative effect on restructuring and performance, and – together with unchallenged monopoly – is viewed as an obstacle to successful transition. According to Kornai (2001: 1591) 'it emerged that the "holy trinity" of stabilization, liberalization and privatization were not sufficient after all. Hardening the budget constraint is a task of equal rank with them, as experience in Russia has shown.'

This chapter has identified a mechanism that has hardened the budget constraint on public enterprises. Extending the federalist approach modelled by Qian and Roland (1998), it has shown that the 'upward devolution' of economic policies to a supranational institution is an effective way of mitigating the time inconsistency problem of national governments by limiting their discretionality, and consequently constraining the budget of public enterprises. Our methodology consisted of a case study of Italian SOEs and the role played by the EU as a supranational institution. We have shown that the devolution of both macroeconomic and microeconomic policies from the Italian government to the European Union restricted the funding of SOEs. On the one hand, the requirements for participation in the EMS and EMU forced the government to reduce its deficit. On the other hand, the competition policy requirements of the Single European Act and direct intervention by the European Commission in the running of these firms severely tightened the budget regime of Italian SOEs in the late 1980s. Hardening domestic firms' budget constraints through supranational pressure is a mechanism that works beyond the context of this case study. It works not only in market economies such as Italy, but also in transitional and emerging ones; not only for members of the EU, but also for applicant countries; not only for state firms, but also for private firms and not only through EU policies, but also through the policies of other international organizations (such as the IMF, the World Bank, the WTO, NAFTA, GATT, the EEA and the EBRD).

The experience of Italian SOEs provides a valuable preview of the financial pressure that will be exerted by the EU on SOEs in EU accession countries.[35] On the macroeconomic side, these countries are reducing their inflation, liberalizing their capital markets and controlling their fiscal policy to satisfy ERM II and the Maastricht criteria (Köhler and Wes, 1999). On the microeconomic side, firms are required to comply with EU competition laws, rules and directives (see Carlin *et al.*, 2000).[36] Other international organizations can have a similar effect on SOE budget constraints. The EU rules on the regulation of state aid have not only been adopted by the European Economic Area and EFTA but have also inspired the GATT–WTO subsidy codes. Many World Bank programmes include structural reforms and most IMF conditionality packages include fiscal tightening.[37] A condition of EBRD loans is that banks must deal with their bad loans, which translates into a harder budget constraint on firms. More generally, the increasingly global and interdependent nature of the capital and product markets, together with the liberalization of trade, have created a global competitive pressure that itself works as a supranational institution.[38]

Supranational pressure works because it eliminates the time inconsistency problem at the domestic level.[39] Supranational institutions, which maximize the welfare of a supranational constituency, impose fixed policy rules that domestic governments have to follow. This prevents governments from reneging on previous commitments in the event of political overturn, a change in political and economic priorities or a fear of voter opposition to restrictive monetary and fiscal measures, especially in countries with coalition governments.[40] However participating in international organizations is costly. For example the supranational welfare function may maximize competition at an interregional level at the expense of domestic employment, as in the EU. In some cases the costs are higher than the benefits, as the UK's decision to stay out of EMU shows. In other cases, just what the supranational welfare function maximizes is debatable, as shown by the discussions on the appropriateness of IMF packages during the 1997 Asian crisis (Stiglitz, 2000).

So, in what circumstances are governments willing to relinquish sovereign rights to supranational institutions? What is the incentive to participate? The incentive is strong when the benefits of membership are substantial.[41] Increased trade flows, increased financial flows and access to loans are the main economic benefits of participating in supranational organizations. Institutions such as NAFTA, EFTA, GATT and the WTO mainly provide the first (increased trade flows), while the IMF and World Bank mainly provide the others (increased financial flows, access to loans). EMU, and this is unique, offers all three.[42] Moreover the incentive is greater when a government is weak (for example a coalition government) and when the budget deficit is large. Indeed the loss of control over some economic policies may be viewed in a different light if upward devolution provides the opportunity to shift budgetary difficulties and unpopular reforms to a supranational authority.[43]

Even before joining a supranational organization the risk of incurring the costs of non-accession can be a powerful incentive. For example linking the success of economic reforms, including reform of the budget regime, to the prospect of access to the EU (as in the case of many Central and Eastern European countries) or to accession to the WTO (as in the case of China) creates the same pressure the Italian government felt when trying to fulfil the requirements for entering EMU. After joining, the economic and political costs of seceding from an international organization or trade agreement are high. Even if some international agreements cannot be legally enforced, as they can within the EU, the threat of retaliatory action is a powerful incentive to comply with the rules (Ehlermann, 1995; Kobia, 1996). Finally, the more integrated that the world economy and financial markets become, the greater will be the incentive to participate in supranational organizations, the more necessary the upward devolution of economic policies and the more likely that SOEs will face a much harder budget constraint.

Notes

1   Maskin and Xu (2001); *Journal of Comparative Economics Symposium,* 26 (1998); *Journal of Economic Perspectives Symposium,* 16, 1 (2002).
2   Even in market economies the *de facto* renationalization of Railtrack in the UK and the collapse of the electricity industry in California suggest that privatization *per se* does not necessarily create the right financial incentives.
3   The word devolution is commonly used to mean 'downward devolution', and in particular the surrender of powers by a central government to local authorities. We use the term in its literal meaning: 'from the Latin *devolvere,* the transference of rights, powers, property, or responsibility to another, in whatever direction' (*Webster's Dictionary*).
4   We use the term state-owned enterprises (SOEs) for firms owned by the government, as is done in the transition literature. However in market economies the terms public firms or public enterprises are more frequently used. We use the term private firms to mean firms not owned by the government (as opposed to firms not quoted on the stock exchange, as in other literary works).

5 Identifying a switch of budget regime for Italian SOEs in the late 1980s challenges the common wisdom that major changes in these firms only occurred with privatization in the 1990s.

6 Among other objectives, the promotion and protection of employment has always been important for SOEs. The new literature on happiness and economics puts this objective in a different perspective by showing how economists tend to miscalculate the benefits of employment overuse when they see it purely as inefficient. Oswald (1997) demonstrates that in western countries well-being rises hardly at all with increases in real GDP, whereas the biggest source of unhappiness is unemployment. Policies aimed purely at increasing growth are unlikely fundamentally to change well-being (and will underestimate the benefits of high employment), whereas reducing joblessness would.

7 Rules rather than discretion are proposed as a solution in the macroeconomic literature. Similarly for SOEs and SBCS, there have been attempts to create rules to constrain SOEs' funding, for example the UK introduced marginal cost pricing (1967), external financing limits (1976) and, more generally, automatic budget rules.

8 Che's (2001) model and its application to the Chinese economy highlights a trade-off between incurring the problems of the soft budget constraint syndrome discussed here and hardening the budget constraint on state firms. The latter solution may indeed have destabilizing macroeconomic effects because it could prevent some of the objectives of state ownership.

9 The fine for not complying is 0.2–0.5 per cent of GDP for a deficit of 3–6 per cent of GDP and 0.5 per cent for a deficit above 6 per cent.

10 Article 92(2)–(3) of the Treaty of Rome lays down exceptions to this rule, including aid of a social character for individual consumers, aid to promote regional economic development or for rescue and restructuring, and aid to reduce the impact of natural disasters, all of which are deemed compatible with the Common Market.

11 Community Directive 80/273, EEC.

12 Directive 85/413/EEC; see CER-IRS (1992).

13 These included frontier controls, national differences in technical regulations, the so-called fiscal frontiers from different tax levels and regimes, and public procurement biases in favour of domestic firms.

14 'As the market integration process progresses, this will naturally entail a strengthening of competition. There is a danger that member states might react to this increased competition by granting more aid to protect or promote national companies.... Therefore the Commission will apply stricter criteria in its aid discipline, otherwise the positive benefits that should be fostered by the market integration will not be fully realised' (European Commission, 1988: 2).

15 Communication GUCE No. C273/1991.

16 European Commission (1995): 15; also in Parker (1999): 24; Cafferata (1995).

17 When in the nineteenth century the government, led by the Count of Cavour, planned the first railway, neither private entrepreneurs nor bankers were willing to invest in the only Italian private rail engineering company. The government had to finance the project with a large bond issue. Thus the government financially supported the newly born 'private' rail stock industry (Scognamiglio, 2001).

18   When the IRI was set up its portfolio included more than 20 per cent of the equity stock of all Italian limited liability companies: 100 per cent of the defence-related steel industry and coal mining, 40 per cent of non-military steel, 90 per cent of shipbuilding, 80 per cent of railway engines, 30 per cent of power generation, the three largest commercial banks and the telephone service (Barca and Trento, 1997).

19   Moreover the ENI and IRI were required to undertake further bail-outs of loss-making private companies in unrelated businesses. The newspaper *Il Giorno* went to the ENI in 1962, the textile company Lanerossi in 1962 and more textile and clothing businesses in the mid 1960s. The IRI acquired a number of companies in the food industry, including the *panettoni* producers Motta and Alemagna.

20   In the meantime new public holdings were created: The EFIM (mechanical and rail engineering and mining) in 1962, and the EGAM (steel and mining) in 1971. In 1962 the electric power industry was nationalized under the new National Electricity Authority (ENEL).

21   A telling example of the conflict between the old guard of professional managers and politicians is the well-known struggle between the general manager of Alfa Romeo, an IRI motor vehicle company, and the political 'masters' in the IRI itself. The dispute was over the marketing strategy for the new car models and the location of a new plant, Alfasud. The manager wanted to locate it in the north, whereas the IRI wanted to locate it in the south of Italy. The dispute ended with the firing of the manager.

22   Profitability and cash flows were eroded by high wages, price controls and regulated tariffs (electricity, gas and telephone), the rescue of loss-making private companies, and rocketing interest rates, which in the early 1970s greatly increased the financial burden (Coltorti, 1990).

23   Law No. 14/1978.

24   For example it was agreed, and became common knowledge, that the IRI management would be the domain of the Christian Democrats, and the ENI the domain of the Socialist Party.

25   The implicit shadow cost of pursuing non-economic objectives was even certified by law (Law No. 675/1977). State firms were thus required to estimate the costs arising from inefficiency (the so-called *oneri impropri*), which were then subsidized by the Treasury, a procedure that lent itself to abuse.

26   Public holdings began to publish consolidated reports around the mid 1970s. However without standardized accounting or auditing principles, these were not informative and were useless for consistent comparisons (Coltorti, 1990).

27   Some interventions indicated ambivalence about the treatment of state aid to SOEs, perhaps reflecting the different attitudes towards state ownership among the member states. Besley and Seabright (1999) call for a revision of the policy and for clearer, more encompassing criteria.

28   Ilva, the steel sector leader set up in 1987, was further restructured and then sold in March 1995 to an Italian private competitor (Riva), as often happened in Italian privatization.

29   Aid to manufacturing is classified into three categories: horizontal aid (R&D, environment, SME), aid to particular sectors (shipbuilding, steel) and regional aid.

30 Over the years the share of transfers to southern Italy for temporary unemployment benefit and aid for exports grew in importance.

31 Political factors, not dealt with in this chapter, also contributed. For example the exasperation of taxpayers with the squandering of public money for party-political purposes also contributed to the bias in favour of privatization.

32 Law No. 218/1990.

33 Law No. 385, Testo Unico Bancario.

34 For the UK see Parker and Martin (1995) and Florio (2002), for Spain see Villalonga (2000), and for a cross-country sample see Dewenter and Malatesta (2001). In contrast, in the case of Mexico Lopez-de-Silanes (1997) finds that government efforts to restructure firms before privatization can destroy value.

35 The pressure may be even greater. For Italian firms, our empirical studies show that the effects of a switch of budget regimes occurred in the late 1980s, before the Maastricht Treaty and EMU conditions were enforced. The ERM and its external exchange rate anchor, together with tough regulations on state aid, were enough to generate the switch and its consequences. However this is no longer possible for today's accession countries as EMU conditions have been attached to EU membership. Financial market credibility, for example, requires that the EMU conditions be met now, whereas in 1989 this would not have been necessary. It has been argued that the strict fiscal conditions are unnecessary and may even be deleterious for countries with high nominal GDP growth (Schelkle, 2003). It would seem more reasonable to require high standards in law enforcement, bankruptcy procedures, and product, labour and financial market institutions, all of which areas have been recognized as major factors in the effectiveness of privatization (see also Estrin, 2002).

36 Other studies have examined other disciplinary effects of EU policies. For example the constraints imposed by the requirements for EU accession can improve law enforcement (Roland and Verdier, 2000).

37 With respect to IMF programmes, the literature on the conditionality of IMF loans address its nature and effectiveness. In contrast to the EU, the IMF's conditions lack legal enforceability and the debate highlights, for example, the desirability for countries to 'own' the IMF programmes if they are to be made to work (Khan and Sharma, 2001; Drazen, 2002).

38 For example Bartel and Harrison (1999) show that public sector enterprises that have been shielded from import competition are inferior performers.

39 Carare *et al.* (1999) discuss the difficulty in Romania of imposing a hard budget constraint and enforcing financial discipline on SOEs. Similarly Berglof and Bolton (2002: 80) describe how the authorities in most of the former Soviet countries, plus Bulgaria and Romania, 'did not, or could not resist the pressures for financial relief', and how 'this pattern of repeated bailouts for both banks and businesses led to a lack of enterprises restructuring, weaker banks, and the need for more inflationary credit bailouts'.

40 As argued by Roland (2002: 35), the best way to prevent reforms from being reversed is 'to design reform packages via adequate sequencing and compensating transfers so as to create broad support', which, as we have discussed, is what EU application and membership does for applicant countries.

41 For example EMU supporters argue that the common currency will eliminate exchange rate risk, reduce interest rates, stimulate investment and create employment.

42 There are other respects in which the EU is unique. The EU's legislative power and the enforcement of regulations and laws through the European Court of Justice are unmatched by any other supranational organization. Moreover its political institutions, slowly constructed over more than four decades, are now more developed than those of any other region in the world. These institutions undoubtedly help to make EU policies effective external anchors, compared for example with the IMF's policies.

43 In Italy, where the budgetary adjustment to meet the Maastricht criteria was impressive, the strong popular support for EMU seemed to falter. Some politicians and representatives of the entrepreneurs' confederation questioned the benefits of, and some fiercely opposed, EMU participation. See for example Letta (1997) and Caracciolo (1997). However, the government, fully aware of the costs and benefits of the upward devolution of monetary policy, stood firm in its commitment to participate.

References

Amato, G. (1994) 'Un Governo nella transizione. La mia esperienza di Presidente del Consiglio', *Quaderni Costituzionali*, 3 (December).

Angelucci, M., S. Estrin, J. Konings and Z. Zolkiewski (2002) 'The Effect of Ownership and Competitive Pressure in Transition Countries: Micro Evidence from Bulgaria, Romania and Poland', William Davidson Working Paper no. 434, Ann Arbor: University of Michigan Business School, January.

Artoni, R. and P. Ravazzi (1986) 'I trasferimenti statali all'industria', in R. Artoni and R. Pontarollo, *Trasferimenti, domanda pubblica e sistema industriale*, Bologna: Il Mulino.

Barca, F. and M. Magnani (1989) *L'industria fra capitale e lavoro*, Bologna: Il Mulino.

—— and S. Trento (1997) 'State Ownership and the Evolution of Italian Corporate Governance', *Industrial and Corporate Change*, 6, 3: 533–59.

Bardhan, P. and J. Roemer (1992) 'Market Socialism: A Case for Rejuvenation', *Journal of Economic Perspectives*, 6, 3: 101–16.

Barro, R. J. and D. R. Gordon (1983) 'A Positive Theory of Monetary Policy in a Natural Rate Model', *Journal of Political Economy Studies*, 91: 589–610.

Bartel, A. and A. Harrison (1999) 'Ownership versus Environment: Why are Public Sector Firms Inefficient?', NBER Working Paper no. 7043, Cambridge, MA: NBER, March.

Benfratello, L. (2001) 'Determinanti ed effetti delle fusioni ed acquisizioni: un'analisi sulla base delle notifiche alle autorità antitrust', *L'Industria*, 3.

Berglof, E. and P. Bolton (2002) 'The Great Divide and Beyond: Financial Architecture in Transition', *Journal of Economic Perspectives*, 16, 1: 77–100.

—— and G. Roland (1998) 'Soft Budget Constraints and Banking in Transition Economies', *Journal of Comparative Economics*, 26: 18–40.

Bertero, E. (1997) 'Restructuring Financial Systems in Transition and Developing Economies: An Approach Based on the French Financial System', *Economics of Transition*, 5, 2: 367–93.

—— and L. Rondi (2000) 'Financial Pressure and the Behaviour of Public Enterprises under Soft and Hard Budget Constraints: Evidence from Italian Panel Data', *Journal of Public Economics*, 75, 1: 73–98.

—— and —— (2002) 'Does a Switch of Budget Regimes Affect Investment and Managerial Discretion of State-owned Enterprises? Evidence from Italian Firms', *Journal of Comparative Economics*, 30: 836–63.

Besley, T. and P. Seabright (1999) 'The Effects and Policy Implications of State Aids to Industry: An Economic Analysis', *Economic Policy: A European Forum*, 28: 13–42.

Borghini, G. and G. Podestà (1987) *L'Intervento pubblico in economia: il caso delle partecipazioni statali*, Milano: F. Angeli.

Bottiglieri, B. (1984) 'Linee interpretative del dibattito sulle partecipazioni statali nel secondo dopoguerra', *Economia Pubblica*, April–May: 239–44.

Brosio, G. and P. Silvestri (1983) 'Uno sguardo d'assieme', in P. Ranci, *I trasferimenti dello Stato alle imprese industriali negli anni settanta*, Bologna: Il Mulino.

Cafferata, R. (1995) 'Italian State-Owned Holdings, Privatization and the Single Market', *Annals of Public and Cooperative Economics*, 66, 4: 401–29.

Caracciolo, L. (1997) *Euro No: Non Morire per Maastricht*, Bari: Laterza.

Carare, O., C. Claessens and E. Perotti (1999) 'Can Government Mandate Hard Budget Constraints? Bank Lending and Financial Isolation in Romania', Ann Arbor: University of Michigan Business School, William Davidson Working Paper no. 241, January.

Carlin, W., S. Estrin and M. Schaffer (2000) 'Measuring Progress in Transition and Towards EU Accession: A Comparison of Manufacturing Firms in Poland, Romania and Spain', *Journal of Common Market Studies*, 38, 5: 699–728.

—— S. Fries, M. Schaffer and P. Seabright (2001) 'Competition and Enterprise Performance in Transition Economies: Evidence from a Cross-country Survey', Ann Arbor: University of Michigan Business School, William Davidson Working Paper no. 376, May.

CER-IRS (1989) *Mercato e politica industriale*, Bologna: Il Mulino.

—— (1992) *Una politica industriale per la nuova legislatura*, Bologna: Il Mulino.

—— (1993) *La trasformazione difficile*, Bologna: Il Mulino.

—— (1997) *Più tecnologia, più concorrenza*, Bologna: Il Mulino.

Che, J. (2001) 'Soft Budget Constraints, Pecuniary Externality and China's Financial Dual Track', mimeo, University of Illionois at Urbana Chanpaign.

Coltorti, F. (1990) 'Le fasi dello sviluppo industriale italiano e l'intreccio tra settore privato e impresa pubblica', *Rivista di Politica Economica*, v (May): 65–131.

Dewatripont, M. and E. Maskin (1995) 'Credit and Efficiency in Centralized and Decentralized Economies', *Review of Economic Studies*, 62: 541–55.

Dewenter, K. L. and P. H. Malatesta (2001) 'State-owned and Privately Owned Firms: An Empirical Analysis of Profitability, Leverage and Labour Intensity', *American Economic Review*, 1, 91: 320–34.

Drazen, A. (2002) 'Conditionality and Ownership in IMF Lending: A Political Economy Approach', Centre for Economic Policy Research Discussion Paper no. 3562, London: CEPR.

Ehlermann, C. D. (1992) 'European Community Competition Policy, Public Enterprise and the Cooperative, Mutual and Nonprofit Sector', *Annals of Public and Cooperative Economics*, 63, 4: 555–71.

—— (1995) 'State aid control: failure or success?', http://europa.eu.int/en/comm/dg04/speech/five/htm/sp95001.htm.

Emerson, M. (1988) 'Regulation and Deregulation in the Labor Market', *European Economic Review*, 32: 775–817.

Estrin, S. (2002) 'Competition and Corporate Governance in Transition', *Journal of Economic Perspectives*, 16, 1: 101–24.

European Commission (1988) *First Survey on State Aid in the European Community*, Brussels: European Commission.

—— (1990) 'One market, one money', *European Economy*, Brussels: European Commission.

—— (1999) 'State aid and the single market', *European Economy*, Brussels: European Commission.

Feldstein, M. (1997) 'The Political Economy of the European Economic and Monetary Union: Political Sources of an Economic Liability', *Journal Economic Perspectives*, 11, 4: 23–42.

Florio, M. (2002) 'The Great Divesture: Evaluating the Welfare Impact of British Privatizations 1979–1997', draft manuscript.

Fraquelli, G. (2001) 'L'attesa della privatizzazione: una minaccia credibile per il manager?', *Sinergie*, 55 (May–August): 211–33.

Goodhart, C. and D. Schoenmaker (1995) 'Should the Functions of Monetary Policy and Banking Supervision Be Separated?', *Oxford Economic Papers*, 47, 4: 539–60.

Grassini, F. (1981) 'The Italian Enterprises: The Political Constraints', in R. Vernon and Y. Aharoni (eds), *State-owned Enterprises in the Western Economies*, London: Croom Helm.

Gross, D. and N. Thygesen (1992) *European Monetary Integration: From the European Monetary System to the European Monetary Union*, London: Longman.

Harbord, D. and G. Yarrow (1999) 'State Aids, Restructuring and Privatization', in European Commission (1999).

Hart, O. and J. Moore (1995) 'Debt and Seniority: An Analysis of the Role of Hard Claims in Constraining Management', *American Economic Review*, 85: 567–85.

—— A. Shleifer and R. Vishny (1997) 'The Proper Scope of Government: Theory and Application to Prisons', *Quarterly Journal of Economics*, 112, 4.

Jensen, M. C. (1986) 'Agency Costs of Free Cash Flow, Corporate Finance and Takeovers', *American Economic Review, Papers and Proceedings*, 76: 323–9.

Khan, M. and S. Sharma (2001) 'IMF Conditionality and Country Ownership of Programs', IMF Working Paper no. 01/142, Washington, DC: IMF.

Kobia, R. A. J. (1996) 'Introduction to the law, practice and policy of state aids in the European Community', http://europa.eu.int/en/comm/dg04/speech//six/htm/sp96007.htm.

Köhler, H. and M. Wes (1999) 'Implications of the Euro for the Integration Process of the Transition Economies in Central and Eastern Europe', EBRD Working Paper no. 38, London: EBRD, March.

Kornai, J. (1998) 'The Place of the Soft Budget Constraint Syndrome in Economic Theory', *Journal of Comparative Economics*, 26: 11–17.

—— (2000) 'Ten years after "The Road to a Free Economy": the author's self-evaluation', paper for the World Bank conference, mimeo, Harvard.

—— (2001) 'Hardening the Budget Constraint: the Experience of the Post-socialist Countries', *European Economic Review*, 45, 9: 1573–99.

Kumar, A. (1993) *State Holding Companies and Public Enterprises in Transition*, New York: St. Martin's Press.

Kydland, F. and E. Prescott (1977) 'Rules Rather than Discretion', *Journal of Political Economy*, 85, 3.

Laffont, J. and J. Tirole (1993) *A Theory of Incentives in Procurements and Regulation*, Cambridge, MA: MIT Press.

Lawson, C. (1994) 'The Theory of State-owned Enterprises in Market Economies', *Journal of Economic Surveys*, 8, 3: 283–309.

Letta, E. (1997) *Euro Sì: morire per Maastricht*, Bari: Laterza.

Li, W. (1997) 'The Impact of Economic Reform on the Performance of Chinese State Enterprises 1980–1989', *Journal of Political Economy*, 105: 1080–106.

Lo Passo, F. and A. Macchiati (1998) 'La ristrutturazione dell'impresa pubblica in Italia negli anni novanta. Il caso di Iri ed Eni', in F. Giavazzi *et al.*, *Liberalizzazione dei mercati e privatizzazioni*, Bologna: Il Mulino.

Lopez-de-Silanes, F. (1997) 'Determinants of Privatization Prices', *Quarterly Journal of Economics*, 112: 965–1025.

Majumdar, S. K. (1996) 'Assessing Comparative Efficiency of State-Owned, Mixed, and Private Sectors in Indian Industry', *Public Choice*, 96: 1–24.

Martimort, D. (1996) 'The Multiprincipal Nature of Government', *European Economic Review*, 40, 3–5: 673–85.

Martinelli, A. (1981) 'The Italian Experience: A Historical Perspective', in R. Vernon and Y. Aharoni (eds), *State-owned Enterprises in the Western Economies*, London: Croom Helm.

Maskin, E. and C. Xu (2001) 'Soft Budget Constraint Theories. From Centralization to the Market', *Economics of Transition*, 9, 1: 1–27.

Megginson, W. L., R. C. Nash and M. Van (1994) 'The Financial and Operating Performance of Newly Privatized Firms: An International Empirical Analysis', *Journal of Finance*, 49, 2: 403–52.

—— and J. M. Netter (2001) 'From State to Market: A Survey of Empirical Studies on Privatization', *Journal of Economic Literature*, xxxix, June: 321–89.

Mitchell, J. (1998) 'Strategic Creditor Passivity, Regulation, and Bank Bailouts', CEPR Discussion Paper no. 1780, London: CEPR.

OECD (1985) 'Italy', *OECD Economic Survey*, Paris: OECD, June.

—— (1989) 'Economies in Transition', *Structural Adjustment in OECD Countries*, Paris: OECD.

Oswald, A. (1997) 'Happiness and Economic Performance', *Economic Journal*, 107, 445: 1815–31.

Padoa Schioppa Kostoris, F. (1998) 'Economic Policy and Reforms in Contemporary Italy', CEPR Discussion Paper no. 1874, London: CEPR.

Parker, D. (1999) 'Privatization in the European Union: A Critical Assessment of Its Development, Rationale and Consequences', *Economic and Industrial Democracy*, 20, 1: 9–38.

—— and S. Martin (1995), 'The Impact of UK Privatization on Labour and Total Factor Productivity', *Scottish Journal of Political Economy*, 42, 2: 201–20.

Persson, T., G. Roland and G. Tabellini (1997) 'Separation of Powers and Political Accountability', *Quarterly Journal of Economics*, 112, 4: 1163–202.

Pinto, B., M. Belka and S. Krajewski (1993) 'Transforming State Enterprises in Poland: Evidence on Adjustment by Manufacturing Firms', *Brooking Papers on Economic Activity*, 1: 213–61.

Posner, M. and S. Wolf (1967) *Italian Public Enterprise*, Cambridge, MA: Harvard University Press.

Prendergast, C. (2000) 'Investigating Corruption', Public Sector Management Working Paper no. 2500, Washington, DC: World Bank.

Qian, Y. and G. Roland (1998) 'Federalism and the Soft Budget Constraint', *American Economic Review*, 88, 5: 1143–62.

Roland, G. (2002) 'The Political Economy of Transition', *Journal of Economic Perspectives*, 16, 1: 29–50.

—— and T. Verdier (2000) 'Law Enforcement and Transition', CEPR Discussion Paper no. 2501, London: CEPR.

Saraceno, P. (1977) 'The Italian System of State-held Enterprises', *Journal of International Law and Economics*, 11: 407–46.

Schelkle, W. (2003) 'Monetary Enlargement Within the Maastricht Policy Regime: A Mixed Blessing', in N. Fuhrmann *et al.* (eds), *Die Europäische Union: Außenbeziehungen und innere Differenzierung* (forthcoming).

Scognamiglio, C. (1981) 'L'Azione Pubblica per il Risanamento della Grande Impresa', in G. De Michelis, *Rapporto sulle Partecipazioni Statali*, Milano: F. Angeli.

—— (2001) 'Le privatizzazioni in Italia a dieci anni dall'avvio della riforma', *Economia Italiana*, 1, January–April: 11–23.

Senato della Repubblica (1990) *La Politica degli Aiuti di Stato alle Imprese, Indagine conoscitiva svolta dalla Commissione Industria e dalla Giunta per gli Affari delle Comunità Europee*, Rome: Senato della Repubblica.

—— (2000) *Rapporto 2000 sugli Aiuti Statali alle Imprese*, Rome: Senato della Repubblica.

Shleifer, A. and R. W. Vishny (1994) 'Politicians and Firms', *Quarterly Journal of Economics*, 109: 995–1025.

Shonfield, A. (1977) *Modern Capitalism*, Oxford: Oxford University Press.

Stiglitz, J. (2000) 'The Insider', *The New Republic*, 17 April, http://www.thenewrepublic.com/041700/stiglitz041700.html.

Sun, L. (2001) 'Economics of China's Joint-stock Cooperatives', WIDER Discussion Paper 2001/24, Helsinki: UNU/WIDER.

—— with E. X. Gu and R. J. McIntyre (1999) 'The Evolutionary Dynamics of China's Small and Medium Sized Enterprises in the 1990s', *World Development Studies* 14, Helsinki: UNU/WIDER.

Tirole, J. (1994) 'The Internal Organization of Government', *Oxford Economic Papers*, 46, 1: 1–29.

Villalonga, B. (2000) 'Privatization and Efficiency: Differentiating Ownership Effects, from Political, Organizational, and Dynamic Effects', *Journal of Economic Behaviour and Organization*, 42: 43–74.

6
Evolving and Functioning Mechanisms of Employee Stock Ownership in China's Township and Village Enterprises

Laixiang Sun

> It is not the strongest species that survive, nor the most intelligent, but the ones most responsive to change (Darwinian proverb).

Introduction

The growth of rural non-agricultural firms, led by township and village enterprises (TVEs), has been the most prominent feature of China's impressive development since the late 1970s. By 1995 industrial TVEs had become China's top industrial producers, taking over this position from state-owned enterprises (SOEs). During 1995–2000 they produced over 30 per cent of the national industrial value-added, profits and output, and non-agricultural TVEs together accounted for more than 15 per cent of China's GDP (Sun, 2000; *Yearbook*, 2000: 113; *Yearbook* 2001: 3–5, 95).[1]

TVEs are typically established and owned by collectives in rural communities, such as townships and villages. Before the recent ownership restructuring TVEs were best characterized as community enterprises with a governance structure controlled by the community government (Che and Qian, 1998; Perotti *et al.*, 1999; Che, 2002). Since the wave of large-scale ownership restructuring in the mid 1990s most small TVEs have been fully privatized (sold to their managers or other private owners), but the larger TVEs are now mostly characterized by joint ownership by employees, the community government and outside equity holders. In this joint ownership, employees typically hold the majority of shares.[2] Although community governments, which were

159

formerly the sole owners and supervisors of TVEs, have continued to be involved in the governance of the restructured TVEs via the community assets management body and the party branch, their role is now similar to that of a major institutional shareholder.

Of the various joint ownership arrangements, the most representative one is the joint-stock cooperative (*gufen hezuozhi*).[3] Joint-stock cooperatives (JSCs) are emerging not only in the TVE sector but also in the state-owned and private sectors. While the performance of JSCs varies widely among individual enterprises, their average performance has been outstanding. First, the adoption of JSCs has addressed the urgent need for TVE capitalization. In provinces such as Zhejiang, Jiangsu and Anhui, which are the leading areas for TVE development, this has led to a reduction of the debt–asset ratio by an average of 10 percentage points. Second, and more importantly, it is widely reported that those TVEs which have transformed themselves into JSCs have typically shown a significant improvement in performance, exhibited more dynamic features and played the leading role in maintaining the TVE miracle (*Yearbook*, 1997: 299–306; *Yearbook*, 1998: 271–80; *Yearbook*, 1999: 4; Wang *et al.*, 1997).[4] According to a recent survey of TVEs in 16 townships (Beijing Survey Group, 2000), among all the restructured TVEs in the sample, those which have become JSCs have clearly outperformed all the others, including the privatized ones (Table 6.1). With regard to the question of how share ownership has

Table 6.1   Comparison of the average performance of the main ownership forms

Major restructuring forms	Firm number	Net assets (Y1000)	Revenue (Y1000)	Total profit (Y1000)	Total profit/net assets (%)	Total profit/ equity (%)
Joint stock cooperatives	24	2137	7873	1106	51.74	35.12
Selling	27	1692	4845	417	24.62	8.10
Leasing	14	2132	4138	292	13.67	7.04
Leasing and selling combined	19	1841	2961	245	13.33	11.16

Notes: The data are based on a survey of 100 restructured TVEs in Tongzhou District, Beijing, in 2000. The performance measures are averaged across the firms in each category and over the period since the second year after restructuring. The majority of the surveyed firms were restructured during 1995–97. Given the differences in firm size and capital structure, the limitations of this comparison must be kept in mind.
Source: Beijing Survey Group (2000: 39).

affected employees' attitudes and behaviour, a 1999 survey of over 1000 employees in 45 enterprises in three counties in Jiangsu and Shandong provinces shows that employee share ownership has generally made a significant contribution in four important areas: job satisfaction, employees' perceived degree of participation in enterprise decision making, their commitment to the firm, and their attitude towards the ongoing privatization process (Dong *et al.*, 2002).

Property rights arrangements are not uniform among JSCs, with variations among regions, industries and the SOE, TVE and private sectors. In China's official statistics, the various forms of JSC have not yet been clearly brought together in a single category. However the typical features of JSCs in the TVE sector can be summarized as follows.

- Managers and employees own the majority of shares and their shareholdings vary on the basis of paid subscriptions.
- Firms are closely held, implying that the shares are not freely marketable, although subscribed shares can be transferred within the community.
- The local government may hold a large number of shares in the name of the community citizens.
- In addition to the shares held by insiders and the local government, some are usually held by outside equity holders and carry one vote per share.
- A representative form of governance is usually employed, based on 'one person one vote', 'one share one vote' or a combination of the two.
- The laying off of cooperative members is common place, but those laid off may continue to hold their shares if they do not choose to sell them back to the cooperative.

There are different types of share, one of which is similar to a pension trust fund – the fund is owned by the employees and benefits from it are mainly distributed according to seniority. The shares that confer the greatest ownership rights are those held by employees as individuals. However because of the relative smallness of the firms concerned, these shares are not freely marketable. This makes them more like a venture capital investment (with a simple profit-sharing scheme) than the shares of Western public companies. In the typical profit-sharing scheme a fixed proportion of net total profits is distributed as dividends.

The fact that managers and employees hold the majority of shares makes JSCs quite similar to firms with employee ownership. The performance of employee-owned firms has been hotly debated and an enormous body of literature has developed. For cooperatives and closely held employee-stock ownership in developed economies, the theoretical and empirical literature suggests that while these arrangements have both advantages and disadvantages in terms of the performance of the firm, on balance – or at least in the industrial sector – the disadvantages seem to outweigh the advantages (Bonin *et al.*, 1993). Recent studies of employee ownership in the former Soviet Union and Eastern Europe suggest that the balance is tipped even further towards the disadvantages (Earle and Estrin, 1996).

Western studies indicate that the relative scarcity of worker cooperatives in the industrial sector is due to their disadvantages in collective decision making and capital financing (Bonin *et al.*, 1993; Craig and Pencavel, 1995; Hansmann, 1996). The transition literature shows that employee-owned firms pay excessive attention to rents or other firm-specific surpluses due to the lack of fair competition and contract enforcement mechanisms. It is relatively easy to argue that China's JSCs have little political power to maintain some kind of firm-specific rent simply because the markets in townships or villages are too small and too limited. However what deserve special attention are the mechanisms developed by the JSCs to avoid the high costs of collective decision making, check insider control, mobilize internal and external finances, diversify risk, harmonize labour–management relations and facilitate development. Because of the sharp contrast between the promising dynamics of the JSCs and the conclusions suggested in the literature, a better understanding of how the JSCs actually work can bring new insights into the debate on the advantages and disadvantages of employee ownership, and into the discussion on the paths that might be taken by JSCs in the future. It could also reveal the roles that alternative forms of ownership and governance could play in an alternative institutional environment.

When a new ownership arrangement emerges, much attention is paid to the question of whether it is transitory or will endure. This chapter puts emphasis on ownership as an evolving process and raises an important and relevant question: can this arrangement facilitate both institutional transition and socioeconomic development? We are already aware of the huge development costs of institutional transition, so a new ownership arrangement that is capable of simultaneously facilitating a smooth transition and creating impressive growth deserves attention and investigation.

The emergence of joint-stock cooperatives in the TVE sector

The spontaneous initiation of JSCs at the grass-roots level occurred during 1982–85 in Wenzhou (Zhejiang province), Fuyang (Anhui province) and several other rural counties. The early JSCs were typically based on joint-stock cooperation among households and small private firms. The use of JSCs as an experimental form for the ownership restructuring of TVEs was initiated in 1987 in the Zhoucun district of Zibo city, Shandong province. However this experiment was seriously constrained by the requirement that the majority of stock should be held collectively by the community or the TVE (Vermeer, 1996). In 1992, following the decisive push for reform by Deng Xiaoping, the official restriction on share distribution between collectives and individuals became increasingly unpopular and was gradually abandoned. The removal of this restriction combined with the renewed momentum for reform has led to the rapid expansion of a new JSC arrangement in which employees as a group hold the majority of shares (*Yearbook*, 1998: 271–80). There are many local variations of the JSC form that have evolved according to the local political and institutional conditions. In order to sketch out the major features of the ownership and governance structures emerging in different localities, we shall classify them into three general groups: community-based, enterprise-based, and those in the broad agricultural sector.[5]

Community-based JSCs

Community-based JSCs emerged in the late 1980s in rich villages with a significant collective capital accumulation and located on the outskirts of rapidly expanding cities such as Guangzhou and Shenzhen. The driving forces for the establishment of community-based JSCs included:

- The need to alleviate the long-standing tension and increasingly sharp conflicts between village government officials and villagers.
- The departure of a large number of villagers following state requisition of their lands.
- The need to meet the high equity capital demand of the village economy.

The tension and conflicts were the result of the increasing bureaucratization of community governments and the corrupt behaviour of community officials. Community officials enjoyed complete control over collective assets but bore none of the risks. Their corrupt business dealings, repeated loss-making decisions and engagement in asset stripping eventually provoked open conflict and forced the higher-level governments to look for solutions. In those villages which suffered from open conflict, the JSC form was at first regarded by the higher-level governments as a way to establish economic democracy (Huang, 1993: 165; Wu and Li, 2001). Enabling every adult villager to become a shareholder and setting up a governance structure similar to that of a shareholding company have brought both economic and political democracy to these communities.

Each household selects its own shareholder representative, and in the assemblies of shareholder representatives the 'one person one vote' principle is maintained. The significant benefits to be had from membership and subscribed shares provide an incentive for households to participate in the equity democracy. The monitoring framework in which shareholder representative assemblies monitor the board of directors and the board of directors monitors the TVE managers provides a mechanism for villagers to exercise democracy regularly and effectively. Although community collective shares continue to exist, the control rights over them are equally shared by the community households, rather than simply being exercised by community leaders. This makes community collective shares quite different from state shares in restructured SOEs, where the state shares are held by local governments (Gu, 1999: 40–5).

In coastal areas many cities are expanding rapidly and many villages on the outskirts of these cities are subject to city government requisition of a large proportion or most of their collective land for city expansion. Although farmers who lose their land can take up urban social status and take a formal job in the urban sector, assigned by the city government, they have the right to claim their share of the community capital accumulation left to the village. In order to address such claims and smooth the process of land requisition, the setting up of JSCs became desirable for all governments from the village to the city level. It was likened to 'returning the shares to their original creators' (*huan gu yu min*) (Huang and Zheng, 1993). Villagers employed outside the village receive dividends from their shareholdings but have no voting rights.

In rich villages, most households had large savings deposited in state banks, while collective village borrowing was catered to by state banks, SOEs and other institutions. Both villagers and village leaders had an incentive to look for a mechanism to link their household savings with the investment demand of their village TVEs. Although this may not have been a direct reason for the initiation of community-based JSCs, it has significantly contributed to their development and improvement (Huang, 1993). Subscribed shares based on cash payment have become increasingly important both as a proportion of total equity and because of the part they play in improving the governance structure. Community-based JSCs typically hold shares in joint ventures with foreign or domestic companies, in their own subordinate companies and in other communities. In all these kinds of shareholding the community-based JSCs act like a typical institutional shareholder or venture capitalist. The internal ownership and governance structures seem to have brought them competitive advantages in respect of establishing joint ventures and of functioning as parent companies (Huang and Zheng, 1993: 117–19; *Yearbook*, 1997: 305; Wu and Li, 2001).

Enterprise-based JSCs

The overwhelming majority of JSCs are enterprise-based and the shareholders typically include the employees, individual members of the community, the community government (in the name of all community citizens) and institutional shareholders outside the community. The desirability of community collective shares has been hotly contested in China, with opponents claiming that collective shares facilitate political intervention by the community government, and that the mechanism for monitoring the community government is far from perfect and differs from that for monitoring enterprises (see for example Han and Zhang, 1993; Wang *et al.*, 1997; Tan, 1998). Meanwhile proponents claim that, at the village level at least, collective shares are crucial for the balanced development of the village economy and are particularly important for supporting agricultural and infrastructural development. They insist that the village should be basically an enterprise organization and that the committee of villagers or villager's representatives is an autonomous organization of villagers rather than a government body, according to the Organic Law of Villager's Committee of the People's Republic of China. They suggest that the separation of government and enterprises at the village level would bureaucratize the village organization and induce organizational conflicts within the village (Policy Research Office, 1997).

While both the opponents and the proponents of community collective shares have brought insights into the discussion and the practical issues concerned, at the village level the proponents' points seem to be more pertinent. In fact village-based JSCs appear to be both socially and economically effective (Han and Zhang, 1993: 141; *Yearbook*, 1997: 3–5).

The existence of collective shares is not a problem for community-based JSCs, as discussed in the previous subsection, but in villages with only enterprise-based JSCs the existence of collective shares may be more of a problem in practice, although it could also facilitate the emergence of village-based JSCs. At the township level and above, the problems highlighted by the opponents may be more relevant. The solutions to these problems have taken a variety of forms. For example in Zhucheng city in Shandong province the city government sold all shares to enterprise employees and managers and leased the land to restructured JSCs (Sun, 1997: 20–2), while in Henggang town in Shenzhen city the township's collective shares are held by the Henggang Joint-Stock Investment Company, which is monitored by the Assembly of Shareholder Representatives from the subordinate villages rather than the town government (Henggang Town, 1993; Wu and Li, 2001).

JSCs in the broad agricultural sector

According to the official Chinese definition, the broad agricultural sector includes crop farming, livestock, forestry and fishery. JSCs in the broad agricultural sector mainly take the form of forest farms, orchards, aquatic farms, irrigation systems and marketing cooperatives (Han and Zhang, 1993: 212–18, 253–320; *Almanac of China's Economy*, 1994: 672–3). The economic rationale for these organizational forms is to a certain extent similar to that for farmer-owned cooperatives in the West that specialize in processing and marketing agricultural products (Hansmann, 1996: ch. 7). In these JSCs, producer-owners have highly homogeneous interests, their products are relatively homogeneous and the ability to achieve economies of scale is beyond the capability of individual households. Moreover, due to the great scarcity of capital and job opportunities in rural China and serious imperfections in all markets, farmers need to accumulate capital, create more jobs using their own capital and increase their production scale and marketing power collectively. As a consequence these JSCs typically match capital shares with job opportunities (*yizi dailao*). There is a division of labour within the cooperatives and the cooperatives engage not only in processing and marketing but also in producing. These features make JSCs in the Chinese agricultural sector quite different from their counterparts in the West.

One China-specific form of farmer-owned cooperative is the 'land share cooperative' (*tudi gufen hezushe*), which has emerged in some of the most developed coastal areas. A basic feature of this type of cooperative is the conversion of the land contract rights held by member households into shares. This is called the 'capitalization of land contract rights'. Villagers who do not work as farmers can convert their land contract rights into shares and become shareholders in a larger farm managed by a specialist farming family. The latter pays a proportion of its revenues as dividends to the shareholders, in addition to paying agricultural taxes to the state and land-use fees to the village government. The share value is usually determined in discussions and negotiations in the village assembly, where the voting procedure and other features of the JSC obtain (*Almanac of China's Economy*, 1994: 672; Chen and Han, 1994).

One might expect that the JSCs in the agricultural sector will sooner or later converge with the Western form of farmer-owned cooperatives and specialize in the processing and marketing of agricultural products and the provision of certain services to producers. However such a convergence would be seriously constrained by the factor endowment of the Chinese agricultural sector, which is characterized by an extreme land scarcity, capital scarcity and labour overabundance that is likely to persist for generations. It is this that makes the responsibilities of China's farmer-owned cooperatives different from those of their counterparts in the West.

Functioning mechanisms of joint-stock cooperatives

Mechanisms to restrain insider control

In this subsection we shall compare the restraint mechanisms against insider control in China's JSCs with those applied in China's semi-autonomous SOEs and large public companies in the United States (Table 6.2). As is well documented in the literature, under the contract responsibility system SOEs enjoy *usus fructus* – the right to control state assets and to enjoy the incomes so generated – but they bear none of the risks. In order to restrain opportunistic behaviour and self-dealing among SOE insiders, government agencies are able to intervene in SOE operations and party organizations have the right to control personnel. However this practice incurs high bureaucratic and political costs and contributes to the inefficiency of the state sector as a whole (Qian, 1996; Jefferson, 1998; Perotti, *et al.*, 1999).

In US publicly held corporations, insiders, particularly managers, control the assets of outside shareholders. Because of the wide dispersion of shareholdings the managers of many large public companies have long been essentially self-appointing and self-policing. The mechanisms that

Table 6.2 Comparative models of insider control

Owner	Model and performance	Restraint mechanisms
The state	SOEs in transition: privatized profits and socialized losses	Government inspection and intervention
Outside shareholders	Large US corporations: competitively strong	(1) Competitive markets for capital, products and managerial labour: • performance comparison and managerial reputation; • threat of takeover, bankruptcy and exit. (2) Shareholders' votes (by show of hands or sale of shares) (3) Legal and institutional constraints, rigorous accounting standards, extensive mandated disclosure, prohibitions on insider dealing, procedural rules facilitating shareholder litigation, a well-developed financial press
Insiders and some outsiders (insiders hold the majority of shares)	Joint stock cooperatives in China: competitively strong	(1) Competitive product markets: continue or exit. (2) Hard budget constraint: threat of liquidation, bankruptcy or exit. (3) Shareholders vote by show of hands (both inside and outside shareholders). (4) Benefits from smallness: information problems are largely internalized. (5) The local government acts as a major institutional shareholder. (6) Revaluation of shares is based on book value, profitability and collective discussions. (7) Portfolio risks are diversified by shareholdings in other community firms and by holding contracting rights over farmland

function to keep managers accountable to the shareholders include mainly the competitive markets of capital, products, and managerial labour, and embedded legal and institutional constraints, as listed in Table 6.2. Although shareholders have the opportunity to vote at annual or extraordinary general meetings, a more effective way of bringing managers to account is for shareholders to sell their holdings.

Compared with SOEs operating under transitional conditions and large US public corporations, insider control in China's JSCs is less problematic. The battle for survival in the highly competitive product markets and hard budget constraints have forced them to cut costs and improve their efficiency. Both inside and outside shareholders have long had cooperative relations and geographic proximity. Their interests in the firm are now measurable and clearly defined in terms of shares. When facing tough market competition the best strategy for them is to acknowledge, safeguard and promote their common interests and to choose cooperation rather than conflict. The community government, by acting as a major institutional investor, has become more helpful because it now acts in a less predatory manner while continuing to mediate market transactions and resolve disputes among the parties involved, particularly between insiders and outsiders.

For China's JSCs, the most challenging issue is deciding who will monitor the monitors in general and the community government in particular. The community government typically holds a large stake in most JSCs in terms of financial capital, land or both. In the ownership restructuring process, the government often plays the triple role of 'coach', 'referee', and 'athlete'. In terms of raising equity capital and mediating credits, the part played by the community government seems to be indispensable, on at least in the near future. In most of the townships and villages with JSCs, the community government acts as the *de facto* representative of local shareholders in the exercise of shareholders' residual control rights. Together these facts indicate that proper behaviour by community governments is and will continue to be crucial to the success of local firms. Although the community's drive to survive in the face of interjurisdictional and market competition can function as an alternative mechanism to keep local officials in check, it cannot replace the internal governance structure. In order to promote the most competent people to the key positions and to prevent officials from opportunism and corruption, political democratization within the community is as if not more important than the equity democratization promoted by JSCs. Unfortunately the pace of political democratization has lagged behind that of equity democratization, particularly at the township level.

Structures to avoid the excessive cost of collective decision making

In comparison with state ownership of SOEs and collective ownership of TVEs before the restructuring, the ownership form of JSCs reduces the costs of both monitoring and collective decision making. First, investing part of personal savings in the firm in exchange for control rights will certainly increase employees' commitment to the firm (Dong *et al.*, 2002) and may encourage self-monitoring and peer-group monitoring. Since employees now have a measurable personal stake in the fortunes of the firm in which they work they are more motivated to engage in consolidated collective action when faced with market competition. Second, employees already know a great deal about the firm simply as a by-product of their employment, but they now have a stronger incentive to acquire information on the effectiveness of managers. The improved flow of information and communication between workers and managers may serve to avoid needless conflict. They can also appoint representatives to monitor managers' handling of the fortunes of the firm, which will reduce the costs of managerial opportunism. Finally, the reduction of government intervention enables the firm to focus on its business criteria, which helps to reduce the costs incurred by conflicting criteria.

However, because workers act as both equity owners and employees in exercising their control rights over JSCs, the interest differences induced by the dual role may increase the cost of collective decision making if mechanisms for resolving conflicts of interest are not put in place. Employees may disagree about their relative wages. They may have quite different opinions about the distribution of the firm's earnings between capital and labour because they have invested substantially different sums in the firm. They may fail to reach agreement on the firm's investment plans due to their different stakes in the investment projects. There may be different attitudes towards technical updating among unskilled, skilled and white-collar workers, and between younger and older workers. In order to avoid some of these conflicts and limit other costs to a tolerable level, appropriate institutional and social mechanisms need to be put in place.

The institutional and social mechanisms to avoid or limit the cost of conflicts of interest that are emerging in China's JSCs include representative governance, formal charter limitations on voting procedures and voting outcomes, review by outside agencies, and the shared norms and urge for survival that are sparked by competition. Representative governance is analogous to that employed in large corporations with dispersed shareholdings, and in large cooperatives such as Mondragón in Spain

(Cheney, 2000; Hansmann, 1996: 98–103). Under this form of governance both inside and outside owners elect representatives to a board of directors, which is responsible for appointing, overseeing and dismissing the firm's managers. Direct employee participation in governance is largely confined to annual meetings and to major constitutional changes such as a merger or splitting the firm, changing the firm's statute (for example to a limited liability company), the issuance of bonds, and increasing or decreasing the number of shares. The members of the board and the managers hold office for a minimum term of three to five years, and the board members cannot be removed during their term without good cause. This arrangement serves to secure professional management and to avoid the biased decisions and high costs of highly participatory governance forms.

Formal charter limitations on voting procedures and voting outcomes means that there are formalized limitations on substantive decisions that may be subject to conflicts of interest. For example the distribution of profits is largely defined by the firm's charter and is based on government regulations. According to the regulations issued by the Ministry of Agriculture on 12 January 1990 (Article 15), rural JSCs should retain 60 per cent of their post-tax profits for investment and capital accumulation. The remaining 40 per cent may be used for dividends, bonuses and employee welfare funds, but it is recommended that dividends should amount to no more than 20 per cent of total post-tax profits.[6] Relative wages are largely determined by piece rate, contracting (for managers) and subcontracting (for teams in workshops). The wage level is based on the firm's performance the previous year and is subject to local government approval, but it is left flexible in order to accommodate changes in market competition. The strong delegation of decision-making power to managers and the chartered attenuation of employee's rights to earnings and control appear to have effectively muted the interplay of political forces among employees, preempting costly conflicts. Criticisms in China tend to focus on the weakness of employees' role in controlling the management. While agreeing that employees should play a more active role in the exercise of democracy, our analysis suggests that it is better to let them play a greater part in the process of community democratization than in the firm.

At present the outside review function is still performed by local government agencies, mainly state asset administration bodies, financial bureaux, local branches of state banks at the county level and above, and the community government at the township and village levels. Although there continue to be certain bureaucratic and political costs, their review and oversight activities seem to bring more benefits and less costs than before. In addition to the roles played by major institutional investors, market intermediaries and dispute arbitrators analyzed above, the community government plays a quite similar part to that of the 'social council' in Spain's Mondragón. The members of the social council are elected by local constituencies and the council serves as a major venue for discussions and negotiations, which serve to smooth relations between employees and management. The effectiveness of the above mechanisms depends on the presence of a hard budget constraint and on the extent of market and interjurisdictional competition. Without competitive pressure and a hard budget constraint they may not function in a positive way. Competition and a hard budget constraint make profits sensitive to the performance of the firm and instil the same urge for survival among inside and outside owners and managers. As a consequence profitability and an urge to survive may become shared norms among stakeholders. Competition also encourages local government agencies to promote and secure better ownership arrangements and to function as a helping hand rather than a 'grabbing hand'.

Channels to raise capital and diversify risk

Apart from the costs of collective decision making, theoretical concerns about employee-ownership include the concentration of risks and the difficulty of raising capital. With regard to risk concentration, when employees invest a significant portion of their wealth in the firm that employs them they bear much more risk than do employees who do not invest. They not only reduce the diversify of their investment portfolio, but also reduce the separation between their financial portfolio and their human capital, their means of earning an income. If the firm fails they lose not only their jobs but also their savings (Putterman, 1993; Hansmann, 1995: 76). With regard to the difficulty of raising capital, because of asymmetric information and interest differences between employee-owners and outside investors, predominantly employee-owned firms may be less attractive to outside investors, resulting in undercapitalization (Craig and Pencavel, 1995; Earle and Estrin, 1996).

However, as pointed out by Earle and Estrin (1996: 12), the risk concentration argument ignores the point that human capital risk may be reduced due to a reduction of the risk of lay-off and the loss of firm-specific investment or rents because investing personal savings in the firm brings employees some control rights. This point is certainly very relevant for SOEs in transitional economies, where capital markets are severely underdeveloped and the highest risk for employees and society is large-scale lay-offs. In addition, if outside funds are difficult to obtain, employee ownership can provide a modest pool of funds to use for the firm's survival and capitalization.

JSCs in the TVE sector have an inbuilt mechanism for risk diversification as from the outset township and village communities have engaged in a range of activities, including manufacturing, agriculture, commerce, construction and transportation (Sun, 1997: section 4).[7] Some JSCs are based on the full range of community activities, that is, households and employees hold shares in the community firms as a whole rather than in single firms. Even in the case of firm-based JSCs, local employees and their households typically hold shares in other community firms and also retain their right to use farmland. As documented by Gu (1999) and Sun (2000), the establishment of JSCs in both rural and urban China has greatly strengthened the capitalization of firms, rather than the opposite. For small and medium-sized firms the possibility of raising equity capital from markets is usually very weak and the cost is often unbearably high, even in an economy with well-developed capital markets. For them the most feasible and efficient way of raising equity capital is to issue shares to employees, community members and relatives and to attract venture capital with the assistance of the community government.

Compared with JSCs in the TVE sector, those emerging from the SOE and private sectors tend to be disadvantaged in terms of risk diversification. To the extent that this can be a serious obstacle to firm development, they have a more urgent need to transform their ownership structure to the limited liability form, with ownership by management or outside investors. The flexibility of the JSC ownership form can facilitate this type of transformation, as shown by the experiences in Wenzhou (Sun, 2000).

The above analysis suggests that for numerous small and medium-sized enterprises in the TVE sector there is no reason to assume that the JSC ownership form will be a transitory arrangement. Some may grow into limited liability and openly held companies, and some may be closed due to business failure. However, many of them will continue to enjoy the advantages of this ownership arrangement and many new firms will adopt it due to its cost and benefit advantages. In fact by the end of 2000 the number of surviving firms that had adopted the JSC form at their start-up stage was 28 168, and the number of surviving JSCs that had been formed by means of a cooperation between household and private firms was 48 542 (*Yearbook*, 2001: 166). However the various parts played by the community government could be transitory. In the near future the role of major institutional investor could be separated from the role of administration and regulator. In the longer term the role of major institutional investor could be transferred to real financial institutions or intermediaries, once they are fully functioning and mature.

Remaining challenges to JSC development and TVE reform

The analysis and evidence indicate that TVE ownership restructuring in general and the emergence of employee stock ownership in particular have been effective in curing TVE mechanism degeneration and in improving TVE capitalization.[8] However the restructuring still has some way to go. First, progress is uneven and there is still a lack of unified and rigorous legal provisions for standardizing the establishment and operation of joint ownership firms and JSCs. Second, the fact that grassroots political democratization lags behind that of equity democratization and has not made progress at the township level is hindering the healthy evolution of joint ownership firms and JSCs. In communities where political democratization has proceeded only in name, the adoption of JSCs has not resulted in a reduction of local government control. Without a democratic balance in the community and proper reviews by outsiders there is a strong possibility that JSCs will degenerate into disguised forms of managerial buy-out, which will result in employees bearing higher risks while managers – often local government officials – enjoy most of the profits and almost all the decision-making power.[9]

As well as these challenges to TVE reform, many other problems that are common in developing economies have surfaced and constrained the development of TVEs. First, in general enterprise management is still far from professional and proficient. The top managers are typically members of the local community and have had a relatively poor education. They may have a strong desire to develop their firms but lack the management skills needed to deal with market competition and improve efficiency. The development of tools for market-based economic decision making has lagged behind the general growth of the TVE sector. For example the company accountant is usually a bookkeeper rather than being an integral part of management, mainly due to the severe shortage of professional accountants. As a consequence many TVE managers have no access to the information flows generated by modern accounting practices, which prevents them from making rational and timely business decisions (*China Daily*, 26 October 1995: 2). The shortage of competent engineers and technicians has also undermined the improvement of TVE technological management.

Second, there is an obvious conflict between the need for risk diversi-fication and the lack of technical economies of scale in production. TVEs are typically locally initiated and locally based. In order to diver-sify business risks it is rational for a township or village to set up several small-scale TVEs in different sectors. However in many industries small-scale production is not profitable in the medium or long term. This casts a shadow over the long-term prospects of many small-scale TVEs.

Third, in many cases the start-up of TVEs has been driven by local resources rather than market demand. In the past there were no marketing problems due to widespread supply shortages, but from the mid 1990s onwards the demand constraint started to dominate the Chinese economy. As a consequence local-resource-based TVEs are confronted with the problem of how to adjust their product structure and update their products in order to meet market demands and main-tain their market shares.

Fourth, almost all TVEs have been collectively initiated by township governments, village governments, households and groups of house-holds, based on local resources and conditions. The benefits of this include very low entry costs into non-agricultural sectors, the ability to exploit local resources, and other comparative advantages. However the constraints on development are significant as well. Rural industrializa-tion has not yet resulted in meaningful urbanization, so in general TVEs will not be able to enjoy the benefits that flow from urbanization for quite some time. In other words the further development of TVEs will be restricted by the continuing lack of infrastructure, market information and strategic services, and by poor transportation and communication networks. Furthermore human capital development will continue to be constrained by local and kinship-based vested interests and by employees' dual role as worker and peasant.

At the macroeconomic level, the overall pattern of TVE distribution suggests three negative factors: (1) the use of scarce land and the existing infrastructure is inefficient; (2) the development of a service sector is restricted by the absence of demand for its products, so the countless jobs that the sector is capable of creating, which are urgently needed in China, will not be forthcoming; and (3) there is a risk that environmen-tal pollution may go unchecked in certain localities. In order to tackle these problems, since the early 1990s the Chinese government has paid greater attention to the establishment of small industrial cities and towns. Some experiments have been conducted and supporting policies issued. The role of both central and local governments in this area is certainly crucial. The challenges linked to the general development problems cannot be addressed by ownership reform alone, although ownership reform will create a sound institutional base for tackling the problems. Ownership restructuring is only one of the major aspects of the TVE development process. Management modernization, urbanization in a form that is compatible with TVE growth, human capital development and the modernization of corporations are all vital tasks facing TVEs and the Chinese government. The challenges from both reform and development will continue to put pressure on all the players in this field, providing them with strong incentives and stimulating them to look for innovative and adaptive solutions.

Concluding remarks

This chapter has considered the progress made in the radical restructuring of TVE ownership in China. Although most small TVEs have been privatized by selling them to private owners, the ownership structure of the typical larger TVE is now characterized by joint-stock ownership by its employees, the community government and outside equity holders. To illustrate how Chinese JSCs differ from industrial cooperatives and closely held employee stock ownership in the West and employee-owned firms in transitional economies in Europe, the chapter has identified and discussed the core mechanisms developed by China's JSCs, including mechanisms to avoid excessive collective decision-making costs, check insider control, mobilize internal and external financial resources, diversify risks, harmonize labour–management relations and provide the flexibility needed for the JSCs' further evolution.

The most striking feature of China's joint ownership forms in general and JSCs in particular is that they combine the incentives that come with individual ownership and capital accumulation with the existing institutional and social capital embedded in the township or village community. They can be regarded as a hybrid between the closely held joint-stock firm and the former collective TVE, and they represent both continuity and dynamic adaptation. These hybrid modes could be transitional in the case where a jointly owned firm or JSC firm grows out of the community and becomes an openly held company. However the fact that the closely held firm is and will continue to be the dominant ownership form in the rural economy suggests that the institutional and social capital embedded in the rural community will continue to be of value to most community enterprises. When firms are closely held their corporate governance problems are fundamentally different from those in the openly held firm. For the closely held firms, their shares are not listed on stock exchanges and governance through the competitive stock market is irrelevant. Their governance problems typically involve the use of mutual class shares and managerial networks, redesigning ownership and control via multilateral negotiations and influence-seeking among different stakeholders. In all these areas the vesting of social and institutional capital in the community provides information advantages and cost-saving potential (Aoki, 2001).

As transition does not involve the immediate replacement of old institutional structures with new ones and the process can be quite lengthy, it is necessary to adopt ownership and governance mechanisms that are adaptively efficient; that is, capable of providing the economic and political flexibility needed for people and organizations to respond to new opportunities, accommodate progress in know-how, pursue knowledge and learning, encourage risk taking and creative activities, encourage trial and error in a world of uncertainty, and undertake a change of course if a particular set of tactics seems unlikely to result in a successful outcome. Judged by these criteria, the ownership and governance mechanisms in China's employee stock enterprises and JSCs can be seen as adaptively efficient. They might be transitional but also have good chance to go beyond China's transition period. What is certain is that they will continue to pursue adaptive efficiency and catch comparative advantages from more than one institutional and social channel so as to strengthen their competence and to meet new challenges. The advantages of pursuing adaptive efficiency via a hybrid form of ownership may be the most instructive lesson China's TVE restructuring can offer to decision makers and entrepreneurs in transitional and developing economies.

Notes

1 In official statistics, rural enterprises are classified into four categories: township-run (*xiangban*), village-run (*cunban*), owned by a group of households (*lianhu*, mainly partnerships), and owned by an individual household (*geti*), that is, a sole proprietorship employing fewer than eight people. The TVEs in this chapter fall into the first two categories. Although household-run and jointly owned private enterprises accounted for about 42 per cent of value added and 56 per cent of employment in the rural non-agricultural sector in 1996, they tend to be much smaller in scale (*Yearbook*, 1997: 121). Furthermore a large number of them are subcontracted subsidiaries of larger TVEs.

2 Employee shareholdings include both individual and collective shareholdings. Typically the collective shares account for only a small proportion of the total shares held by employees.

3 By the end of 2000, of the approximately 802 000 TVEs that remained in the collective ownership category 163 000 (20.3 per cent) were JSCs, 25 000

(3.1 per cent) were joint-stock companies and the others had either retained the more conventional collective form of ownership (with leasing or management-responsibility contract arrangements) or registered themselves as limited liability companies (*Yearbook*, 2001: 3).

4   During 1992–98 the TVE sector continued to grow strongly. TVE value added increased from 299 billion yuan in 1992 to 997 billion yuan in 1998, representing a real growth rate of 13.6 per cent per annum. In 1999 the growth rate of TVE value added was still about 9 per cent, despite the fact that many small TVEs were being transferred to private ownership and despite the negative impact of the deflation and export difficulties caused by the East Asian economic crisis (*Yearbook*, 1996: 102–8; *Statistical Yearbook of China*, 1999, 2000: table 9.2).

5   The broad agricultural sector includes farming, forestry, animal husbandry and fishery.

6   In August 1997 this profit-distribution framework was adopted for urban JSCs by the State Commission for Restructuring the Economic System, which issued guidelines (*Zhidao yijian*) to the urban JSCs (*Economic Daily*, 7 August 1997).

7   At the end of 1996 China had 45 500 townships and 740 100 villages. On average, each township with a population of about 24 000 possessed nine township-run non-agricultural firms, and each village with a population of about 1200 had 1.54 village-run non-agricultural enterprises.

8   TVE mechanism degeneration refers mainly to increased bureaucratization in communities with successful TVEs, softened budget constraints among TVEs in the same community, and other moves towards SOE-type mechanisms.

9   The author thanks one of the referees for this interesting observation.

References

Almanac of China's Economy (various issues), Beijing: Almanac of China's Economy Press.

Aoki, M. (2001) *Toward a Comparative Institutional Analysis*, Cambridge, MA: MIT Press.

Beijing Survey Group (2000) 'Evaluating the Quality of TVE Restructuring in Tongzhou District', *China's Rural Economy* (*Zhongguo Nongcun Jingji*), 6 (June): 37–42 (in Chinese).

Bonin, J. P., D. C. Jones and L. Putterman (1993) 'Theoretical and Empirical Studies of Producer Co-operatives: Will Ever the Twain Meet?', *Journal of Economic Literature*, 31, 3: 1290–320.

Che, J. (2002) 'From the Grabbing Hand to the Helping Hand: A Rent Seeking Model of China's Township-Village Enterprises', WIDER Discussion Paper 2002/13, Helsinki: UNU/WIDER.

—— and Y. Qian (1998) 'Institutional Environment, Community Government, and Corporate Governance: Understanding China's Township–Village Enterprises', *Journal of Law, Economics, and Organization*, 14, 1: 1–23.

Chen, J. Y. and J. Han (1994) 'On China's Rural Reform and Deng Xiaoping's Ideas about the Development of China's Agriculture', *China's Rural Economy* (*Zhongguo Nongcun Jingji*), 10 (October) (in Chinese).

Cheney, G. (2000) *Value at Work: Employee Participation Meets Market Pressure at Mondragon*, Ithaca and London: Cornell University Press.

China Daily (various issues) (English newspaper published in China) http:// www.chinadaily.com.cn/.

Craig, B. and J. Pencavel (1995) 'Participation and Productivity: A Comparison of Worker Cooperatives and Conventional Firms in the Plywood Industry', *Brookings Papers on Economic Activity: Microeconomics 1995*, Washington, DC: Brookings Institution: 121–74.

Dong, X.-Y., P. Bowles and S. P. S. Ho (2002) 'Does Employee Share Ownership Matter? Some Evidence on Employee Attitudes in China's Post-Privatization Rural Industry', unpublished manuscript, Department of Economics, University of Winnipeg.

Earle, J. S. and S. Estrin (1996) 'Employee Ownership in Transition', in R. Frydman, C. W. Gray and A. Rapaczynski (eds), *Corporate Governance in Central Europe and Russia*, Vol. 2, Budapest: Central European University Press.

Economic Daily (Jingji Ribao) (various issues) http://www.economicdaily.com.cn/.

Gu, E. X. (1999) 'Local Government and Ownership Reform of Small and Medium SOEs', in L. Sun with E. X. Gu and R. J. McIntyre, *The Evolutionary Dynamics of China's Small and Medium-Sized Enterprises in the 1990s*, World Development Studies 14, Helsinki: UNU/WIDER: ch. 3.

Han, J. and Q. Zhang (eds) (1993) *Joint-Stock Cooperative Economy in Rural China: Theory, Practice and Policy*, Beijing: Economic Management Press (in Chinese).

Hansmann, H. (1996) *The Ownership of Enterprises*, Cambridge, MA: The Belknap Press.

Henggang Town Party Committee and Town Government (1993) 'Co-operation at Three Levels and All Based on Shares', in Han and Zhang (1993): 142–51.

Huang, R. and B. Zheng (1993) 'Community-Based Joint-Stock Cooperatives: The Experiment in Tianhe District of Guangzhou Municipality', in Han and Zhang (1993): 107–22.

Huang, S.-G. (1993) 'The Development and Improvement of Rural Joint-Stock Cooperatives in Bao-an County', in Han and Zhang (1993).

Jefferson, G. H. (1998) 'China's State Enterprises: Public Goods, Externalities, and Coase', *American Economic Review*, 88, 2 (May): 428–32.

Perotti, E., L. Sun and L. Zou (1999) 'State-Owned versus Township and Village Enterprises in China', *Comparative Economics Studies*, 41, 2 (Summer): 151–79.

Policy Research Office of Yichang County Party Committee (1997) 'Discussion on "Integration of the Village and its Enterprises into One Organisation"', *China's Rural Economy (Zhongguo Nongcun Jingji)*, 8 (August): 36–9 (in Chinese).

Putterman, L. (1993) 'Ownership and the Nature of the Firm', *Journal of Comparative Economics*, 17, 2 (June): 243–63.

Qian, Y. (1996) 'Enterprise Reform in China: Agency Problems and Political Control', *Economics of Transition*, 4, 2: 427–47.

Statistical Yearbook of China (various years) edited by the State Statistical Bureau, Beijing: China Statistics Press.

Sun, L. (1997) 'Emergence of Unorthodox Ownership and Governance Structures in East Asia: An Alternative Transition Path', *Research for Action*, 38, Helsinki: UNU/WIDER.

—— (2000) 'Anticipatory Ownership Reform Driven by Competition: China's Township–Village and Private Enterprises in the 1990s', *Comparative Economic Studies*, 42, 3 (Autumn).

Tan, Q. (1998) 'Determining the Orientation of Property Rights Reform of Township and Village Collective Enterprises in Light of the Nature of the Enterprise', *China's Rural Economy (Zhongguo Nongcun Jingji)*, 3 (March): 13–20 (in Chinese).

Yearbook of China's Township and Village Enterprises (various issues) edited by the Editorial Committee of the TVE Yearbook, Beijing: China Agriculture Press.

Vermeer, E. B. (1996) 'Experiments with Rural Industrial Shareholding Co-operatives: The Case of Zhoucun District, Shandong Province', *China Information*, 10, 3–4: 75–107.

Wang, T., H. Yang and C. Qiao (1997) *China's Joint-Stock Cooperative Economy*, Beijing: Enterprise Management Press (in Chinese).

Wu, Y. and S. Li (2001) 'The Evolving Trend of the Property Rights Structure and Governance Mechanism in the "Henggang Model"', *China's Rural Economy (Zhongguo Nongcun Jingji)*, 7 (June): 56–60 (in Chinese).

7
Network Externalities and Cooperative Networks: Stylized Facts and Theory

Stephen C. Smith

Introduction

This chapter argues that cooperatives may benefit from being in a region with other cooperatives, or in a sector in which there are many cooperatives, or within a supply chain (that is, having significant forward or backward linkages) in which cooperatives are common. In other words there are network externalities or complementarities of organizational type, at least when it comes to organizational form. As a result organized networks can serve to internalize some key externalities that might pose significant problems for individual cooperatives operating in isolation. This chapter sets out a theory of the role of cooperative networks, which is then applied in Chapter 8 to a comparative case study of the La Lega and Mondragón networks. The possibility that reaction functions may shift with changes in the available institutions is introduced, and is applied to the presence and activities of cooperative leagues. The theory is broader in its potential application; for example it may shed light on the large differences between the performance of industrial districts in developing countries.

The need for a theory of cooperative success in networks is clear. The economic literature provides a wide range of strong arguments against the viability of cooperatives. Although there are counterexamples of and counterarguments for each of these claims, taken together the arguments against cooperative viability are very strong. Indeed they appear to have the weight of evidence on their side, for industrial cooperatives are rather rare. Yet worker cooperatives are far from rare and employ hundreds of thousands of workers around the world. On the other hand, in practice cooperatives are almost always grouped together in clusters. This fact strongly suggests that progress in understanding the conditions under which cooperatives can be viable will require a better theory of the advantages of cooperative clustering. The remainder of this introduction features a brief review of some of the main claims for the inefficiency of cooperatives, as well as some of the counter-arguments.

The literature on worker cooperatives identifies numerous sources of their potential failure (some of the arguments below are reviewed in greater detail in Bonin *et al.*, 1993). First, if workers hold a property right to their jobs they will substantially lose the incentive to work. Efficiency wage benefits are effective if there is fear of dismissal. Although in principle workers could hire supervisors to ensure that no worker is shirking, in effect these supervisors would be the employees of the workers and it is unclear whether they could really pose a credible threat. There is a counterclaim in the literature that workers who own their firm have an incentive to work hard and even monitor one another, but while this is certainly possible, many organizational and free-rider problems would still have to be overcome. Second, there is the time horizon problem: workers may have an incentive to invest in the firm until they retire or otherwise depart from the cooperative, but not afterwards as pure worker cooperatives do not give members the right to sell their membership to the highest bidder.[1] Hence there is an expectation that cooperatives will be unable to raise the efficient level of capital investment internally. Even if cooperatives could guarantee a full return of capital gains to worker-investors, workers might well find it difficult to obtain sufficient funds to take advantage of this opportunity (and if the firm is to remain a cooperative, the next gener-ation of workers might be faced with an insurmountably high cost of buying a membership).

Third, and related, cooperatives will also have a hard time raising capital externally because of the concern that workers might take out profits in the form of higher wages, or if this is legally or contractually prohibited, will find a way to take out profits through 'gold-plating', such as recreational facilities, fancy furniture, fancy dining arrange-ments and the like. Fourth, workers are inadequately diversified if they own the firm in which they work, a fact that corporate collapses – such as that of Enron – bring to the fore. Even when there is no obvious management malfeasance such as that found at Enron, the recent bankruptcy of majority-worker-owned United Airlines, with a substan-tial loss of workers' assets, shows that concerns about risk are not to be dismissed lightly. Fifth, there is the basic problem of entrepreneurship. If each worker receives only a fraction of the profits of the cooperative, say one *N*th in the case of a cooperative with *N* members, then there is little incentive to play an entrepreneurial role to establish the firm; this is an example of what is known as the 1/*N* problem in the literature. Finally, as Hansmann (1996) stresses, democratic decision making runs into major obstacles in a firm where voting workers have non-homogeneous preferences.

Moreover it is argued in the literature that even if such problems are overcome, cooperatives will be subject to subsequent degeneration. It is argued that such firms will not take on additional members but will hire outside workers instead. If they are able to do so, the majority members will layoff minorities in order to concentrate the profits among a smaller number of claimants. If they cannot, members will nonetheless become a smaller and smaller proportion of the workforce when some among their members retire or otherwise exit the firm. In addition, highly profitable cooperatives may be purchased by outside firms, providing a windfall for the members. Moreover there will be a strong tendency for underinvestment, leading to uncompetitiveness. Finally, while some of the problems of establishing a firm in the first place are overcome because there is an ideological commitment to cooperative ideals, in many cases it can be expected that subsequent generations of workers will not share the same commitment.

The literature on cooperatives and the labour-managed firm has a wide variety of counterarguments for each of these points. For example, to some extent outside financing problems can in principle be solved with the use of specialized financial instruments (Waldmann and Smith, 1999), but establishing such instruments in the first place may be subject to coordination failures. One might of course observe cooperatives with smoothly functioning voting procedures in cases where the workforce, and hence worker preferences, are more homogeneous, but this would surely leave out a large fraction, probably a majority, of the sectors in an economy. Further, one can imagine that some of these problems could be prevented with constitutional prohibitions on actions that might lead to degeneration, but the question is what authority could or would impose and enforce such prohibitions? And even so, as long as there was an incentive not to attract new members when market conditions called for hiring members, or to undertake other actions that could undermine efficiency, the long-term institutional stability of cooperatives would remain in question. Yet as we shall see in Chapter 8, some well-performing cooperative industries do exist, and although they are a distinct minority in every economy they appear to be more stable and long-lived than conventional firms. Clearly something is lacking in the special case, *ad hoc* counterexamples to the arguments against the viability of cooperatives.

There are other purported advantages to worker cooperatives, such as higher morale, more cooperative labour relations and better information sharing, but the case of United Airlines shows that such benefits are not always forthcoming in majority-worker-owned enterprises; and such explanations of the potential success of cooperatives do little to explain why they are grouped together in geographic clusters, one of the most important stylized facts of the successful cooperatives that exist in the world today. Further progress in understanding the conditions under which cooperatives could be viable will require an understanding of the causes and effects of cooperative clustering.

This is largely neglected in the literature and the analysis in this chapter is aimed at helping to redress this neglect. Thus we have strong arguments as to why worker cooperatives should not work, or at best be rare and found only in a few specialized industries; but at the same time we have important examples of their long-term success in a highly diversified range of industries, especially in Spain and Italy.

The potential role of cooperative clusters

The famous market test of efficient organizational forms – that if an organization is efficient it will thrive in the market but not otherwise – must be qualified when market failures are present. The market test has been used by various authors when seeking to explain the relatively low number of cooperatives, notably Hansmann (1996; see also the discussion in Bonin *et al.*, 1993). The importance of this test was emphasized by Mario Nuti (2000) when making use of an old Italian proverb: *'se sono rose, fioriranno'* (if they're roses, they'll bloom). Although this metaphor is very colourful, the (metaphorical) reply proposed in this chapter is that a single rose may not necessarily bloom alone: it may need to be part of an ecosystem in which other roses are present, and in which supporting actors and elements (for example bees, fertile soil, rainfall) are also found.[2] Coordination failure can result from strong complementarities among firms (see for example Murphy *et al.*, 1989; Kremer, 1993), and this chapter argues that there are significant complementarities among firms of a similar organizational type, or at least in the case of cooperatives.[3] Their presence suggests that even if barriers to entry are overcome and a cooperative is established it may not survive, not because of intrinsic inefficiencies but simply because of the lack of other cooperative entries, and perhaps also because of a lack of coordination among the cooperatives that do enter the market. The hypothesis of this chapter is that cooperative leagues can help to internalize these externalities.

We shall now consider ten examples of areas in which network externalities may be present in groupings of cooperatives. (Other specific areas are described in Chapter 8, where two case studies of cooperative networks are presented.) First, new managers are likely to have had experience with cooperative management when they take a new managerial job at a cooperative. Second, employees will encounter similarly empowered counterparts in joint ventures, sales or other market activities, maximizing the benefits of decentralized authority.[4] Third, banks will have experience of lending to such firms. Lending transaction costs are always highest when a bank first lends to a borrower with a far from normal structure or set of internal or external governing regulations,[5] and a similar argument could be applied to insurance and other services. More generally, private firms in a region may well be hostile to cooperatives when cooperative density is low. Business associations may, for example, lobby the government to restrict them. But when the cooperative sector reaches a sufficiently large size, cooperatives are more likely to gain acceptance by the private sector and business relations such as subcontracting can begin. Indeed precisely this historical pattern has been identified by the Mondragón Co-operative Corporation (MCC), reviewed in Chapter 8.[6]

Fourth, governments will have experience providing a legal framework and other services, as well as taxing such firms. Fifth, there are more examples of cooperative organizational and other relevant experiments from which to absorb lessons ('learning by watching') in the region or sector. Sixth, in addition to pure spillovers, such as tips learned when having lunch with counterparts from other firms, a pool of consultants in organizational development and other fields and with relevant cooperative experience will be available: there will be a 'thick market' of suppliers to cooperatives, improving the probability of a good match. Seventh, in the case of involuntary separations it will be easier for cooperatives and workers with relevant cooperative experience to find each other, thus lowering training costs.[7] Eighth, backward and forward linkages can provide additional complementarities, which is particularly important when increasing returns are present (Todaro and Smith, 2003: 167–8), and similar organizational forms across these linkages may matter. The La Lega cooperative (see Chapter 8) makes extensive use of such linkages across sectors. Ninth, trust and shared values in business arrangements is another sphere in which history matters (Adsera and Ray, 1998), and complementarities may play a part in this. For example it is probably no accident that cooperatives are strong in north-central Italy where social networks are dense but weak in Il Mezzogiorno where they are thin (Putnam, 1994). These advantages are separate from traditional economies of scope; the argument is not (only) that the costs of production are lower within a single organization or with a shared collective good, but rather that costs are lower across organizations of a similar type as a result of their presence in the market. Moreover a cooperative league such as La Lega can facilitate the internalization of such benefits. Tenth, some process innovations may fit with the organizational comparative advantage of cooperatives, such as non-Tayloristic operations that utilize knowledge and skills embedded in the work team, that is, unobservable to management. Such innovations are selected against when workers have an incentive to shirk; but if cooperatives can overcome this problem, through a combination of direct financial ownership incentives augmented by mutual peer monitoring, these innovations can be used efficiently. The more cooperatives there are, the greater the incentive to invest in such innovations.[8] Moreover – to the extent that cooperatives are more risk-averse than conventional firms – the information role of cooperative innovation consortia could be more significant for productive efficiency than is the case with similar consortia of conventional firms.

The latter observation can be viewed as a special case of the argument by Conte (1986) that one function of a supporting structure such as Mondragón is to reduce subjective uncertainty about the profitability of cooperative enterprises. This uncertainty could include unfamiliarity with the institutional structures of cooperatives, such as their legal structure, as well as imperfect information on the applicability of a new technology, as noted above, in addition to conventional income risk. If this subjective uncertainty is greater than that for, say, individual proprietorships, cooperatives may not be formed due to a simple lack of information. Beyond this, it can be conjectured that two of the functions of consortia, such as those devoted to innovation or finance, as observed in Mondragón and La Lega (see Chapter 8), is to reduce members' uncertainty about the value of the existing innovations, and to contribute original innovations of special relevance to cooperatives.

The economic theory of labour-managed firms and producer cooperatives highlights a number of other areas in which a league may play a significant role. As suggested above, one major concern is that cooperatives have special problems achieving entry because there are too few incentives for entrepreneurial activity (Bonin *et al.*, 1993). In the pure cooperative form each member receives an equal share of the profits, so a single worker-entrepreneur has only a small financial incentive to start a cooperative, a situation known as the $1/N$ problem in the literature. In addition, it is argued that once a cooperative is formed it might encounter what is called the 'heterogeneous voter problem', and experience high decision-making costs or even impasses if the workers' preferences are very different (Hansmann, 1996). Finally, cooperatives have some incentive to degenerate into a non-cooperative form even if entry is achieved, because unless contracts are well specified it may be more profitable to hire new workers as conventional employees rather than admit them as full members. A cooperative league can circumvent such problems by playing the entrepreneurial role, taking into account such potential problems as voter heterogeneity in the initial decision on the scope of the individual cooperatives' activities and setting constitutional constraints on what they may do. Aside from the issues that are particular to cooperatives, many of the principles outlined here also apply to other types of firm, such as small enterprises with strong complementarities within an industrial district (for an overview of the related issues and applications to developing countries, see Schmitz and Nadvi, 1999).

In sum, there may be strong complementarities among cooperatives in a region, sector or industry group, implying that there are increasing returns at the cooperative network level. In this case (Pareto-ranked) multiple equilibria may be present; that is, some of the outcomes may clearly be better than others from a social welfare standpoint, but the market may be unable to provide the better outcomes.[9] Put differently, the system as a whole may suffer from coordination failure; but the establishment of cooperative leagues or cooperative umbrella corporations may be an effective strategy for resolving the problem.

Some basic models

To formalize these ideas, consider the following stylized model. Suppose that some cooperatives are prepared to enter the market even if no others do so. This would follow from a very strong organizational comparative advantage[10] among cooperatives in some fields that would make it privately efficient for members to opt for entry, although they would gain higher incomes (or utility) if other cooperatives entered. This corresponds to a positive vertical intercept for privately efficient cooperative density against the horizontal axis – (expected) cooperative density (Figure 7.1). As drawn, the privately efficient cooperative density function at first exhibits increasing returns, reflecting the network externalities among the cooperatives proposed above.[11] Additional cooperatives that consider it privately efficient to enter the market only because other cooperatives have done so have what we call a 'weak organizational comparative advantage'. Where the function first cuts the 45° line from above, at D_1, a low cooperative density equilibrium is found. However it is implausible that network externalities will grow at an increasing rate until density reaches its maximum value (unity). In particular there are likely to be sectors in which conventional firms have a strong organizational comparative advantage. This will lead to diminishing returns at the network level, and eventually the privately efficient cooperative density function may cross the 45° line from above again, as at D_2, providing a high cooperative density equilibrium. The intermediate point where the curves cross, D_3, is an unstable equilibrium. If these conditions are present, both low and high cooperative densities may be sustained as equilibria, and in this regard an economic role of a cooperative league is to increase cooperative density past the critical level D_3, at which the higher density cooperative incidence can be sustained as an equilibrium. Put differently, part of the problem

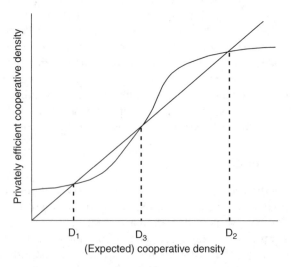

Figure 7.1   Privately efficient cooperative density function and multiple cooperative density equilibia

is solved simply by higher density rather than by the presence of a cooperative league *per se*, although the league may play a key role in expanding and maintaining that density. There is, however, a second role for the league: to increase the privately efficient cooperative density for any given (expected) cooperative density.

There is an analogy here to the literature on industrial districts. As Nadvi (1999) has stressed, some of the benefits of a firm's location within a district of enterprises in a sector or a small group of related sectors are gained simply by the fact of location; Nadvi calls this 'passive collective efficiency'. However other benefits can only be achieved through collective action, such as developing joint training facilities or promotional activities, or lobbying the government as an industry rather than as individual firms (Porter, 1990). Nadvi (1999) calls these benefits 'active collective efficiency'. One factor determining the dynamism of an enterprise district is the ability of its constituent firms to find a mechanism for collective action. While the government can provide financial and other important services to facilitate cluster development, social capital is also essential, especially group trust and a shared history of successful collective action; but this takes time to develop.[12]

The active role of the cooperative league is reflected by a shift of the privately efficient cooperative density function, as shown in Figure 7.2.

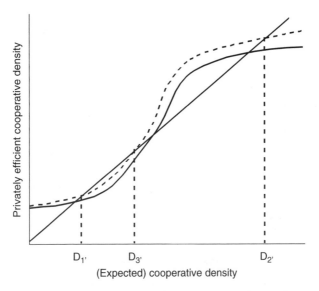

Figure 7.2 The shift of the privately efficient cooperative density function

However the cooperatives may also benefit from active cooperation among themselves (as suggested below). If coordination failures make such cooperation difficult, a cooperative league could efficiently shift up the schedule in Figure 7.2 through coordination activities in consortia and other arrangements (though more information would generally be needed to provide welfare comparisons). The result would be to increase the return to members from establishing a cooperative, increasing the equilibrium cooperative density (at both high and low density equilibria). The general suggestion is that reaction functions may shift when changes in the available institutions are introduced. While applied here to the presence and activities of cooperative leagues, the idea should have broad applications when assessing the role of institutional reform in economic development, a subject that is widely discussed but insufficiently formalized.[13]

A cooperative league could shift the privately efficient cooperative density function even if there were a single-equilibrium density, as would occur if the function exhibited diminishing returns throughout. This is illustrated in Figure 7.3, in which there is a positive number of cooperatives in the single initial equilibrium. The presence of the league shifts the cooperative density function upwards, leading to a new

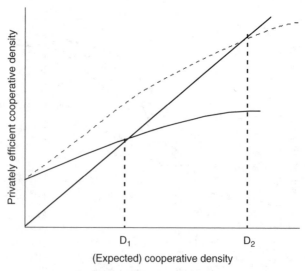

Figure 7.3 The presence of the league shifts the cooperative density function upwards

equilibrium with a larger number of cooperatives (with a cooperative density function starting from the origin, the presence of a league could lead to a positive number of cooperatives where none could exist without it). In any case, the argument that cooperative leagues can play an efficiency-enhancing role does not depend on the presence of multiple equilibria. Of course it is possible that this shift may not be the result of efficiency gains; it could reflect private gains due to rent seeking, such as successfully lobbying the government for special advantages. This possibility, and more generally a cost–benefit appraisal, would have to be considered before one could conclude that the effect is an unambiguous Pareto improvement from the economy-wide point of view. Another issue faced by an efficiency-enhancing cooperative league is that the degree to which it can shift the curve will depend on its resources, which will in turn depend on cooperative density and the fraction of cooperatives joining the league (paying dues and commissions). To this extent there may be free-rider problems in addition to a coordination problem.

In a recent application of this general analytical approach, using a more rigorous but necessarily narrower modelling framework, the present author and a colleague (Joshi and Smith, 2002) modelled the establishment of cooperatives and the emergence of cooperative leagues as a process in the endogenous formation of coalitions. We employed this approach to analyze the strategic incentives for individual players to establish labour-managed cooperatives and for these cooperatives to organize themselves into cooperative leagues. In our model, coalitions emerged endogenously as the Nash equilibria of an announcement game. A two-stage game was set up and solved by means of backward induction techniques. We addressed the issues in the context of non-cooperative games of coalition formation. While at first it may seem odd to study cooperative formation as a non-cooperative game, we think it is highly appropriate: while successful cooperatives are likely behave internally in ways that are better modelled as a cooperative game, the difficulty of establishing cooperatives in the first place involves numerous problems that are better conceptualized as elements of a non-cooperative game.

We shall briefly review some of the results of the exercise (for full details see Joshi and Smith, 2002). For the purposes of the argument of this chapter, if the cooperative league is formed through an open membership game, which is the second stage of our game, there can be two Nash equilibria. In one equilibrium a cooperative league is formed; in the other it is anticipated that no cooperative league will be formed, and hence no cooperatives are formed. In this case the former equilibrium with a cooperative league Pareto-dominates the latter, in which no league is formed.

In the first stage of our game we examine the formation of the individual cooperative firms. We begin with *ex ante* identical players who decide either to work in a conventional firm in return for an exogenously determined payoff (the market wage) or to participate in a labour-managed cooperative in return for an (uncertain) share in the revenue, net of capital costs. We allow multiple, symmetrically sized cooperatives to be formed endogenously. We allow for the fact that a cooperative member may face uncertainty on the demand side and thus a risk to net income (we assume away employment risk in the conventional sector); this uncertainty may be a function of the size of the cooperative. In line with the discussion earlier in this chapter, we also allow for the fact that the formation of cooperatives may generate a (positive) externality, or spillover, for other cooperatives.

We then show that, when payoffs to potential worker-members from joining a cooperative initially increasing with the number of members and then decreasing, the outcome of the game depends on the rules of cooperative formation. If the payoffs to individual members are less then the conventional wage, then all three of the rules of cooperative formation examined yield the outcome that no cooperatives will be formed. If the payoffs are exactly equal to the alternative wage at a single, unique membership size, then the open membership and exclusive membership rules of the game yield the same outcomes: either no cooperative will be formed or all the cooperatives formed will have the same number of members. On the other hand, in this case the coalition unanimity game has a unique outcome: only cooperatives of that unique size will be formed.

But if the payoffs to the members exceed the alternative wage for some membership sizes, then the three alternative rules of cooperative formation examined yield different outcomes. In particular, in the open membership game, if at least some workers continue to work for conventional firms, then cooperatives will be formed at the largest size for which the payoffs are equal to the alternative wage. However if the payoffs exceed the conventional wage only when all workers join cooperatives, then the equilibrium cooperative size can potentially include a wide range of membership sizes. In the exclusive membership game all cooperative sizes, in the interval when the payoffs are at least as large as conventional wages, are equilibria. Finally, in the coalition unanimity game only cooperative sizes at which the highest income per member is achieved are equilibria. Only the latter result corresponds closely to the traditional neoclassical Ward–Vanek literature (though not necessarily with its comparative statics implications).

Each of our three games generally corresponds to alternative traditions in the literature and institutions. The open membership game conforms to Mondragón's first principle of open admission, and can be traced to an important tradition in the cooperative movement that is sometimes associated with Theodor Hertzka's utopian novel *Freeland* (1891). The exclusive membership game reflects the way in which many cooperatives are formed in practice: a group of potential members self-select themselves as a group to form a cooperative without knowing with certainty what the payoff to their coalition will be; a long as the payoff, determined after the group is formed, at least matches the alternative (conventional firm) wage, the outcome is a stable firm (an equilibrium). In the coalition unanimity game players are in a position to choose a membership size that maximizes their assumed objective – their (equal) share of net income – so this game solution concept corresponds to the Ward (1958) and Vanek (1970) neoclassical analysis of the labour-managed firm, or some variants of it, such as the 'inegalitarian' cooperative type introduced by Meade (1972). Among other things this shows that our framework is flexible enough to incorporate each of the major perspectives in a highly diverse body of literature.

When examining the incentives for individual labour-managed cooperatives to create a cooperative league, we take it as given that a subset of the workers in the economy have already formed symmetrically sized cooperatives with a given number of members, as just described. This allows us to focus on the endogenous formation of a league. We assume that a dominant coalition of cooperatives can be formed via an open membership game of the type introduced by D'Aspremont *et al.* (1983), in which any player can join the league by announcing their intention to do so. The dominant league is a Nash equilibrium of this game and is internally stable (no cooperative that has announced its intention to join has an incentive to withdraw) and externally stable (no cooperative that has announced its intention not to join has an incentive to announce a decision to join). For the sake of modelling simplicity, only one league is allowed to form; multiple leagues are ruled out by assumption. Despite this restriction we are still able to show the potential for multiple Nash equilibria in league formation, some of which may be inefficient: even when we restrict ourselves to the formation of one dominant league there are two Nash equilibria in the league formation game, one of which – failure to form a league – is inefficient. This result would hold even if multiple leagues were allowed to form, and indeed in general a larger set of equilibria are likely.

Gross payoffs to a member in the league will depend on the number of players who have agreed to participate in the cooperative sector, and/or the number of players in each cooperative. In other words, spillovers or externalities are generated by having more players in the cooperative sector and each cooperative in the sector being larger. Thus we write gross payoffs quite generally as $\Pi(L;h,m)$, where h denotes the number of members in each cooperative, m is the total number of players who have agreed to form cooperatives, and L is the number of cooperatives in the league. In Figure 7.4 these gross payoffs to a member cooperative is charted as a function of the number of cooperatives participating in the league.[14] The only modest restriction we impose is monotonicity: gross payoffs to a league member weakly increase as more cooperatives join the league; no restrictions are imposed on the rate at which gross payoffs increase. We also assume that payoffs to cooperatives may increase when more cooperatives are formed, even if they do not join the league.

With regard to costs, it is assumed that the formation of a league requires some initial fixed investment; as the league expands this fixed cost will be distributed equally among all members. Thus the cost per member decreases as the size of the league increases. In Figure 7.4 the costs to members as a function of league size is shown to be

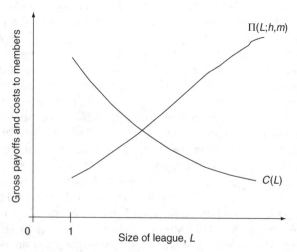

Figure 7.4 Gross payoffs and costs to members

monotonically decreasing. But our analysis also holds for the case in which there is a minimum efficient league size after which the cost per member increases. For example administrative costs may rise as the league expands and becomes a more complex organization. Figure 7.5 charts the net payoff to a member of the league and compares the payoff for a cooperative member with that for a non-member. Three points should be noted here. First, for a non-member we do not have to distinguish between gross and net payoffs because the non-member does not share any of the costs of league formation. Second, non-member payoffs may depend on the number of members in each cooperative, h, and the total number of players who have agreed to form cooperatives, m, because of the presence of spillovers. Third, non-member cooperatives may gain from the presence of a league due to strategic complementarities. These payoffs are shown in Figure 7.5. Since non-members enjoy positive spillovers from the formation of a league, and the spillover benefits are presumably smaller than the direct benefits from participating in a league for small league size, the function Φ may intersect Π at least twice. In Figure 7.5 there are two Nash equilibria: no league is formed at all, or a league of size $L_2(h,m)$ is formed.

With multiple Nash equilibria, payoffs to players in one equilibrium dominate those in another. Only one Nash equilibrium is efficient:

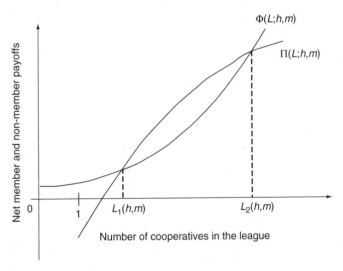

Figure 7.5 Net payoffs to members and non-members

that in which a league of size $L_2(h,m)$ is formed. However our analysis shows that an inefficient equilibrium could arise if all cooperatives expected that no league would be formed. Even if an efficient league were formed it is possible, given the parameters of the model, that not all cooperatives would participate in the league. In the case being considered, $L_2(h,m)$ cooperatives are members of the league and $(m/h) - L_2(h,m)$ cooperatives are non-members. Depending on the values of h and m and the shape of the functions Π and Φ, the equilibrium league size could be small and there could be a large number of free-riding non-member cooperatives. Finally, in the original study (Joshi and Smith, 2002) we examined other possible equilibria and analyzed the first stage of the game, the endogenous formation of cooperatives. In particular we developed in detail the case in which, because of a failure to anticipate league formation, no cooperatives are formed even though their formation would be socially efficient. Thus the multiple equilibria anticipated from an examination of incentives to form cooperative leagues were entirely consistent with recent concepts of game theory employed in the modelling of endogenous group formation.

The existence of cooperatives may depend on the roles played by a cooperative league, but a cooperative league requires payments from its constituent cooperative members to offset its costs. Hence cooperatives and their supporting structure face something of a chicken-and-egg situation that is common to many cases of multiple equilibria, such as that posed by Acemoglu (1997), where workers' investment in skills depends on the firms' investment in technology, which in turn depends on the availability of skilled workers. This general result can be established under a variety of modelling strategies.

Implications

This framework has several empirical implications. First, everything else being equal, successful cooperatives will exist where cooperative density is high. Second, successful cooperatives that began as isolated firms are more likely to develop strategies to encourage the entry of similarly organized firms than will unsuccessful cooperatives in similar circumstances (however one would have to be careful to account for selection bias in empirical work on individual cooperatives, because when network externalities are present presumably only exceptionally efficient cooperatives will enter an area with low cooperative density). Third, successful cooperatives are more likely to form leagues and umbrella groups or corporations of similarly organized firms to help preserve cooperative density by, among other things, providing temporary support to ailing firms during restructuring, as occurred in Mondragón, or support mergers structured to preserve employment and market share, as seen in La Lega (see Chapter 8).[15] The evidence presented in Chapter 8, taken as a whole, strongly suggests that these conditions do hold for the networks of Mondragón and La Lega. Indeed one of the central points of that chapter is that the mere creation of these cooperative networks was their most important innovation and adaptation. Virtually all of the other innovations studied required the existence of networks as a necessary precondition.

As further evidence of the significance of clustering, the cooperatives in La Lega are highly concentrated in the heartland of north-central Italy.[16] Emilia-Romagna, which is one of Italy's 20 regions, can almost be viewed as a cooperative industrial region in itself.[17] La Lega's cooperatives alone account for about one eighth of Emilia-Romagna's GDP, and a far greater share in some cities and towns in the region. In the case of Mondragón, the systematic development of cooperatives in the town of that name and subsequently throughout the region was part of a policy to create jobs in an area of high unemployment, and to encourage the spread of a set of deeply felt values; but it is also significant that the economies of scale and scope thus realized also provided substantial benefits to the individual cooperatives that had existed before the network was set up (for example marketing cooperatives). This framework and the evidence supporting it also has a clear policy/managerial implication: a league of cooperatives will want to support cooperative entrepreneurship for reasons that go beyond direct financial return (and beyond any philosophical motives) in that the presence of additional cooperatives will provide external benefits to each. On its own a single cooperative will generally be unable to internalize such an externality (unless it is very large in relation to its reference markets).

For regional governments, if there are a number of cooperatives of sufficient scale or scope to constitute an important part of the regional economy but their survival is as at some risk, a regional development strategy aimed at establishing other cooperatives may be of value. For example the minimum efficient density may increase with certain forms of technological change. The framework also leads to testable hypotheses for cases outside the scope of this study. For example La Lega has put much effort into developing new cooperatives in Il Mezzogiorno in southern Italy, but these have been viewed as less successful than those in north-central Italy. If this is the case, one explanation could be that they have a less dense set of networked relationships and are more scattered geographically. If so, a policy measure for La Lega would be to place greater emphasis on the creation of many cooperatives in concentrated local areas, such as a small city.

In conclusion, it is worth stressing that more than coordination failure may be at work here: prisoners' dilemmas are also involved. The fact that some cooperatives thrive outside formal networks that are in close geographic proximity to them suggests that not all externalities are internalized in the league, and that geographic and economic proximity to other cooperatives or to the league itself attracts at least some of the benefits. Hence there is a potential free-rider problem; if many cooperatives were to secede from their networks they might save on the payment of dues, but they could deteriorate in the long term. An alternative hypothesis is that, despite the evidence presented, the key is not the league, but simply the degree of cooperative density.

The framework developed in this chapter leaves quite abstract the types of service efficiently provided by a cooperative league. Clearly these are likely to be services with some economies of scale and scope in their provision, larger than the efficient productive scale of the constituent cooperatives. The range of services might be relatively large because cooperatives tend to be small, probably reflecting their organizational comparative advantages. But which of these services should be procured from standard suppliers on the general market and which by a league or consortium specializing in selling to cooperatives is clearly an empirical question. The strategy used in the next chapter to identify relevant services is to characterize the common functions of the two most successful cooperative networks, La Lega and Mondragón, which otherwise are organizationally and historically different entities with dramatic internal organizational differences.

Notes

1   However, Bartlett *et al.* (1992) could find no difference between the La Lega cooperatives and matched conventional firms in their time horizon criteria. On the other hand these cooperatives had a lower capital to labour ratio than did conventional firms.

2   The Italian expression is already plural: if they are roses, they will bloom.

3   It is hoped that the present analysis will help to provide a basis for a more generally applicable theory of network effects in organizational forms, but the focus here is exclusively on worker cooperatives.

4   For a detailed discussion in the context of high-performance workplaces, see Levine (1996).

5   Interview with Renee Jakobs of the National Co-operative Bank (NCB) Development Corporation, Washington, DC, 2001.

6   Interview with MCC officials, 17 April 2001.

7   Such training costs could include learning how to function effectively as a cooperative member rather than a hired worker. For an applicable formal search model, see Acemoglu (1997). Involuntary separations include the death of workers and company bankruptcies.

8   For an applicable formal model, see some of the works by Gregory Dow, for example Dow (1993).

9   For an overview of the economics literature see in particular Murphy *et al.* (1989), Kremer (1993) and Banerjee and Newman (1993); for a partial survey see Ray (1998, ch. 5).

10 The concept of organizational comparative advantage is introduced and applied to industrial cooperatives in Smith (1994).

11 The relevant measure of density will depend on the issue: for some applications density refers to the fraction of enterprises organized as cooperatives; for others, measures such as the share of value-added, the share of the labour force or the share of finance accounted for by cooperatives will be more relevant. In some of the cases described below, the most relevant measure is the fraction of an output (which could include an innovation) purchased for use as an input by cooperatives.

12 See Schmitz and Nadvi (1999), especially the Introduction and the contributions by Dorothy McCormick and Hermine Weijland. For a brief introduction to industrial districts in the context of developing country urbanization, see Todaro and Smith (2003, ch. 8). For relevant experimental evidence see Gachter and Fehr (1999).

13 See for example World Bank (2002).

14 To normalize for convenient graphical interpretation, if $L = 1$ then there is one cooperative in the league (incurring all the costs of league formation); if all cooperatives choose not to join, then $L = 0$.

15 Other inferences are possible but are beyond the scope of this chapter. For example cooperative formation rates are highly uneven across time, for instance there was a dramatic upsurge in cooperative formation across Europe in the 1970s. We might reasonably hypothesize that a successful cooperative network will capitalize on such periods by drawing in many of the new cooperatives and providing crucial services to ensure the survival of the cooperative form as well as of the individual cooperatives. The uneven rates of expansion over time also suggest that a dynamic version of this analysis would prove fruitful, and have applications in related areas, such as industrial districts, which appear to evolve over time in a series of identifiable steps.

16 This chapter focuses on the cooperatives in this region, particularly those in Tuscany and Emilia-Romagna, not only because that is where the strongest concentration of cooperatives is found, but also because this is the region in which the author conducted most of his research (Bartlett *et al.*, 1992; Smith, 1994).

17 Italy is known for its Marshallian industrial district organization of manufacturing production – see for example Porter (1990).

References

Acemoglu, D. (1997) 'Training and Innovation in an Imperfect Labor Market', *Review of Economic Studies*, 64 (July): 445–64.

Adsera, A. and D. Ray (1998) 'History and Co-ordination Failure', *Journal of Economic Growth*, 3: 267–76.

Ammirato, P. (1996) *La Lega: The Making of a Successful Co-operative Network*, Brookfield: Dartmouth, Ashgate.

Banerjee, A. V. and A. Newman (1993) 'Occupational Choice and the Process of Development', *Journal of Political Economy*, 101, 2: 274–98.

Bartlett, W., J. Cable, S. Estrin, D. Jones and S. C. Smith (1992) 'Labor-Managed Co-operatives and Private Firms in North-Central Italy: An Empirical Comparison', *Industrial and Labor Relations Review*, 46: 103–18.

Bonin, J., D. Jones and L. Putterman (1993) 'Theoretical and Empirical Research on the Labor Managed Firm: Will the Twain Ever Meet?', *Journal of Economic Literature*, 31, 3: 1290–1320.

Conte, M. (1986) 'Entry of Worker Cooperatives in Capitalist Economies', *Journal of Comparative Economics*, 10, 1: 41–7.

D'Aspremont, C. A., A. Jacquemin, J. J. Gabszewicz and J. Weymark (1983) 'On the Stability of Collusive Price Leadership', *Canadian Journal of Economics*, 16: 17–25.

Dow, G. K. (1993) 'Why Capital Hires Labor: A Bargaining Perspective', *American Economic Review*, 83, 1: 118–34.

Ellerman, D. (1984) 'Entrepreneurship in the Mondragon Cooperatives', *Review of Social Economy*, 42, 3: 272–94.

Gachter, S. and E. Fehr (1999) 'Collective Action as a Social Exchange', *Journal of Economic Behavior and Organization*, 39, 4: 341–69.

Hansmann, H. (1996) *The Ownership of Enterprise*, Cambridge, MA: The Belknap Press.

Hertzka, T. (1891) *Freeland: A Social Anticipation*, London: Chatto & Windus.

Hey, J. D. (1981) 'A Unified Theory of the Behavior of Profit-Maximizing, Labor-Managed and Joint-Stock Firms Operating under Uncertainty', *Economic Journal*, 91: 364–74.

Joshi, S. and S. C. Smith (2002) 'An Endogenous Group Formation Theory of Cooperative Networks', WIDER Discussion Paper 2002/87, Helsinki: UNU/WIDER.

Kremer, M. (1993) 'The O-Ring Theory of Economic Development', *Quarterly Journal of Economics*, 108, 3: 551–75.

—— (1997) 'Why are Worker Cooperatives So Rare?', Working Paper 6118, Cambridge, MA: NBER.

Lerman, Z. and P. Claudia (1993) 'Financing Growth in Agricultural Co-operatives', *Review of Agricultural Economics*, 15, 3: 431–41.

Levine, D. I. (1996) *Reinventing the Workplace: How Business and Employees Can Both Win*, Washington, DC: Brookings Institution.

Martin, T. (2000) 'The Impact of Worker Ownership on Firm-Level Performance: A Comparative Study', PhD dissertation, Yale University.

Meade, J. E. (1972) 'The Theory of Labour-Managed Firms and of Profit Sharing', *Economic Journal*, 82, 325: 402–28 (supplement).

Miyazaki, H. (1984) 'On Success and Dissolution of the Labor-Managed Firm in the Capitalist Economy', *Journal of Political Economy*, 92, 5: 909–31.

Morley-Fletcher, E. (1992) 'Questa "piccola rivoluzione"', *Rivista della Co-operazione*, March–April.

Murphy, K. M., A. Shleifer and R. W. Vishny (1989) 'Industrialization and the Big Push', *Journal of Political Economy*, 97, 5: 1003–26.

Nadvi, K. (1999) 'Collective Efficiency and Collective Failure: The Response of the Sialkot Surgical Instrument Cluster to Global Quality Pressures', *World Development*, 27, 9: 1605–26.

Nuti, M. (2000) 'Employee Participation in Enterprise Control and Returns: Patterns, Gaps, and Discontinuities', in V. Franicevic and M. Uvalic (eds), *Equality, Participation, Transition*, New York: St Martin's Press.

Porter, M. (1990) *The Competitive Advantage of Nations*, New York: Free Press.

Putnam, R. D. (1994) *Making Democracy Work: Civic Traditions in Modern Italy*, Princeton, NJ: Princeton University Press.

Ray, D. (1998) *Development Economics*, Princeton, NJ: Princeton University Press.

Schmitz, H. and K. Nadvi (1999) 'Special Issue on Clustering and Industrialization', *World Development*, 27, 9.

Smith, S. C. (1994) 'Innovation and Market Strategy in Italian Industrial Co-operatives: Econometric Evidence on Organizational Comparative Advantage', *Journal of Economic Behavior and Organization*, 23, 3: 303–21.

—— and M.-H. Ye (1987) 'The Behavior of Labor-Managed Firms under Uncertainty: Product Diversification, Income Insurance and Layoff Policy', *Annals of Public and Co-operative Economics*, 57: 65–82.

Todaro, M. P. and S. C. Smith (2003) *Economic Development*, 8th edn, Reading, MA: Addison-Wesley.

Vanek, J. (1970) *The General Theory of Labor-Managed Market Economies*, Ithaca, NY: Cornell University Press.

Waldmann, R. and S. C. Smith (1999) 'Investment and Supply Effects of Industry-Indexed Bonds: The Labor Managed Firm', *Economic Systems*, 23, 3: 245–68.

Ward, B. (1958) 'The Firm in Illyria: Market Syndicalism', *American Economic Review*, 48, 4: 566–89.

Whyte, W. F. and W. Kathleen (1991) *Making Mondragon*, 2nd edn, Ithaca, NY: ILR Press.

World Bank (2002) *World Development Report 2002*, New York: Oxford University Press.

8

Network Externalities and Cooperative Networks: A Comparative Case Study of Mondragón and La Lega with Implications for Developing and Transitional Countries

Stephen C. Smith

Introduction and approach of the study

The Mondragón Co-operative Corporation (MCC)[1] in the Basque region of Spain and La Lega[2] cooperative network in Italy are arguably the most striking examples of globally competitive, worker-managed cooperatives. This chapter makes a systematic comparison of the innovative and evolving mechanisms developed by these networks to mitigate the disadvantages inherent in the typical cooperative structure, but without substantially forgoing or compromising too much on the offsetting advantages and attractive features of cooperative forms of organization. The comparison is motivated by the theory of cooperative networks introduced in Chapter 7. The chapter examines recent institutional responses within these networks to increasing global competition and the need to accelerate the pace of innovation[3] and improve quality, and considers their applicability to other cooperative clusters. Implications for developing and transitional economies are also explored. It should be noted that although the two networks now operate in advanced economies, this was not the case in their formative stage, which is partly why their experiences are relevant to developing countries. (An appendix available from the author provides further details of the historical and institutional background of these networks for readers who are unfamiliar with them.)

The systematic comparison of these two networks is presented along nine dimensions, selected either for their importance in the theoretical literature on cooperatives and similar enterprises, or for their prominence in the formal structures of one or both networks. In each case the role of cooperative networks, whether through consortia or industrial, regional or national associations, is highlighted. The nine dimensions are:

1. The entry problems experienced by individual cooperatives.
2. The problems associated with exiting, including the cooperative 'degeneration' problem.
3. Decision-making procedures, with an emphasis on the role of worker's 'voice'.
4. Consortia and second-level cooperatives, and their role in solving management and organizational problems.
5. The role of and policies towards joint ventures and interfirm alliances.
6. Innovation and technology transfer strategies.
7. Finance and investment instruments and institutions.
8. Institutions and instruments for risk mitigation.
9. Employment policy.

The concluding section sums up the findings and explores the implications of institutional innovations for restructuring enterprises in transitional economies with substantial employee ownership, such as Russia, for cooperatives in developing countries with significant cooperative systems, such as India, and for other countries that would like to encourage the development of cooperatives or employee ownership.

The extensive networks of worker cooperatives of La Lega in Italy (employing nearly 80 000 members) and Mondragón in Spain (employing approximately 40 000 at the end of 2000) are probably the OECD countries' most important and successful groups of worker cooperatives, or firms featuring full employee ownership and self-management. This chapter examines the reasons for the continued success of these unusual clusters of firms in the face of significant shocks and growing competitive pressures, and provides insights into the comparative advantages of this form of organization. These networks can be seen as an important laboratory to address several important issues for developing countries and regions.

First, widespread (and apparently long-term) employee ownership has become a central feature of the transitional economies since privatization.

However too little is known about how to maximize the net benefits from this arrangement. In this regard the experiences of the most successful Western examples of long-term, full-employee ownership offer important insights. Second, a significant and growing number of workers in developed countries such as the United States (Blasi and Kruse, 1991) and developing countries such as Korea (Cin and Smith, 2002) now participate in some form of broad-based employee stock plan. This has produced benefits, but has also led to an undiversified concentration of risk. Some of these firms are located in relatively disadvantaged areas. The experiences of Mondragón in particular offer lessons for risk management strategies when workers' wealth is largely concentrated in the firms in which they are employed.

Third, agricultural cooperatives play an important role in many developing countries, and these countries also feature other forms of organization with implicit employee ownership – from ESOPs in East Asia to worker cooperatives in South Asia, social enterprises in Latin America, common property resources in Africa and, or at least until recently, township and village enterprises in China. Fourth, Mondragón and La Lega offer unique opportunities for testing theories of organizational behaviour and organization that may be applicable to a number of institutions in developing countries. The two cases studied here are quite distinct: many of their institutional details differ significantly and there seems to have been almost no economic interaction between the Lega and Mondragón systems. However there has been a striking convergence of their functions if not their organizational structures.

It is hypothesized that the cooperatives in La Lega and Mondragón and the associated networks have adapted and specialized in ways that accentuate the benefits and diminish the costs of their organizational forms, which are effectively exogenous. The working assumption is that if functional convergence is found in the organizational and market strategies of these two successful cooperative groupings, generalizations from the examples of convergence will provide a useful basis for working hypotheses of cooperative strategies that may be generally applicable to cooperatives and majority-employee-owned firms in developing and transitional countries. Hence this study identifies areas of convergence and goes on to present them in a systematic manner. It should be noted that this strategy is a method of hypothesis generation, not a rigorous method of hypothesis testing in its own right.

Legal statutes and regulations on cooperatives, and – in the Italian case – even cooperative law written into the national constitution, can and have been changed – explicit cooperative bylaws have been modified in both La Lega and Mondragón at the network and individual cooperative levels. However bylaws and laws for which cooperative groups lobby codify certain features and effectively serve to keep them exogenous over long periods of time.[4] The somewhat informal strategy followed in this study is to identify aspects of organization that are exogenous, or at least for the 1945–2000 period covered by this study, by determining which principles have never been altered internally or through any external legal or other environmental change supported by the cooperative or cooperative group.

The evidence suggests that effective, ultimate control by worker-members is the most fundamental and unchanging feature. In the case of La Lega, the national constitution (Article 49 on cooperatives), the national laws on cooperatives and individual cooperative bylaws have changed (including major revisions in 1992) but the principle of majority voting control by the employees of the firm has never been altered. In each case the principle does not follow from obviously internal cultural features, but rather has been imported from the cooperative movement. La Lega, for example, has demonstrated a willingness to give a minority vote to capital (even if in practice there have been almost no cases since the law was modified in 1992 to allow for this), but there has never been any willingness to consider outsider or capital majority voting control. Again, legal changes lobbied for by the cooperative networks serve to codify values and keep certain features exogenous. Institutions, such as cooperative networks, that promote specific social values in addition to seeking private profits are likely to exhibit a complex relationship between the law and exogenously given structures. Law on employee ownership almost always reflects broader social goals beyond efficiency alone (Smith, 1994b).

In the case of Mondragón, the exogenous features are primarily embodied not in the law (although Spanish cooperative law is applicable) but in ten internal principles (these are described in detail in an appendix available from the author). These principles were instituted by Mondragón's founder, Arizmendi, from the beginning to prevent the cooperatives from degenerating into conventional firms. For example Arizmendi was an articulate opponent of Taylorist (deskilled) production processes, and the principles reflect an attempt to codify this stance, among other things. To a significant extent this can be taken as a constraint, around which an organizational comparative advantage had to be found in order to adapt and survive in the market. The interpretations and applications of the principles were modified as external conditions changed and the need for more formal corporate structures became apparent. In fact various organizational adaptations came and went during the timeframe of this study. The initial development of the Caja Laboral Popular (CLP), Mondragón's credit union, was an endogenous response to the need to attract more capital once the investment capacity of the members and the retained earnings were exhausted, but attention was paid to maintaining the ten principles in the process of acquiring the required capital. The CLP subsequently grew to become one of Spain's largest financial institutions and was required by Spanish regulations to service non-cooperatives, but it still provides loans to cooperative firms and members. Although these loans are not subsidized, there is a clear advantage in having an intermediary that understands the cooperative form of organization and has extensive experience of lending to cooperatives and their members.

For many years the CLP took on the role of providing overall guidance and direction to the Mondragón group. However when the group reorganized itself into a cooperative corporation, much of the directing role of the CLP was removed and it became a more narrowly specialized and independent financial intermediary with much looser ties to the overall Mondragón network. So the directing role of a financial institution cannot be taken as exogenous, though one might not have guessed this from some of the literature on Mondragón. But in the view of Mondragón strategists at least the essence of the principles has remained inviolate. Analogously, some of the organizational adaptations in La Lega described below represent alternative strategies to deal with the same need to raise large blocks of capital while maintaining exogenous features, perhaps most notably majority control by members.

This study argues that many innovative Mondragón and La Lega institutions and strategies, including the evolving organization of the networks themselves, represent an endogenous response to the need to remain competitive while maintaining exogenously given characteristics. In effect the active strategy at the network level has served to build on the advantages and limit the effects of the disadvantages of the cooperative form of organization. To the extent that these networks have been successful in these aims, the lessons from their experience may have a very wide applicability.

Cooperative adaptation and organizational innovation in Mondragón and La Lega

This section makes a systematic comparison of the institutions and mechanisms that have been developed by Mondragón and La Lega to mitigate the disadvantages of the typical cooperative organizational structure and market position, but without losing its critical advantages and attractive features. The nine strategic areas selected for the comparative analysis are considered in turn. The issues and key responses of the two networks across these nine areas are summarized in Table 8.1.

Table 8.1 Schematic view of responses to strategic issues in Mondragón and La Lega

Strategic area	Nature of market or organizational failure	Response of Mondragón (Spain)	Response of La Lega (Italy)
1 Entry problems experienced by individual cooperatives	Collective action problems, or the '1/N problem'. Heterogeneous voter problems. Uncertainty about cooperative organization and other characteristics	Use internal entrepreneurial division (later reformed as a specialized cooperative). Use constitutional restrictions: accepting the clear principles established by the league lowers bargaining costs among potential members, makes initial decision making easier and reduces uncertainty	Second-level cooperative Promosviluppo charged with starting new cooperatives and conducting feasibility studies. Offer assistance to newly joining nascent cooperatives
2 Strategy towards the degeneration problem and other cooperative exit problems	Incentive for firm to shed members to enable a larger profit share for the remaining members. Other forces leading cooperatives to degenerate into conventional firms	Put constitutional restrictions on actions that Mondragón cooperatives can take. Encourage high membership rates. Foreign subsidiaries not cooperatives, a problem under active discussion	Bankrupt cooperatives encouraged to merge with other cooperatives. Constitutional restrictions placed on cooperatives' ability to convert to conventional firms

Table 8.1 (continued)

Strategic area	Nature of market or organizational failure	Response of Mondragón (Spain)	Response of La Lega (Italy)
3 Joint policies towards special issues in decision making	Slow, inefficient decision-making processes under workplace democracy, compounded by the large size of the network	Use representative structure in cooperatives and in the Mondragón Co-operative Corporation (MCC)	Use membership-based consortia
4 Collective solutions to shared internal organizational problems	Cooperatives naturally of small size; small firms increasingly disadvantaged	Set up Lagun-Aro social insurance scheme, Ularco (legal/adminstrative group), Ikerlan, Ideko (R&D), Lankide (export group)	Set up over 30 specialized institutes and consortia, e.g. ICIE (R&D), SMAER (organizational development consulting), Conco-op (subcontracts large orders), ACAM (a purchasing consortium), SINNEA (management training)
5 Strategy towards joint ventures and interfirm alliances	Conventional firms increasingly dependent on joint ventures; cooperatives may be disadvantaged	MCC itself effectively a large alliance. Works with foreign affiliates	Active policy of developing joint ventures with both cooperatives and non-cooperatives
6 Specialized market niche and innovation and technology transfer strategies	Scant market for innovations oriented towards cooperative organizational comparative advantage	MCC member cooperative specializing in innovation and other research for MCC members	Second-level consortia focused on innovation, such as ICIE. Specialize in high-skill, low-capital processes
7 Cooperative finance and	Cooperatives subject to moral hazard problems	Develop strategy of working with in-house credit	Push for legal reforms to enable outside capital

investment instruments		union. Innovative internal capital accounts. Specialized financial cooperatives. Actively search for new financing sources, may lead to innovation.	membership. Sponsor several specialized financial intermediaries focusing on cooperative financing issues
8 Specialized risk mitigation strategies	Employee-owners have high concentration of financial and human capital assets, so more risk averse than conventional firm owners; may limit effectiveness in market competition	MCC highly diversified, possibly a response to risk. Some profit sharing across divisions. Other temporary assistance for troubled cooperatives. In-house retirement fund	Set up specialized consortia in finance and insurance sectors. Risk mitigation through strategies to lower exit rates. La Lega regional and sector leagues use modest risk reduction mechanisms, but this is an apparent strategic gap
9 Employment strategy	Conventional labour-managed firms have incentive to admit too few members and to exhibit perverse supply responses	Set up entrepreneurial division charged with creating new cooperatives. Growth from splitting existing cooperatives. Use of a buffer of non-member labour (about 20 per cent)	Strong influence of unions with incentive to expand member employment, subject to union wage

The entry of individual cooperatives

There is clearly a collective action problem when starting a cooperative firm. Unlike an entrepreneur with a conventional firm, only a small share of the benefits of playing the entrepreneurial role accrue to the founder of a cooperative; and despite their many achievements, the administrative structures of La Lega and Mondragón may have failed thus far fully to internalize this externality. Even in Spain and Italy, new cooperatives constitute only a small fraction of newly entering firms. The conclusion that conventional firms will remain dominant is qualified but not reversed by the observation that exit rates are low or that a large fraction of entrants are individual proprietorships that never intend to approach the scale of the Mondragón and La Lega cooperatives.

Cooperative entry rates are highly uneven and appear to be far more variable than for conventional firms. Cooperatives seem to have brief periods of exceptionally rapid growth in terms of number of firms and employment, followed by long periods of relative stasis or slow decline. Sometimes the periods of greatest decline are clearly attributable to exogenous political forces. Both Italy and Spain had a large and vibrant cooperative sector in the years preceding and following the First World War, but both sectors were systematically decimated by the fascists in each country (for the case of Italy see Ammirato, 1996; for Spain see Whyte and Whyte, 1991). In the postwar era La Lega had two periods of remarkable expansion: in the mid 1940s, in the aftermath of liberation, and in the 1970s, a period of economic dislocation and rapidly rising unemployment. In Mondragón the greatest upsurge of new cooperatives was also in the 1970s. Indeed in Europe as a whole the mid to late 1970s and early 1980s was a period of employment stagnation and cooperatives accounted for a very high percentage of net job creation in several European countries, including France as well as Italy and Spain (Estrin, 1985).

Entry with the institutional support of a league has other potential advantages. For example, having a set of clear principles established by the league lowers the cost of bargaining among members or potential members and makes initial decision making easier, overcoming in part the Hansmann (1996) heterogeneous voter problem.

In the 1940s and 1970s La Lega cooperatives were generally formed from scratch. Some were formed by the members of an existing cooperative who wished to branch out into a new sector and tended to be committed to the ideals of cooperation, even to the point of wage cuts to make the venture a success (Ammirato, 1996). Others were created to take advantage of state funding for job creation programmes, including special unemployment insurance funds. Unions also promoted a number of new cooperatives – unions clearly had an incentive to expand the demand for union wage employment. The central La Lega bodies themselves set up new cooperatives and assisted workers in troubled conventional firms who wished to buy out those firms. In fact, over a period of two decades up to half of new industrial cooperatives in La Lega were created from failing firms. Typically, the relevant trade union would approach the regional La Lega association on the matter. La Lega then performed a feasibility study, and if the project appeared promising the conversion of the firm to a cooperative was financed. Since the early 1980s La Lega's Promosviluppo consortium has worked systematically with plant and other conversions. Under the 1992 cooperative law, for which La Lega lobbied, 3 per cent of the profits of every registered cooperative has to be put in a solidarity fund in order to set up new cooperatives in new sectors or less well-served regions, with special emphasis on southern Italy. As a direct result the number and share of cooperatives in Il Mezzogiorno has grown substantially in recent years, but these continue to perform less well than their northern counterparts and the future of many appears doubtful.

The supporting networks and institutional arrangements of La Lega have been highly effective in preventing cooperative deaths (see below), but so far they have had more limited success at promoting the establishment of new cooperatives. However a comparison with other countries shows that far more cooperatives have been established in southern Italy than in any other comparable country or region of the world (outside Spain and Italy). In recent years the majority of recorded cooperative start-ups have been spinoffs from existing cooperatives, with a significant number of others deriving from the purchase of conventional firms, often plants facing closure. This represents a change from the period prior to 1980.

The cooperative entry profile of Mondragón is strikingly similar to that of La Lega. There was a rapid increase in cooperative start-ups in the 1959–82 period, when more than 100 sizable industrial cooperatives were formed. This number may seem small, but bear in mind that the average employment level is about 300 and that the cooperatives are concentrated in a small geographic area. The process ultimately led to the MCC becoming by far the largest employer in the Basque region and among the top eight in Spain as a whole, before even considering other Mondragón-spawned cooperatives and the impact made by the CLP. The expansion rate was especially rapid during the 1970s.

A key player in this expansion was the CLP Entrepreneurial Division (a kind of internal consulting firm), which in 1991 became an independent MCC cooperative, the LKS. When groups of existing cooperative members or other community residents wished to start a cooperative in a new sector the division would perform a feasibility study. The prospective cooperative group would elect one of its own as manager, and the latter then worked in-house at the CLP while the project was being studied. At other times the original idea came from the division itself. The division also provided a range of services that would normally be provided by a venture capitalist firm, including technical and organizational consulting services as well as financing. Its funds came from loans from the CLP, membership fees from new members and fees for other services.

The expansion process slowed dramatically in the early 1980s with the severe recession and problems arising from increased competition when Spain's trade barriers were lowered. From 1982 Mondragón entrants were primarily spin-offs from existing cooperatives that had experienced rapid growth or wished to diversify, or derived from takeovers of conventional firms, rather than being completely new ventures as in earlier years. Today, most new entrants appear to be conversions from traditional firms, and in recent years fewer than 25 per cent of all affiliated cooperatives have been initiated by the LKS entrepreneurial cooperative, which is responsible for promoting start-ups. This pattern of growth through takeovers is generally typical of larger and more mature corporations.

It is worth investigating the impetus for cooperative entrepreneurial behaviour more closely. Clearly the individual financial return from starting a cooperative is generally low, but the returns are not zero. For an individual who lacks formal management credentials, organizing a cooperative may enable him or her to establish a sufficiently good reputation among the members to be elected general manager, thereby earning a higher salary (and enjoying a more interesting job) than would otherwise be possible. Even with credentials such as an MBA or an engineering degree, the process of organizing a cooperative and becoming manager can be far swifter than slowly working one's way up through the ranks of a conventional firm. There are also clear external rewards, such as the esteem of one's friends, neighbours and fellow citizens. Moreover interviews with non-managerial cooperative members have revealed that they greatly value their membership, as well as the camaraderie and solidarity with their neighbours that joint membership and the sharing of a joint destiny engenders. This is so valuable to some people that they help to organize cooperatives in which they can only expect to participate as rank and file members.[5]

However it is important to compare the opportunity costs. If a person has the talent to organize a cooperative it is probable that he or she could also organize a conventional firm, and become not only the manager but also a claimant for a share of the net income of the firm. Moreover it is not clear that the resultant social standing and esteem would be much less than from organizing a cooperative. A typical utility ranking might be manager–income claimant, followed by cooperative manager, cooperative member and worker in a conventional firm.

Hence the incentive to be a cooperative entrepreneur is not as great as might be thought. An alternative that would enable the capture of a much greater share of the rents would be for a private entrepreneur to establish a firm and then sell shares to the workers. Several US plywood cooperatives were originally organized in this way. However there appear to be no cases in the literature of firms being started by private entrepreneurs specifically in order to sell them to La Lega or Mondragón organizations or turn them into cooperatives. If the firm is valuable, why sell it? If it is not valuable, Mondragón or La Lega would presumably discover this during the valuation exercise.[6]

In conclusion, despite their low failure rate and proven long-term stability, the Mondragón and La Lega forms of organization will remain a small minority unless or until the problem of new start-ups is successfully resolved in the current conditions of faster private sector employment growth, intensifying competition and an accelerating need for innovation.

Strategy towards the degeneration problem and other cooperative exits

Studying the exit rates of firm types is important when tracking the growth or decline rate of an organizational form in general. However the study of exit rates among cooperatives is especially important because of the theoretical prediction of the labour-managed firm literature that life-cycle processes will lead either to extinction of the firm or to its degeneration into a conventional firm (see for example Miyazaki, 1984). The exit rate is very low in both La Lega and Mondragón – indeed extraordinarily low compared with conventional firms. Whilst the life-cycle theory of labour-managed firms predicts cooperative exit and degeneration in both bad and good market conditions over the business cycle, both networks, and the firms within these networks, have maintained their cooperative character over many decades. It will thus be instructive to consider how cooperative life-cycle problems have been successfully avoided by the MCC and La Lega.

La Lega generally responds to impending failure by merging a failing cooperative with another cooperative without incurring job losses (however workers are frequently reassigned to different tasks and/or sectors). This approach fits well with La Lega's long-term strategy of encouraging the development of very large, or what might be termed flagship, cooperatives. Mondragón provides temporary subsidies during times of cooperative distress. To avoid moral hazard, this support requires the pain to be shared, with reduced wages and a reduced value of the internal capital account, and it is not uncommon for some members to be temporarily transferred to other cooperatives. Sometimes permanent transfers are arranged, and systematic efforts at reorganization, changes in the product mix and even a switch to an entirely new product line are frequent practices. Inevitably some cooperatives fail and are dissolved, where upon the workers are transferred permanently to other cooperatives. Most, but certainly not all, of those which have failed were converted ailing conventional firms, in which case failure could have been partially expected (although not fully so because the MCC would have conducted feasibility studies). Failure among new cooperative start-ups is relatively rare. Up to 1992 about eight industrial cooperatives failed out of some 120 from-scratch start-ups.[7] At least some of these were attempts to start a cooperative in a town some distance from Mondragón where there had been few if any cooperatives previously. One example was the Zarauz cooperative in an isolated coastal town where all the factories had closed – this looked promising for a few years but then failed (Whyte and Whyte, 1991: 78–80). There have been a handful of failures since 1992, most of which subsequently merged with other cooperatives.

Although conventional exit is rare in both La Lega and Mondragón, and when it does occur it is likely to result in a merger, there is exit of a different kind: degeneration into a conventional firm. There has also been a case in which the members of a Mondragón cooperative sold their shares to an outside bidder. While degeneration is not an exit in the conventional sense, it does constitute what could be called an 'organizational exit'. The issue here is not whether degeneration can or does occur, but of explaining its extreme rarity.[8] One could suggest that La Lega's 'new capital' membership, which allows for 30 per cent outside votes by shareowners, is a form of degeneration. However majority worker voting is maintained, and the system merely allows greater access to the capital needed to survive in a changed market place without compromising the essential character of the cooperative. It could also be suggested that the creation of consortia, in which workers are employees rather than members, is also a form of degeneration; but once again the ultimate control is retained by the member cooperatives, which in turn are controlled by ordinary workers.

In Mondragón there have been numerous reorganizations and other organizational changes since the 1980s, and critics have claimed that the changes have given the MCC more of the character of a corporation (as its name implies) rather than a network of cooperatives. However, people interviewed at Mondragón have consistently stressed the inverted-pyramid nature of the MCC, meaning that while the official corporate chart of the MCC might resemble that of an ordinary holding company, in reality all the authority is held by the individual cooperatives, so that the apparent base of the pyramid is really its functional apex. In practice the MCC directors are a committee of cooperative directors, and any cooperative that does not consider that the MCC corporate offices are adding value to its operations may secede at any time. Although there have been some secessions, in 2001 the seven-cooperative ULMA group was seeking to return to the MCC fold (the MCC offered a proposal, which was duly studied by ULMA).[9] This is a clear sign that there is a strong incentive for the centre to add value.

This is another area in which the lessons from Mondragón may have a much wider application than thought. The majority of large conventional corporations have a similar structure, with several enterprises grouped under a holding company and run from a corporate headquarters, but some are struggling to make the model work (note for example the recent reorganization at Boeing) and might learn from the incentive structure of the MCC, in which the centre must add value to the component parts or face their spin-off.

There are now about 20 per cent non-member workers in most of the industrial cooperatives, and one might ask whether this too is a form of degeneration or organizational exit. However, as evaluated later, such a conclusion cannot be supported in the Mondragón case. Another feature of Mondragón is that it has a rapidly growing number of foreign subsidiaries with non-members who are simply employees of a corporation wholly owned by the MCC. Although the MCC is not currently planning to reorganize these firms as cooperatives, there is active discussion of alternatives such as profit-sharing, which would give the workers the same profit share as the members of the parent cooperative, but without membership rights. The anomaly of a cooperative owning a conventional subsidiary is acutely felt in Mondragón, and is the subject of a vigorous internal debate. But whatever the outcome for the foreign subsidiaries, the strategy does not appear to constitute degeneration because the cooperatives in the main MCC complex are unaffected. As being a major supplier to a number of multinational firms is a crucial part of its business, the MCC must often locate where its purchasing firms locate; indeed this is a contractual requirement under many 'preferred supplier' agreements. Without overseas subsidiaries in production and marketing, and given the realities of the competitive environment, Mondragón would have been very adversely affected and might have been unable to survive without taking this step.

In most of the foreign countries in which the subsidiaries are established, the cooperative form of organization is almost unknown and employees would have to be educated about its benefits, procedures, risks and responsibilities, including the need to make an extra effort and endure sacrifices in times of adversity. The response of workers and managers to such changes would be highly uncertain, even if costly conversion and training was undertaken. In addition, one of the major ways of dealing with financial distress in a cooperative is to transfer workers to other cooperatives, an option that is not available in a foreign subsidiary. In Mondragón it is viewed as tragic that some jobs must be moved to overseas subsidiaries in order for the MCC to remain competitive. The desire is to return these jobs to the Basque region when the MCC's technological sophistication is sufficiently developed to justify this on competitiveness grounds; offering foreign workers membership is viewed as delaying this process. Moreover if, as argued above, a single rose cannot bloom alone, converting an individual firm into a cooperative in a foreign country where no other cooperatives exist could well put the jobs of the workers at risk. In practice there is no known case of workers in these non-cooperative subsidiaries asking to become members or changing to a cooperative form of organization, and there is certainly no evidence that the MCC has ever turned down such a request. The MCC has an explicit commitment to follow labour law scrupulously in each of the countries in which it operates. In sum, there is no basis for considering that these foreign subsidiaries constitute a form of degeneration; instead it is clear that they represent an innovative adaptation in the fight for survival.

Another form of perceived degeneration could be the establishment of cooperative stores in other regions of Spain, with the workers being non-members. However such consumer cooperatives could equally be seen as a kind of hybrid between conventional consumer cooperatives and labour cooperatives, in which case their establishment could be viewed as an innovation rather than degeneration. In the core cooperatives themselves, the trend in recent years has been towards greater decision-making participation by ordinary workers in the workplace. To some extent this parallels the trend towards team self-management and similar developments in the United States since the 1980s.

In conclusion, evidence reviewed so far in this chapter suggests that both networks have maintained the majority employee ownership and control and democratic management that is special to the cooperative form of organization while making necessary, even remarkably innovative adaptations to adjust to the realities of the changing market place.

These adaptations reflect the impressive resilience and organizational innovation that is possible in the cooperative sector when it is organized into effective networks that can help internalize externalities and take advantage of economies of scale and scope. The conclusion, then, is that, contrary to the life-cycle hypothesis, cooperatives need not degenerate or exit over time, or at least not when they are part of an effective cooperative network.

Decision-making procedures/workers' voice

Decision making in La Lega and Mondragón is considered in some detail in the appendix available from the author. Here the economic costs and benefits of democratic decision making are reviewed, and innovations in decision making are examined in light of the ways in which the cooperatives have sought to lower these costs without compromising the essentially democratic character of themselves and the networks of which they are a part.

The advantages of workplace democracy are obvious, especially to academics in universities with a high degree of faculty self-governance: most guard their self-governance prerogatives jealously. (On the minus side, most prefer to avoid committee service – democracy requires participation in a lot of meetings, and this uses up time that could be valuably used for other purposes. With a decision by fiat, a lot of time is saved.) Tenured professors in universities have some features in common with cooperative members. Like cooperative members, they cannot divide the assets of the organization, but they do benefit from guaranteed employment, control over their workplace environment, the right to elect department chairs and the right to play a significant part in the selection of presidents, deans and other key administrators. Decisions about the core activities of the university – teaching and research – are made by those in the best position to understand the issues. And it is not insignificant that almost no professor gives up a tenured position unless it is to accept another tenured position at another university. However there are limits to the analogy. For example academic staff generally cannot vote to remove a key administrator. The main point is that a democratic workplace need not be inefficient, and if it is, the benefits of innovation and decentralization may outweigh the inefficiencies. Finally, as the knowledge economy takes shape, comparing a faculty to an industrial firm will become increasingly plausible.

Other advantages of democratic decision making include avoiding opportunism of owners against workers who have invested in firm-specific human capital, better aggregation of employees' preferences over working conditions, adding an additional channel of management monitoring in the face of agency problems, and better incentives for small-scale innovation.[10]

Given the foregoing, and bearing in mind that there are costs as well as benefits, we may state as a working hypothesis that cooperatives are more likely to be found in sectors in which democratic decision making is less costly or where its benefits are large, and in which the voters are more homogeneous (Hansmann, 1996). Further, when a cooperative or cooperative group is located in a sector or a group of sectors in which the direct voters are less homogeneous, this cooperative or cooperative group will find it advantageous to distribute the various functions to separate entities in order to make the basic decision-making groups more homogeneous. Indeed in La Lega and Mondragón highly educated professional workers, whose pay and preferences are likely to differ from those of unskilled workers, are often found clustered in their own cooperatives or working as conventional employees (or are placed in special membership categories) in consortia or other forms of second-level cooperative. Finally at higher levels of the organizational structure, representative democracy rather than direct democracy may be used to facilitate 'logrolling' and other familiar processes from voting theory.

The foregoing can be expressed somewhat differently, as follows. The need to economize on transaction costs is a significant factor in the organizational decisions of a firm; among these are the costs of decision making. The decision-making process can be divided into two parts: the initial making of the decision, which tends to favour conventional (ultimate) authority; and the practical implementation of these decision throughout the organization, which in some important respects favours highly participatory regimes, including employee-owned firms with internal democracy. The decision-making process in La Lega may be characterized as follows. The individual cooperatives practise self-management, with the general assembly being supreme and day-to-day authority being vested in managers, who serve at the pleasure of the general assembly. On the shop floor there is much greater democracy than in conventional firms.[11] At the network level decision making appears to be relatively slow, due to democratic representation through successively higher-level cooperative bodies. It is worth reiterating here that the authority of the central structures ultimately comes from reputation and persuasion, not formal powers.

In Mondragón the workers in the individual cooperatives hire their managers and elect the board and social council through the general assembly. However, at the MCC corporate level there is more central authority than exists in La Lega, following the individual cooperatives' 1984–85 reorganization into a cooperative group governed by a cooperative congress. This was an explicit response to increasingly rapid technological and market changes (1985 MCC internal document, cited in Cheney, 1999). It is difficult to gauge the precise extent of the MCC's corporate authority in practice – while those interviewed insisted on the dominance of the inverted-pyramid organizational schema outlined earlier, the prestige and practical influence of the MCC corporate offices was palpable.

In Mondragón the size of the basic cooperatives have been kept relatively small, in part to encourage participation. This is in some contrast to La Lega, where cooperative mergers have been systematically encouraged and supported to provide the network with some relatively large firms in order to establish a strong position in the market, facilitate exporting, achieve quantity discounts in purchasing inputs, meet the public relations goal of showing that cooperative organization can be successful for large as well as small enterprises, and play a leading role in *ad hoc* bidding consortia. The annual general assembly is still the highest decision-making body in all of the Mondragón cooperatives. These assemblies elect the council of directors, which is in charge of day-to-day decision making and selecting the manager. There is also a management council in medium-sized to large cooperatives, consisting of top managers appointed by the council of directors. The role of the management council appears to differ between the various cooperatives, but its recommendations are usually followed.

Finally, most of the Mondragón cooperatives have a social council, which in purposes and tasks resembles works councils in Germany and elsewhere. The social council focuses on the concerns of ordinary workers. In some respects its power is limited because it does not hold codetermination rights and the council of directors often treats its views as purely advisory; indeed the social councils have less formal power than do works councils in Germany and other European countries (see Smith, 1991, and the references therein). However ultimately their power is quite strong as they can influence the general assembly (which they represent on a day-to-day basis) to vote to overturn decisions taken by top management and the council of directors. In practice management ignores the advice of the social council at its own peril. The general assemblies of the Mondragón cooperatives have the power to fire their top managers, and some have actually done so. Many of the most important organizational innovations in Mondragón were made, or at least initiated, in response to the very serious recession of the early

1980s. For example the Cooperative Congress was created to address controversial issues such as productivity targets and social matters that required significant MCC-wide adjustments and needed to be democratically legitimated. Other innovations included the consolidation of management functions, spinning off the Entrepreneurial Division from the CLP, placing a temporary moratorium on the creation of new cooperatives in order to conserve the cash flow, transfering redundant members to other cooperatives, and even making unprecedented layoffs.

In sum, Mondragón has adjusted the details of its participatory decision making in response to crises and to improve efficiency, but without sacrificing its essentially democratic character.

The part played by consortia and second-level cooperatives in solving organizational problems

In La Lega many functions are delegated to consortia and second-level cooperatives,[12] and some 30 specialized institutes and consortia are affiliated with La Lega. Inforco-op coordinates these activities, and also raises funds from public sources for activities such as special training classes, seminars and workshops. SMAER is an in-house organizational development consulting group that helps the large cooperatives to maintain a participatory style and cooperative labour–management relations. The large size of some of La Lega's cooperatives is in part the result of the network policies, so a special responsibility may be felt to keep these cooperatives functioning smoothly and in line with La Lega's traditions. Comunicazione Italia, the public relations arm of La Lega, both promotes the image of La Lega as a whole and serves as an advertising agency for cooperatives and consortia in the network. It also offers an additional arena for the coordination of marketing strategies. The SINNEA group focuses on training cooperative managers. Editrice Co-operativa is La Lega's publishing group and its name will be familiar to anyone who even casually follows events in La Lega, for it appears on the back of innumerable La Lega publications, such as external promotional materials, internal studies, and congress and conference proceedings. It also publishes the prestigious cooperative periodical *La Co-operazione Italiana*.

Il Consorzio Nazionale Approvviggionamenti (ACAM) is primarily a purchasing consortium and is oriented towards lowering the cost of intermediate goods by negotiating on behalf of consortium members. As well as obtaining the usual declining purchase price with larger orders, ACAM works to secure additional discounts, partly by negotiating long-term relationships with suppliers who agree to such discounts.

The benefit of this to suppliers is that they save the time usually spent interacting with individual buyers. Other *quid pro quo* arrangements include, according to Ammirato (1996), the placement of advertisements at La Lega construction sites and earlier payment for supplies received in exchange for larger discounts. ACAM has 14 local offices throughout Italy and a headquarters in Bologna.

Conco-op is an industrial consortium that engages in subcontracting across cooperatives when large orders are received; it is financially self-supporting as it charges a 2 per cent commission on the value of subcontracted work. ICIE, the innovation and technology transfer group, is described in greater detail below. Promosviluppo (Development Promotion) is a second-level cooperative charged with starting new cooperatives. It conducts feasibility studies on the conversion of private firms to La Lega cooperatives. It also works extensively in the less developed Mezzogiorno regions, promoting cooperative organization as a development strategy in underserved areas.

La Lega consortia have paid professional staff, which could be seen as a form of contracting out some management functions. These professionals may be paid at a higher rate than the maximum within the cooperatives, but it is usually less than they would receive in the private sector; many are committed to the ideals of cooperation, and there are participatory aspects of the work in consortia that compensate for the salary differential. The largest cooperatives often play a leading role in bidding and consortium activities, so in some respects they may be considered part of the specialized network organizations, although they are still individual cooperatives in their own right.

In Mondragón, nowadays the CLP credit union is primarily a financial intermediary, but prior to the reorganization in the 1980s it performed many of the specialized functions undertaken by La Lega consortia, including new-project feasibility studies. More recently the corporate bodies at the MCC level began to perform many of the tasks undertaken by the specialized La Lega consortia. Indeed the MCC may be viewed as a multifirm joint venture writ large. Mondragón has of course supported the famous technical training school, and played an active part in organizing the new Mondragón University,[13] which it continues to support. Within the MCC, Lagun-Aro operates the social insurance scheme (including unemployment insurance, the pension system and health care); Ularco, founded in 1965, handles legal, administrative and some financial functions; Ikerlan, founded in 1973, undertakes research and development, and also provides services to conventional firms throughout Europe; Ideko provides R&D for the machine tool grouping and now receives about 25 per cent of its revenue from outside contracts; and Lankide is the export group. The consumer durables group FAGOR grew out of Ularco, which was an early (mid 1960s) experiment in extensive intercooperative cooperation. Also significant is the role of FAGOR as a consolidated brand name, reducing marketing costs and allowing all to benefit from joint efforts to improve quality – an area in which cooperatives can take advantage of strong complementarities.[14] According to Clamp (2000), substantial strides have been made in the joint quality-upgrading campaigns. She reports that all of the Mondragón cooperatives have achieved ISO 9000 certification, and that a number have received quality awards; as she rightly points out, this is an exceptional achievement given that many of the cooperatives experienced significant quality problems in the early 1980s crisis period. Some of the Mondragón cooperatives, along with the ULMA group and the MCC, have increasingly exploited their natural comparative advantage in team- and participation-based approaches to total quality management (Cheney, 1999). However it appears that the brand name 'Mondragón' has never been used, which is inexplicable given the colossal international reputation of the group.

The nature of cooperatives is to remain small as this facilitates democratic decision making. However the fact that few worker cooperatives grow to a large size can result in competitive disadvantage in some industries. The restructuring of Mondragón into the MCC was the consequence of explicit recognition of this problem, and it was thought that grouping the individual cooperatives into a larger corporate structure would enable them to take more systematic advantage of economies of scale and scope. As noted earlier, La Lega has taken a different approach and actively encourages the merger of cooperatives. The large cooperatives so formed have played an increasingly important role, ironically at the expense of the already comparatively weak La Lega authority, the very source of encouragement for amalgamation. Finally, it may be noted in passing that the presence of many cooperatives in certain areas gives them the appearance of industrial districts, which is a general feature of Italian organizational comparative advantage in general (see for example Porter, 1990).

Joint ventures and interfirm alliances

Firms form joint ventures to gain access to new markets, acquire technology and realise economies of scale. This has been an increasingly important strategy by firms of all types and size to deal with globalized competition and the need for accelerated innovation. It can be hypothesized that strategic alliances to promote innovation, research and development and/or marketing are now crucial to the market success of worker cooperatives in advanced economies, with different types of advantage being offered by alliances with other cooperatives or with conventionally organized firms. Although strategic alliances are widely considered to be crucial for all firms, they are particularly important for cooperative firms because of their naturally smaller size and comparative advantage in small-scale forms of innovation (Smith, 1994a).

There are two reasonable working hypotheses about the type of partner that would most benefit an industrial cooperative in that there are trade-offs between the benefits of joint ventures with other cooperatives, with conventional firms and with consortia. The first view is that strategic alliances for innovation and technology transfer will be more successful when the partner company is a conventional firm. This is because other cooperatives are likely not only to have a similar history, but also to have acquired similar technology and company strategies (including market segments) over time. Forging a strategic alliance with another cooperative would therefore bring only limited benefits in terms of drawing on the partner's organizational assets. This is especially true in networks such as La Lega and Mondragón, where knowledge is shared through consortia and in the due course of business. Alliances with non-cooperatives would be especially helpful in respect of cooperatives establishing themselves in new market segments.

The second view is that it is strategically more beneficial to form an alliance with other cooperatives, especially within a cooperative league, as other cooperatives are likely to have established processes and organizational innovations that benefit cooperatives most, and will tend to have a similar organizational structure and style of work. Moreover they are less likely to behave opportunistically towards alliance partners; indeed there are explicit and implicit sanctions in La Lega and Mondragón against violating cooperative and league principles, with penalties ranging up to and including expulsion. In effect the members of cooperative leagues have already engaged in joint ventures with league and consortia partners for a long time and therefore have extensive experience of working jointly with other cooperatives. However this can be a double-edged sword as there may be much more to learn from forming an alliance with conventional firms. More speculatively, as interfirm alliances grow in importance the La Lega and Mondragón cooperatives may enjoy some advantage in the general market place because their experience of interfirm alliances is likely to be substantially greater than that of conventional firms of a similar scale, and therefore their learning requirements will be less. Note that the above observations apply only to cooperatives in networks, not to isolated cooperatives; this is another area in which cooperative leagues, not merely cooperative density, is what matters.

In sum, the trade-off is between the greater 'gains from trade' innovations that are possible with alliances with non-cooperatives, and the potentially greater 'productive relevance' of innovations generated in other cooperatives. Of course there is nothing to exclude both types of alliance from being advantageous (or disadvantageous), depending on the circumstances. To some extent participation in new forms of consortia that include both cooperatives and non-cooperatives could provide some of the benefits of each strategy while lowering costs. Nascent examples include La Lega's ICIE and the MCC's Ikerlan, both of which now also work for conventional firms and the government, enhancing not only their profitability but also their ability to transfer productive knowledge to the member cooperatives. There is evidence in Smith (1994a) that La Lega cooperatives with joint ventures have higher productivity. But there are greater productivity advantages to be had from domestic joint ventures among non-cooperatives than among cooperatives, and there is some evidence that cooperatives with joint ventures with other cooperatives have even lower productivity than cooperatives with no joint ventures. However it should be noted that selection bias may be present: only the most efficient and technologically advanced cooperatives would be selected by conventional firms for joint ventures; and it is reasonable to assume that ailing cooperatives commonly form alliances with each other, perhaps as a precursor to merger. Unfortunately there is no evidence explicitly relating consortia strategy to joint venture strategy, so this would be a useful area for further research. There is also the possibility of foreign joint ventures in direct foreign investment, as commonly used by the MCC, which will be another useful area for research as experience accumulates.

Yet another form of interfirm alliance is outsourcing. Our working hypothesis is that outsourcing is conducted less by cooperatives than by comparable conventional firms. Outsourcing poses a potential threat to cooperative organization in that it may be viewed as the disguised hiring of non-member labour; and as an increasing share of the work that was once done in-house is outsourced, job security may be lower, as unions frequently complain. However a significant amount of domestic outsourcing may be conducted through other cooperative enterprises within the league. For example there is some sharing of orders among the cooperatives in the MCC's Donovat machine tools group, and a sharing of orders among smaller La Lega cooperatives in the Emilia-Romagna region, but more systematic evidence is needed. In La Lega, strategic alliances continue to develop among Italian cooperatives, and intriguingly are now being developed in a systematic way in the social services cooperative sector; this may provide new insights and have possible implications for developing countries. The MCC conducts a substantial amount of international outsourcing, including to conventionally organized, wholly owned subsidiaries.

Innovation and technology transfer strategies

Cooperatives are more likely to foster small innovations (see Vanek, 1970: 294–6) but are probably less likely to foster large innovations than are conventional firms. Small innovations are those which improve individual or group workers' productivity, improve the quality of existing products or generate minor product variations, while large innovations generate new products or radically different production processes. Thus in a competitive market environment it can be hypothesized that labour cooperatives will have a comparative advantage in choosing an innovation strategy that focuses on minor innovations in which the experience and practical knowledge of production and line employees take centre stage (Smith, 1994a).[15] On the other hand cooperatives will be reluctant to introduce innovations that might result in job losses.[16] Italian industrial cooperatives tend to employ more workers than are needed to maximize income per head (Smith, 1984). The implicit weight thus placed on employment as an objective is consistent with either above-median or below-median innovative activity; successful innovations in products, processes or organization in an imperfectly competitive market may lead to increased sales and employment and this could more than compensate for the introduction of labour-saving techniques.

Cooperatives might be reluctant to introduce labour-saving (skill-limiting) innovations, which would detract from specializing in products of a more artistic nature, or at least products of high quality and high craftsmanship.[17] Cooperatives should have a comparative advantage in production processes that require a conscientious group effort on the part of production workers, but information is internal to such teams and hence is difficult to monitor. Certainly production quality is more difficult to monitor than quantity of output and it can depend on ordinary employees having a strong personal commitment to the success of the enterprise. Thus cooperatives tend to specialize in craft-intensive manufacturing operations, using production methods that make use of experience, training, attention to detail and conscientious-ness, but not necessarily a high level of formal education. This is a testable hypothesis, supported by anecdotal evidence, but no data appear to be available to test it formally at this stage. Certainly Mondragón has been successful in improving the quality of its products since the early 1980s; but of course many conventional firms have as well. Cooperatives will also find it necessary to achieve larger-scale tech-nology transfers and innovations. Since, as argued above, individual cooperatives probably do not have an organizational comparative advantage in these activities, it would make sense to contract out such work to consortia. This is exactly what has happened in La Lega and Mondragón.

The Institute for Cooperative Innovation (Istituto Co-operativo per L'Innovazione, ICIE) describes itself as La Lega's national institute for applied research and technology transfer. The ICIE has two regional centres and a headquarters in Rome; publishes an elegant quarterly peri-odical on innovations of interest to cooperatives, including information on patents that have become available through public sources; and promotes grant applications at the individual cooperative and consortia levels for public funds for innovation and technology development. In addition to funds from La Lega and its affiliated cooperatives, the ICIE also receives funds from public sources for contract innovation work. For example it currently has a large contract to develop innovative technol-ogy for housebound disabled and elderly people. The ICIE was originally formed in the early 1970s as a research and consultancy group for the construction cooperatives, with which it has worked to develop improved ceramics, glass, insulating bricks and energy efficiency innov-ations for housing cooperative complexes. It expanded its activities in the mid 1980s and since then has conducted research in an astounding variety of fields in which La Lega cooperatives work, including historical and artistic preservation, pollution abatement, recycling and applied laser technologies.

In addition to engaging in original innovation and encouraging innovation among the member cooperatives, the ICIE publicizes innov-ations developed elsewhere by public or private institutions that it believes may be of special relevance to La Lega cooperatives (Ammirato, 1996). In this way it improves the information flow to cooperatives, and perhaps reduces uncertainty about the applicability of innovations that cooperatives near of themselves. To the extent that cooperatives are more risk-averse than conventional firms, the information role played by cooperative innovation consortia could be more significant for productive efficiency than is the case with similar consortia among conventional firms. The construction cooperative consortium (CCC), which was one of the earliest consortia, dating back to 1912, conducts some of its own research, as do other smaller consortia.

Historically the La Lega cooperatives have produced highly crafted products embodying considerable artisan skill, and some of these products are popular export items. However the flip side is that the cooperatives have remained distinctly low-tech and only a minority have found a niche in the high-craftsmanship artistic market. In order to compete, many have found it necessary to upgrade their technological levels substantially. The ICIE has performed an invaluable service in this regard, not only providing sorely needed expertise but also in changing attitudes towards technology among many of the stubbornly traditional industrial cooperatives.

At Mondragón, R&D and technology transfers are largely handled by Ikerlan, a cooperative that has generated an internal profit each year. Currently the MCC is developing, with Basque government and private enterprise support, a large research complex – to be known as Garaia – in a greenfield site near the hilltop head quarters of the MCC, CLP and Ikerlan.[18] These research establishments will support both cooperatives and conventional firms. Ikerlan will have to redefine its function to some extent when the planned establishments begin operations. The MCC also views its foreign direct investment strategy as a way of absorbing the best foreign techniques and transfering them to its home base in the Basque region (Clamp, 2000), supplementing the group's traditional reliance on licensing-based technology transfers.

Finance and investment instruments and institutions

Credit market failures can mean that good-quality borrowers (able and honest workers) who lack collateral cannot capitalize cooperatives, thus curtailing this type of entrepreneurial activity (for an applicable formal model see Banerjee and Newman, 1993). While this can be a problem for potential entrepreneurs, the problem is especially severe when financial intermediaries lack experience of lending to cooperatives. This suggests a need for financial institutions that specialize in cooperatives, especially if they also have detailed information on credit risks among cooperative borrowers.

In La Lega a major financial role is played by Fincooper, whose motto and purpose is 'efficient financial services for the cooperative firm'. Fincooper is a finance consortium that for the 30 years since its founding has played a central part in the financing of La Lega cooperatives.

It plays many of the roles of traditional financial intermediaries, including conventional commercial banking, investment banking and financial advice. It uses advanced information technology and sophisticated financial instruments. Currently more than 1500 worker cooperatives participate in the consortium. The advantage of Fincooper is that it has specialized human capital – as it states to new potential members:

> Fincooper is knowledgeable and specialized in problems of cooperatives and their markets because it is always working side by side with member cooperatives, and has developed a vast and structured network of relationships to carry out its work. The consortium also specializes in providing financial as well as technical support in addressing firm reorganization and consolidation in times of financial distress, as well as major development and expansion projects.[19]

Participation is voluntary so Fincooper has a strong incentive to live up to its promise of providing highly efficient financial services. Another major La Lega arm, Unipol, provides all forms of insurance for cooperative enterprises. In addition there are specialized financial intermediaries such as the merchant bank FINEC (National Cooperative Finance Company) and the retail credit union BANEC (Cooperative Movement Bank), which lends to households and small enterprises, both cooperative and conventional. There is also a network of locally based La Lega financial intermediaries. In short La Lega has a diverse and relatively sophisticated set of financial intermediaries in virtually all fields of finance but equity.

However La Lega is even beginning to move into a form of quasi-equity finance through the recent introduction of minority *soci sovventori*, which literally means 'backer members' but might be better translated as 'capital memberships'.[20] These are permitted under the 1992 Italian cooperative legal reform lobbied for by La Lega. One class of such shares provides some minority voting rights to outside capital, while a second class confers no voting rights. By law the latter shares receive a 2 per cent higher return than the voting shares, and strict accounting and disclosure requirements are imposed on larger cooperatives. The adoption of a *soci sovventori* strategy might enable cooperatives to raise capital more efficiently without sacrificing their cooperative character and giving away decisive control. It might also facilitate strategic alliances with conventional firms. Such instruments could be subject to moral hazard, however, so it remains to be seen how they will be received by the market.[21]

Unlike La Lega, Mondragón has not publicly indicated the need for new sources of finance, but this does not necessarily mean they are not required. Cooperatives may have enough finance for projects they intend pursuing, but may be dismissing others as beyond their scope or not worth considering because of an instinctive understanding that there are financial limitations. One Mondragón official stated in an interview that 'there are no projects that go wanting for funding that the members are willing to risk their own funds on', and that 'managers say they do not face a shortage of capital'.[22] However the failure to pursue worthy projects in which members do not want to invest may be because of workers' risk profiles; the official's comment may indicate a need for financial innovation rather than the absence of need. Indeed one of the highest ranking MCC officials has indicated that a search is already under way for effective ways of raising outside capital. There is of course a moral hazard issue here, as indicated by a recent failed attempt to develop a strategy to tap the equity markets; but some instrument, perhaps an information assurance policy board or something similar, could be helpful.

Mondragón's innovative internal capital accounts, which hold the financial stakes of the members, are important sources of capital and a symbol of the members' commitment to their cooperatives. The members' stakes are refundable upon retirement or other severance, provided the cooperative in question is sufficiently solvent. Although the funds are fully fungible with the rest of the cooperatives' financing needs, the accounts earn interest. Of great importance in the past was the relationship with a large credit union, the CLP, which played an active part in the management of the Mondragón group until it became sufficiently advanced to become more independent. The decision to spin off the CLP when the MCC was formed a decade or so ago was highly controversial at the time but now seems a courageous and far-sighted move. While maintaining 'captive' financial intermediaries, or at least including a large bank in an industrial group, may be useful in the early stage of development, once a certain level of development has been achieved, it may serve to slow progress. The earlier relationship between the CLP and the Mondragón cooperatives was perhaps not so very different from the cosy finance–industry combines in Japan, which have kept the country mired in stagnation for more than a decade. In contrast Mondragón has continued to grow, becoming the eighth largest industrial group in Spain, and has maintained its position on the frontier of technology. The CLP's freedom to lend where the returns are highest has aided the growth and development of the Basque region, which in turn has increased the demand for many

Mondragón products, including those sold through its large Eroski retailing group as well as consumer durables and other goods. The rapid development spurred in no small part by the CLP has also led to other less tangible benefits, such as the continued development of a market for highly skilled labour.

Institutions and instruments for risk mitigation

Workers who own the firm in which they work face potentially large risks. Making reasonable assumptions about the typical wealth portfolios of members, it can be hypothesized that workers in Lega and Mondragón face a substantially higher retirement income risk than workers in comparable conventional firms. To some extent this risk is probably mitigated by the much lower exit rates in Lega and Mondragón; that is, there is a much lower risk of job loss in cooperative firms and measures may be taken to mitigate the risk of plant closure or layoffs. Fully endogenizing this effect is an important avenue for future research. This source of risk aversion may be an important part of the explanation for the very low failure rate of these cooperatives. It is worth noting again that the extensive diversification undertaken in the early years of the Mondragón group was in effect a strategy for diversifying against risk (Smith and Ye, 1987). To some extent this may have resulted from the need for portfolio diversification by the CLP credit union; but it may also have been directed at the reduction of employee risk. As noted previously, Conte (1986) has argued that one function of support structures such as these in Mondragón may be to reduce the uncertainty felt by prospective members, thus promoting entry; as evidence Conte notes that cooperative entry is much more frequent in areas where support structures are strong. Moreover some of the operations of consortia, such as those devoted to innovation or finance, as described in previous sections, may be to reduce members' uncertainty about the value of existing innovations, as well as to contribute original innovations of special relevance to cooperatives.

In Mondragón all cooperatives that belong to a regional group or a sectoral subgroup allocate part of their gross surplus or all of their net dividends to a central fund, which is then distributed among all the cooperatives. The Lagun-Aro group operates a social insurance scheme covering unemployment insurance, pensions and health care (note that cooperatives in Spain are not covered by a national social security scheme). Many cooperatives that do not belong to the MCC, including the ULMA group, individual local cooperatives and cooperatives from other regions, participate in Lagun-Aro.

Cooperatives trade-off some forms of risk for others. While the risk of job loss is low, the risk of wage variability can be high. In addition there is more insurance against shocks to ability (Kremer, 1997). The successful cooperative (or league) will balance these risks while mitigating moral hazard. One way of doing this is to require a probationary period before full membership is granted. Although this is an imperfect mechanism, it can be compared with the tenure process in a university. Indeed a typical private university is in some ways like a cooperative; tenured faculty staff come as close to a group of 'owners' as one could find. One of the risks of tenure is that even after a fairly long probationary period (six years), a professor's fundamental character may not be known to her or his colleagues. If this is a significant danger, there must be some way in which a successful cooperative can overcome it. The explanation suggested here is that in general most new cooperative members are known by some of the existing members as personal friends, fellow parishioners, club members and so on; it is much more common for new employees in a conventional firm not to know the owners, managers or employees well or at all. The social network utilized by cooperatives in this way can be viewed as another form of network effect. The implication is that successful cooperatives are less likely to be found in cities where anonymity reigns and social networks are less developed. To the best of our knowledge this hypothesis has never been tested formally.

Employment strategy

There is no conventional 'short term' in a purely worker-managed firm where all workers are members, because membership comes with certain property rights, even if the members are indifferent (or worse) about laying off their colleagues. Though labour is variable in the long term through attrition, it is no more variable than capital stock. However the use of non-member labour introduces an element of short-termism to the practical analysis of La Lega and Mondragón. The standard theory of the worker-managed firm includes the view that full or majority employee ownership is inherently transitional: either the firm will fail or it will become a victim of its own success, with workers selling their shares for substantial capital gains. However the La Lega and Mondragón stories show that neither outcome is inevitable. In fact these cooperatives have prospered and successfully adapted to significant shocks, notably increased competition following national deregulation and international integration in the EU and rapid technological change. The available information suggests that the number of cooperative exits is well below the industry averages, although additional evidence is needed. Moreover these complexes have maintained the cooperative employee ownership and decision-making character of their member cooperatives through decades of dramatic change in the European economy. However this does not indicate organizational stasis: in both La Lega and Mondragón significant organizational adaptations have been made in recent years, and these are certainly important factors in the cooperatives' continued success. The networks and administrative support structures in both organizations have been crucial in keeping the member firms in business and maintaining their cooperative character. They have also played an important role in ensuring that the Ward effect (described below), and the predictions of firm deaths or transformation to conventional firms found in the literature on the labour-managed firm have not prevailed in practice. The practice of cooperatives starting other cooperatives in order to benefit from network externalities, which appears to have happened in both La Lega and Mondragón, would certainly have included the establishment of mechanisms to safeguard the cooperative character of these firms. Obviously these would include measures to counteract the Ward effect and to protect employment in and the viability of the cooperative sector.

Clearly successful cooperatives and cooperative networks will have prevented the Ward effect, whereby members lay off colleagues in good times in order to share the surplus with as few claimants as possible (see Ward, 1958; Vanek, 1970). If they had not, according to the theory, they would have become extinct, either by degeneration or by systematic loss of market share, or by outright closure. While there is no evidence that the Ward effect has ever occurred in practice, given the preoccupation of the economic theory literature with variants of this effect it is worth exploring why it has not been observed in La Lega or Mondragón. Interviews with La Lega officials suggest that the Ward effect does not occur because the system as a whole acts as if its objective is to maximize employment by paying union wage rates; this reflects the close relationship of La Lega to the Italian unions (however more evidence for this hypothesis – particularly in respect of the way it is worked out in practice – is needed). Some econometric evidence that the Ward effect does not apply in La Lega cooperatives can be found in Smith (1984).

In the case of Mondragón, employment generation has long been an explicit objective of the system. In fact Martin (2000) shows that the Mondragón cooperatives exhibit greater flexibility than conventional firms in terms of pay, hours worked and output, and in the conventional (that is, non-Wardian) direction. This is partly due to Spain's rather rigid labour law and the industrial relations practices in conventional firms. The Ward effect does not appear if there is an effective membership market (Sertel, 1987). Although a significant membership fee has to be paid to join a Mondragón cooperative (approximately equal to the annual salary), it cannot be said that there is a membership market because these fees are in proportion to the firms' incomes, which in turn are set in reference to prevailing market rates. Instead the mechanisms to ensure a normal long-term supply response in Mondragón appear to be enshrined in the 'ten principles' (especially the open membership principle), with built-in organizational incentives to increase the number of firms and their total employment. Workers' willingness to take temporary pay cuts is partly determined by their confidence that the losses will eventually be recouped, or at least in part. Of course short-term flexibility in hiring and firing non-member labour also creates an incentive for normal supply behaviour. However there are some caveats to the above. First, even if the Ward effect is not found in practice, this does not mean that the underlying incentive for it does not exist. At a later time, perhaps when the authority of the network administration is weaker, the Ward effect might rear its head. Second, even if cooperatives do not lay off members when prices rise, they may not have as many workers as a conventional firm of the same size; and this in itself could be seen as a moderate form of the Ward effect. Indeed Smith's (1984) results for La Lega cooperatives are consistent with a null hypothesis that no workers will be hired at all when there is an output price rise.

This again raises the degeneration issue: one could ask whether the growing proportion of workers who are temporary members, or non-members is not itself a form of degeneration from the cooperative form. But there remain strict limits on the number of non-members who are employed and on the period for which they can work before attaining member status. Since the wrenching reorganization required by the Europe 1992 integration initiative, which resulted in unprecedented lay-offs of members, the Mondragón cooperatives have been determined to prevent this happening again. To this end most have adopted a policy of keeping about 20 per cent of workers in non-member status. However interviews revealed that this policy is held in universal distaste, and that the goal of virtually all the cooperatives is to offer membership to as many non-member workers as possible as soon as prudence allows. There is no short term consideration in a worker-managed enterprise in which all workers are members, because the membership level is no more easily adjusted than the capital stock. The presence of some non-members is viewed, probably correctly, as sometimes required in the interest of competition with conventional firms, but there are many examples of growing cooperatives extending their membership while remaining consistent with the 20 per cent non-member policy. Our conclusion is that Mondragón's employment policies are geared to protecting the employment status of members, and not to exploiting non-members in order to increase the profits per member. Finally, the strategic alliances seen in both La Lega and Mondragón may also be viewed as a partial remedy for the Ward effect, as subcontracting to partner firms offers an alternative to increasing employment (Sacks, 1977).

So why has no strong Ward effect ever been found? The reason is probably that there is no incentive to create a firm that would carry out such a practice. Moreover even if some fluke created such a firm, it would very quickly metamorphoze into something else or be extinguished. That is, the arguments against the creation of cooperatives, or for their degeneration if they already exist, apply specifically to firms that behave in a Wardian fashion, but not necessarily to cooperative of the types found in the La Lega and Mondragón networks. Again, this is not to deny that there are incentives for the Ward effect, but it is just one force among many, and for structural reasons it is rarely likely to become significant in the cooperatives we are studying.

It should also be pointed out that beyond the reasons due to the organizational behaviour of cooperative networks, the Ward effect may not be observable in individual cooperatives because of the basic fact of human solidarity – as Joan Robinson (1967) has pointed out, cooperative members would not lay off their brethren for a few extra dinars. Her argument has been given greater weight by the findings of studies of cooperative behaviour under familiarity plus social sanctions, such as those conducted by Gachter and Fehr (1999). As the most effective constitutions reinforce the collective aspirations of those who live under them, group solidarity is an important explanation of why constitutional restrictions against Wardian behaviour might prove successful. In summary, the perceived absence of the Ward effect is partly because there is no incentive to create Wardian-type firms, partly because cooperative networks actively work against the Ward effect, and partly because of the very short longevity of any Wardian-type firms that might emerge.

We may conclude that the employment policy in both Mondragón and La Lega has been to expand both the number of workers and the share of workers who are members while employing a sufficient number of non-members to avoid the trauma of having to lay off members, or at least in most circumstances. With this framework, normal supply responses can be expected in theory, and the available evidence suggests that they are found in practice as well.

Conclusions and implications for development policy

The creation of cooperative networks has probably been the most important innovation to take place in La Lega and Mondragón. This innovation may be viewed as a means of internalizing the network externalities examined in this chapter. For virtually all the other innovations studied in this chapter the presence of a network is a necessary precondition, and the associated consortia, second-level cooperatives and administrative departments in such fields as innovation, technology transfer, marketing, finance and insurance all owe their existence to the presence of La Lega's network and Mondragón's CLP and MCC central offices. Among other contributions the consortia have brought about technological progress and quality upgrading, lowered input costs, improved financial intermediation, reduced perceived risks, coordinated marketing strategies, facilitated other strategic alliances and encouraged the development of professional services with experience in the cooperative sector. In La Lega the role of the large cooperatives has also been very important, but this has been encouraged and nurtured by La Lega itself. For example La Lega has encouraged mergers when efficiency gains have been apparent, and La Lega's consulting group has helped cooperatives to continue to function smoothly as participatory bodies as they have grown in size.

The Mondragón and La Lega networks offer important lessons for transitional and developing economies in terms of strategies to help employee-owned firms to grow, diversify, protect employment, mitigate risk, innovate and develop appropriate support structures. However their experiences offer relatively little guidance on how to promote the entry of new firms because in both Spain and Italy success in establishing new cooperatives has been limited in recent years; for this, other strategies will have to be employed. Despite their low casualty rates, Mondragón and La Lega styles of organization will remain rare unless the problem of launching new firms is resolved. It should also be noted that both networks have benefited from existing social capital, most importantly the presence of a high degree of trust, as well as contributing to new social capital. It is likely to be much more difficult to establish such networks in areas where there is substantially less trust and other social capital than was found in the Basque region and north-central Italy prior to the establishment of Mondragón and La Lega.

The support structures in Mondragón and La Lega have helped to buffer individual cooperatives from short-term market forces that could have led to exit, sale or degeneration to a non-cooperative form. This buffering has taken the form of risk mitigation, social insurance, innovation in financial intermediation and institutions, the encouragement of joint ventures and interfirm alliances, and far-reaching technical-innovation and technology-transfer strategies. However the buffering has generally not been offered in the absence of viable business reorganization plans, so the support identified is not analogous to the subsidies given to inefficient state-owned enterprises in developing countries. The provision of similar support could be encouraged for the cooperative network Kerala Dinesh Beedi in India, or individual cooperatives that are finding it difficult to 'bloom alone' in other parts of India, or in Latin America and elsewhere. Consortia could be established with the technical assistance of those in the best position to offer guidance, namely experts from La Lega and Mondragón. The provision of United Nations funds to enable the La Lega consortia and Mondragón groups to help to develop cooperative networks elsewhere might yield high returns. Because of the typical free-riding problem in initiating a cooperative network, and the lack of a way for entrepreneurs to get a return from financing such a system, if cooperatives and their advocates are not already working to establish such a network, this may have to be initiated with public support. Such support could include organizing specialized consortia to address the most pressing needs (binding constraints, or limiting factors) of the typical cooperative.

Another clear lesson for enterprises in transitional economies with substantial employee ownership, such as Russia, and developing countries with significant cooperative systems, such as India, is the value of establishing formal institutions to solidify, develop and expand the networks of cooperatives. It is significant that the services available to the Mondragón and La Lega cooperatives are provided by independent and self-managed cooperatives within the two networks, and not by government or state-sponsored entities. This is in sharp contrast to the situation in many developing countries. The problem is to determine how to support the development of such institutions while ensuring their autonomy from the state and their responsibility to the constituent cooperatives. Clearly such institutions should eventually be supported by the cooperatives themselves. This has been successfully achieved in Mondragón and La Lega largely because the movements are indigenous and autonomous from the Spanish and Italian governments.

Another finding of policy significance is that both the networks studied provide services that are specific to the needs of *worker* cooperatives; that is, the cooperatives are not treated as merely an unusual form of the more common agricultural marketing cooperatives, consumer cooperatives or credit unions. Abell (1988) has found that of the worker cooperatives in developing countries that are linked to a network or support structure, those which perform poorly are either government run or are run as branches of broader cooperative organizations. The observations in this chapter may be viewed as corroborating Abell's conclusion from case studies in Sri Lanka, Tanzania and Fiji that independent institutions specific to the needs of worker cooperatives are needed if they are to be effective.

Government agencies lack the incentive and the necessary expertise to develop new cooperatives and help existing ones to thrive, and organizations that deal with other forms of cooperative have different economic interests and incentives from those which pertain to worker cooperatives. Moreover the network services needed by worker cooperatives differ from those of other cooperatives, so more specialized consortia are required. For example independent worker cooperatives are interested in increasing their own profitability, not that of their input suppliers. This is not to say that cooperatives of different forms, including agricultural marketing cooperatives and worker cooperatives, could not benefit from belonging to a common organization as there would clearly be network efficiencies; rather it is to say that worker cooperatives need fully independent consortia or other second-level organizations that will put the needs of worker cooperatives first.

As Abell (1988) argues, in areas that do not have a significant number of cooperatives the government will have to develop and support fully independent cooperative umbrella groups. Although it may be doubted whether any government has the desire to create a genuinely independent agency, the National Co-operative Bank in the United States offers a partial model, in which a one-time appropriation created an endowment for an independent financial institution which has the development of new cooperatives, including worker cooperatives, as part of its charter. It is only a partial model, however, because by design worker cooperatives have only a minority role in the Co-operative Bank (they are restricted to a holding not exceeding 10 per cent of its lending) and it is dominated by other forms of cooperative, particularly consumer and housing cooperatives. In addition the bank lacks the incentive and the resources to initiate a worker cooperative network. These shortcomings could have been prevented if the government had aimed from the beginning to support worker cooperatives rather than consumer, housing or other forms of cooperatives. Both Mondragón and La Lega have intranetwork sources of finance, but despite discussions of alternatives, particularly in La Lega, financing has generally taken the form of conventional loans, often short-term ones, so thus far they have not addressed the need for specialized financial instruments.

This chapter has identified many areas in which cooperatives can benefit from cooperation, and shown the distinct but functionally parallel ways that these have been addressed in La Lega and Mondragón. Elsewhere it is unclear which consortium areas should be developed first as the most pressing needs (binding constraints) will differ between countries, but included will be areas such as finance, innovation, marketing, the resolution of labour disputes and achieving economies of scale in purchasing inputs. It makes sense to start with activities that are likely to bring the greatest initial rewards with the smallest effort and expenditure. Having seen the benefits to be had from specialized consortia, cooperatives will be more willing to embark on larger, riskier ventures. Once the consortia are well established an umbrella group can be created, either a loose alliance, such as La Lega's networks, or a more centralized system, such as the MCC. There will of course be many obstacles – including lack of funding and expertise, insufficient ideological commitment and government intervention – standing in the way of groups similar to the MCC and La Lega arising in the developing world and transitional economies, but in many regions the key step would be to establish independent umbrella networks. Many other constraints could be resolved if this step were taken.

Cooperative start-ups seem to emerge in clusters in time and space, often in times of economic dislocation. The conditions in many developing and transitional countries may be analogous to those in Italy in the mid 1940s and 1970s, and in Spain in the 1960s and 1970s. If so, cooperative development may be an effective way of rapidly expanding employment, especially in regions recovering from conflict and other crises; and this process could be facilitated by the UN in a number of ways, including the provision of technical assistance.

Notes

1   For further details see the Mondragón website: www.Mondragón.mcc.es.
2   For further details see the La Lega website: www.legaco-op.it.
3   In this chapter the term innovation, when used broadly or without qualifiers, refers to any product, process or organizational innovation needed to adapt to increasing market competition and pressure for a higher rate of technological improvement.

4 In this interpretation, law is created by actors with a set of goals and values they wish to keep exogenous, and in this sense the role of cooperative law differs – in degree rather than kind – from conventional business and contract law, or values and management styles in a conventional company.

5 Fraternity can be viewed as 'the missing leg of the three-legged stool' of the French Revolution – *liberté, egalité, fraternité*. Indeed to participate, as one does fully in a democratic cooperative, is to partake in a fraternity, or solidarity. Not to participate (to be excluded from the fraternity) is a form of poverty (see Sen, 1999, 2000). Those who are disenfranchised because they have no voice in the firm are at least partly cut off from the social body in which they need to participate if they are to become fully actualized. Being excluded from the fraternity is a form of poverty that can be as real as malnourishment. It has real effects: it can make people physically as well as mentally ill, and can lead to social pathologies (for a partial survey see Smith, 1991, 1994b). Professors tend to grumble about faculty meetings, but the loss of control over the working environment in teaching and research would be sorely felt if meetings were taken away. That is how many cooperative members appear to feel about their cooperatives: a difficult and at times exasperating form of organization in which to work, but better than the most likely alternative for most – working as an employee in a conventional firm without participation rights.

6 In fact this may help solve the mystery of how the process worked in the US plywood cooperatives; in some cases workers may have been overcharged for their shares, as some writers suggest.

7 Interview with MCC officials, 17 April 2001. Note that the figure of eight failures is far higher than the single failure cited by Whyte and Whyte (1991) and often quoted in the literature, but the MCC officials could find no basis for this smaller estimate.

8 It could be argued that the fact that degeneration and exits do occur on occasion, but are very rare, is more impressive than a perfect record. With a perfect record one would wonder whether artificial, costly support, such as local government subsidies, effectively precluded failure, in which case the theory has not been put to the test at all.

9 Interviews at MCC, April 2001. The details of the discussions were reported in the local press.

10 Each of these is also an argument for works councils, as well as employee-owner voting (Smith, 1991). Of course there may be a concern that workers with codetermination rights will behave opportunistically, to the detriment of employers, and this might outweigh their positive role in providing a check against management opportunism towards shareholders as well as workers. However, in cooperatives the workers are effectively self-employed.

11 This is visible among the production teams, and sometimes reinforced by symbolic means. One La Lega cooperative visited by the author proudly displayed signs around the factory proclaiming '40 years of self-management!'

12 This section draws on interviews by the author and on Ammirato (1996).

13 Interview with Professor Fred Freundlich, Mondragón University, 19 April 2001.

14 See Kremer (1993) for a relevant formal model.

15   Vanek (1970) argues that large-scale innovation is invariant across economic
     systems, but individual cooperatives lack the scale and expertise to make
     this practical for them. Certainly some economic systems have proven more
     adept at innovation than others: compare Western mixed economies with
     the former Soviet system.
16   Interview with officials at the Istituto Cooperativo per L'Innovazione (ICIE)
     Rome, 12 April 1990.
17   It is difficult to separate these forces from historical influences, for example,
     the centuries-old artisan and artistic traditions in north-central Italy, where
     most of the La Lega fieldwork was carried out.
18   *Garaia* has a dual meaning in Basque: 'summit' and 'perspective'.
19   For further details see the Lega and Fincooper webpages: www.legaco-op.it
     and www.legacoop.it.
20   Legge N. 59 del 1992. For a discussion see Marco Sigiani's preface (which is
     available in English translation in typescript form) to *Libertà, Uguaglianza ed
     Efficienza* (Liberty, Equality and Efficiency) (Milan: Feltrinelli, 1995) and
     several writings by Edwin Morley-Fletcher, especially Morley-Fletcher (1992).
21   This raises the issue of whether new financial instruments need to be
     developed for cooperatives more broadly, which I examine in a recent paper
     with Robert Waldmann (1999). We propose a financial instrument ('industry
     average performance bonds') that pays variable funds based on the perform-
     ance (for example value-added) of the industry in which the cooperative is
     situated. This allows for greater use of bond finance for two reasons. First, by
     carrying a variable interest rate it carries less risk for the cooperative; for
     example payments will be reduced in recessions and increased in booms.
     Second, being based on industry-wide performance it is relatively immune
     to moral hazard problems, so investors should be more willing to purchase
     such bonds (at a lower interest rate). The adoption of this instrument would
     also have the advantage of reducing Wardian incentives.
22   Interview with Carmelo Urdangarin of Mondragón's Donovat machine tool
     group, 17 April 2001.

References

Abell, P. (1988) *Establishing Support Systems for Industrial Co-operatives: Case Studies
     from the Third World*, Brookfield: Gower.
Ammirato, P. (1996) *La Lega: The Making of a Successful Co-operative Network*,
     Brookfield: Dartmouth, Ashgate.
Banerjee, A. V. and A. Newman (1993) 'Occupational Choice and the Process of
     Development', *Journal of Political Economy*, 101, 2: 274–98.
Blasi, J. and D. Kruse (1991) *The New Owners: The Mass Emergence of Employee
     Ownership in Public Companies and What it Means to American Business*, New
     York: HarperCollins.
Cheney, G. (1999) *Values at Work: Employee Participation Meets Market Pressure at
     Mondragón*, Ithaca, NY: ILR Press.
Cin, B.-C. and S. C. Smith (2002) 'Employee Stock Ownership and Participation
     in South Korea: Incidence, Productivity Effects, and Prospects', *Review of
     Development Economics*, 6, 2: 263–83.
Clamp, C. (2000) 'The Internationalization of Mondragón', *Annals of Public and
     Co-operative Economics*, 71, 4: 557–77.

Conte, M. (1986) 'Entry of Worker Co-operatives in Capitalist Economies', *Journal of Comparative Economics*, 10, 1: 41–7.

Estrin, S. (1985) 'The Role of Producer Co-operatives in Employment Creation', *Economic Analysis and Workers Management*, 19, 4: 345–84.

Gachter, S. and E. Fehr (1999) 'Collective Action as a Social Exchange', *Journal of Economic Behaviour and Organization*, 39, 4: 341–69.

Hansmann, H. (1996) *The Ownership of Enterprise*, Cambridge, MA: The Belknap Press.

Kremer, M. (1993) 'The O-Ring Theory of Economic Development', *Quarterly Journal of Economics*, 108, 3: 551–75.

—— (1997) 'Why are Worker Co-operatives So Rare?', working paper 6118, Cambridge, MA: NBER.

Martin, T. (2000) 'The Impact of Worker Ownership on Firm-Level Performance: A Comparative Study', PhD dissertation, Yale University.

Miyazaki, H. (1984) 'On Success and Dissolution of the Labour-Managed Firm in the Capitalist Economy', *Journal of Political Economy*, 92, 5: 909–31.

Morley-Fletcher, E. (1992) 'Questa "Piccola Rivoluzione"', *Rivista della Co-operazione*, March–April.

Porter, M. (1990) *The Competitive Advantage of Nations*, New York: Free Press.

Robinson, J. (1967) 'The Soviet Collective Farm as a Producer Cooperative: Comment', *American Economic Review*, 57: 222–3.

Sacks, S. R. (1977) 'Transfer Prices in Decentralised Self-Managed Enterprises', *Journal of Comparative Economics*, 1: 183–93.

Sen, A. (1999, 2000) *Development as Freedom*, New York: Knopf.

Sertel, M. R. (1987) 'Workers' Enterprises are not Perverse', *European Economic Review*, 31: 1619–26.

Smith, S. C. (1984) 'Does Employment Matter to the Labour Managed Firm? Some Theory and an Empirical Illustration', *Economic Analysis and Workers Management*, 18: 303–18.

—— (1991) 'On the Economic Rationale for Codetermination Law', *Journal of Economic Behavior and Organization*, 16: 261–81.

—— (1994a) 'Innovation and Market Strategy in Italian Industrial Co-operatives: Econometric Evidence on Organizational Comparative Advantage', *Journal of Economic Behavior and Organization*, 23, 3: 303–21.

—— (1994b) 'On the Law and Economics of Employee Ownership in Privatization in Developing and Transition Economies', *Annals of Public and Co-operative Economics*, 65, 3: 437–68.

—— and M.-H. Ye (1987) 'The Behavior of Labour-Managed Firms under Uncertainty: Product Diversification, Income Insurance and Layoff Policy', *Annals of Public and Co-operative Economics*, 57: 65–82.

Vanek, J. (1970) *The General Theory of Labour-Managed Market Economies*, Ithaca, NY: Cornell University Press.

Waldmann, R. and S. C. Smith (1999) 'Investment and Supply Effects of Industry-Indexed Bonds: The Labor Managed Firm', *Economic Systems*, 23, 3: 245–68.

Ward, B. (1958) 'The Firm in Illyria: Market Syndicalism', *American Economic Review*, 48, 4: 566–89.

Whyte, W. F. and K. Whyte (1991) *Making Mondragón*, 2nd edn, Ithaca, NY: ILR Press.

Index

@Home 92(n5)
Abell, P. 237
ACAM *see Consorzio Nazionale Approvviggionamenti*
accounting 131, 152(n26), 174
Acemoglu, D. 196, 199(n7)
acquisition and development (A&D) 73
adaptive efficiency 25–6, 177
Africa 204
agency problems 37, 40, 42, 52, 53, 58, 99, 124, 127, 128, 145–6
Aghion–Bolton model 74–5, 92–3(n7)
agricultural cooperatives 204, 237
Alemagna 152(n19)
Alfa Romeo 135f, 138, 141, 152(n21)
Alfasud 152(n21)
Alitalia 140, 141
allocational inefficiencies 127, 129
Almazan, A. 43, 64
Amato Law (1990) 144, 153(n32)
Amdahl, G. 82
American Electronics Association 8
Ammirato, P. 210, 221, 239(n12)
Anderson, C. W. 62(n5)
Andreatta, B. 141
angel investors 92(n3)
Angelucci, M. 147, 154
Anhui province 160, 163
Aoki, M. 10, 69, 71, 83–5, 87–9, 92(n4)
Applebaum, E. 102
Arizmendi 205
Arthur Anderson 107
Artoni, R. 142
Assembly of Shareholder Representatives 166
assets
  inanimate 18–19, 75
  intangible 113
Association for Quality and Participation 8

Atanasov, V. 56
Australia: equity ownership 96
Austria 54

backward and forward linkages 181, 185
Baldwin, C. Y. 69–70, 77–83, 87–9
Banca Commerciale Italiana 135f
BANEC (Cooperative Movement Bank) 228
Banerjee, A. V. 199(n9), 227
Bank of Italy 12, 137
bankruptcy 153(n35), 168t
banks/banking 41, 46, 52, 54, 56, 57, 62(n5), 125, 128, 133, 144, 149, 152(n18), 153(n39), 185
  central 14
  pressure-sensitive investors 43
  state-owned 14, 164, 171
Bartel, A. 153(n38)
Bartlett, W. 198(n1), 200
Basque region 211, 216, 227, 229, 235
Baumol, W. J. 31(n7)
Becht, M. 54
Beijing: Tongzhou district 160n
Bekaert, G. 58, 64
Belgium 54
Ben-Ner, A. 101, 119(n3)
Benfratello, L. 146
Berg, P. 102
Berglof, E. 125, 128, 153(n39)
Berle, A. 38, 40, 53
Bertero, E. xii, 12, 13, 145–6
Besley, T. 152(n27)
Bethel, J. 40, 64
Bhagat, S. 63(n13)
Bhide, A. 44–5
Blaauw, G. 82
Black, B. S. 62(n9), 63(n13)
Blair, M. M. 30(n2)
Blasi, J. R. xii, 8, 32, 109, 116, 119(n5), 120

block ownership   54, 55, 58
block-holders   61
board of directors   61, 72, 164, 171
board rights   74
Boehmer, E.   41
Boeing   215
Bolton, P.   74, 92(n7), 153(n39), 154
bonds   14, 59, 137, 142, 151(n17), 171
Bonin, J. P.   x, 30(n2), 32, 182, 184, 200
Borokhovich, K.   43, 62(n7), 64
brand names   222
Brazil   54, 60
Breda Fucine Meridionali   141
Bresnahan, T.   89, 92(n2), 93–4(n15)
Brickley, J.   42, 43, 64
British Telecommunications Pension Scheme   51
broad agricultural sector   163, 166–7, 178(n5)
broad-based stock option plans   7t, 7n, 8, 117–18, 204
  company characteristics   108–9
  dilution effect   112
  impact on performance   111–14
  incidence   106–8
  pro forma effect on net income and earnings per share   108
Brooke, B.   44
Brooks, F.   82
Brosio, G.   136, 142
Brown, K.   44
Brynjolfsson, E.   81, 93(n12), 94
budget constraints   11–15
  hard   12, 13, 15, 28, 133, 143, 145–50, 153(n39), 168t, 169, 172
  soft   12, 13, 29, 134–7, 146–8, 178(n8)
budget deficits   130, 132, 137, 138, 150, 151(n10)
  Italy (1980–99)   139t
Budget Law (China, 1995)   14–15
Bulgaria   38, 39, 56, 57, 147, 153(n39)
Bushee, B.   43
business associations   185
business groups   63(n19)

Cadbury Committee code of best practice (1992)   51
Caja Laboral Popular (CLP)   206, 212, 221, 227, 229–30, 235
  CLP Entrepreneurial Division   211, 220
California Public Employees Retirement System (CalPERS)   5, 49, 59, 60, 63(n25)
Campbell, T. L.   62(n5), 63(n19)
capital   58, 59, 169, 172–4, 182, 229
  accounts: internal   209t, 229
  accumulation   30, 166, 171
  financing   162
  gains   231
  intensity   106
  markets   54, 55, 173
  scarcity   167
  stock   233
car industry   86–7
Caracciolo, L.   154(n43)
Carare, O.   153(n39), 155
Carleton, W.   49, 65
Carlin, W.   63(n26), 148, 155
cash flow   54, 74, 145–6, 152(n22), 220
  free cash flow hypothesis   124
causality   110, 115, 119, 119(n11)
Cavour, Count of   151(n17)
Cecchini Report (1985)   131
Central Bank Law (China, 1995)   14
Central and Eastern Europe   105, 150
CER–IRS annual reports   142
chaebol   63(n19)
Chandra, P.   105
Che, J.   151(n8)
Cheney, G.   219
Chidambaran, N.   42
Chief Executive Officers (CEOs)   44, 47, 51
Chief Financial Officer (CFO)   47
Chile   30, 39, 53, 54
China   13–15, 19, 21, 57, 59–60, 63(n22), 104, 125–6, 150, 151(n8)
  non-agricultural firms   178(n7)
  tax and fiscal reforms (1994)   14
  townships and villages   178(n7)
  Ministry of Agriculture   171
Choe, H.   58, 65

Christian Democratic Party (Italy) 134, 152(n24)
CIPE (Interministerial Committee for Economic Planning, Italy) 134, 135f, 140
CISL (trade union) 134
Claessens, S. 54, 55, 65
Clamp, C. 222
Clark, K. B. 69–70, 77–83, 87–9
CLP *see Caja Laboral Popular*
Co-operazione Italiana (periodical) 220
coalition formation 191
codetermination 219, 239(n10)
Coffee, J. 44
collective action 99
collective efficiency (Nadvi) 189
common property resources (Africa) 204
communication 81, 170
community collective shares 165–6
comparative advantage 175, 177, 225
    organizational 187–8, 198, 199(n10), 205, 222, 226
competition 21–3, 28, 130–2, 138, 140, 141, 143, 145, 147, 148, 149, 151(n14), 162, 169, 171, 203, 231
    perfect 21
competitive advantage 165
competitiveness 216
Completion of the Internal Market (Cecchini Report, 1985) 131
computer industry 9, 71, 73, 93–4(n15)
Comunicazione Italia 220
concentration (of ownership) 46, 53
Conco-op 208t, 221
Confederation of Italian Industry (Confindustria) 133
consortia 203, 208t, 220–2, 224, 226, 230, 235–8
Consorzio Nazionale Approvviggionamenti (ACAM) 208t, 220–1
construction cooperative consortium (CCC) 227
consumer cooperatives 216, 237–8
Conte, M. 186, 230
contract cost perspective 19–21
contract enforcement 162

contract innovation work 226
contracting rights 168t
control 44–5, 52, 70, 93(n7), 119(n3)
cooperative alliances and networks 17
cooperative clusters 197, 202, 238
    potential role 184–7
Cooperative Congress 220
cooperative density 188–91, 196–8, 199(n11)
cooperative entry problems 203, 207t, 209–13
    response of La Lega 207t, 210–11
    response of Mondragón 207t, 211–12
cooperative exit problem 203, 213–17, 236, 239(n8)
    response of La Lega 207t, 213
    response of Mondragón 207t, 213–14, 215
cooperative formation rates 199(n15)
cooperative industrial regions 197, 199(n16)
cooperative networks 202–41
    appendices available from author 202, 205
    decision-making 203, 208t, 217–20
    degeneration problem 183, 187, 203, 207t, 213–17, 232–4, 236, 239(n8)
    employment policy 203, 209t, 231–5
    entry problems 203, 207t, 209–13
    exit problems 203, 207t, 213–17, 230, 236, 239(n8)
    facts and theory 181–201, 202
    finance and investment instruments 203, 208–9t, 227–30, 240(n21)
    further research required 224, 230
    hypothesis 204
    implications 196–8, 199(n15), 235–8
    innovation and technology transfer strategies 203, 208t, 225–7
    joint ventures and interfirm alliances 203, 208t, 222–5

cooperative networks – *continued*
  models 187–96
  nine dimensions of comparison
    203, 207–9t
  organizational behaviour 234
  organizational problems 203,
    208t, 220–2
  response to strategic issues
    (Mondragón/La Lega) 207–9t
  risk mitigation 203, 209t, 230–1
  size 194–6
cooperatives 1, 15–17, 162
  Chinese joint-stock 148
  dissolution 214
  endogenous formation 196
  exit 183, 203, 207t, 213–17, 231–2
  hybrid 216
  low casualty rates 235
  new members 183
  sale 236
  second-level 203, 207t, 208t, 220–2
  size 208t, 219
  start-ups 214, 238
  success in networks/clusters
    181–2, 184
coordination 77, 93(n12), 185
  interfirm/intrafirm 81
  interteam/intrateam 81, 82,
    93(n11)
coordination cost reduction 79–82
coordination failure 184, 187, 190,
    191, 198
corporate governance viii–ix, 72, 75,
    90–1
  anxiety 4–5
  definitions 37
  dismissal of CEO 44
  exhilaration 3–4
  global perspectives 36–68
  hybrid forms 27, 176–7
  impact of shareholder activism 48,
    63(n20)
  Italian public enterprises 135f
  JSCs 161–3, 165
  overview 1–35
  ownership and control (three-way
    separation) 3
  structure 49, 61
  theoretical perspectives 17–26

corporate governance problem 19
  four channels to lessen severity
    of 5–7
corporate ownership 19–21,
    93(n7), 101
  collective 178(n3)
  differences across countries 53–4
  evolution 21–3, 59–60
  global perspectives 36–68
  institutionalization 7
  interaction 58–9
  restructuring 27
  sharing 96–123
  structures 53–60
  transitional economies 54–8
corruption 163–4, 169
council of directors 219
Craig, B. 15
credit 21, 128, 208–9t, 227, 237
Crédit Lyonnais Securities Asia:
    Emerging Markets Division 61
Crémer, J. 85
Cull, R. 56, 65
cunban (village-run rural enterprise)
    177(n1)
Czech Republic 11, 38, 55–6, 57, 147

D'Aspremont, C. A. 193, 200
Dahya, J. 51
Darwinian proverb 159
data 119(n9)
  causality 110, 119
  cross-sectional 105, 119
  longitudinal comparisons 114
  panel 105, 106, 110, 119
  selection bias 110, 196, 224
debt 12, 63(n23), 124, 129–30,
    136–8, 138f, 144–5, 160
decision-making 101, 111, 115–16,
    119(n3), 161–2, 171, 174, 183,
    216, 232, 239(n5)
  annual general assembly 219
  cooperatives 203, 208t, 217–20,
    239(n10)
  hypothesis 218
  response of La Lega 208t, 218, 219
  response of Mondragón 208t,
    218–20
  two-part process 218

degeneration problem 183, 187,
    203, 207t, 205, 213–17, 232–4,
    236, 239(n8)
  'innovative adaptation' 216–17
  response of La Lega 207t, 214
  response of Mondragón 207t,
    214, 216
Del Guercio, D. 63(n14)
Delors Report (1989) 130, 144
Déminor ratings 61
democracy/democratization 164,
    169, 171, 174, 218
Demsetz, H. 6
Deng Xiaoping 163
Denis, D. K. 62(n1)
devaluation 137, 138
developing countries 26, 27–30,
    39, 76, 91, 177, 202, 204, 225,
    235–8
Dewatripont, M. 128
Dewenter, K. L. 153(n34)
directors: independent 49,
    63(n13)
disclosure 45, 60 61
'divided technological leadership'
    (Bresnahan) 89
dividends 54, 161, 164, 167, 171
Djankov, S. 55
Donovat machine tools group (MCC)
    224, 240(n21)
dot com bubble 69, 88
Dow, G. K. 199(n8), 200
Drago, R. 102
Dube, A. 115
dynamic commitment
    problem 127

e-commerce 24, 88, 89, 94(n16)
Earle, J. S. 56, 172
East Asia 54
East Asian crisis (1997) 60, 149,
    178(n4)
Eastern Europe 162
EBRD (European Bank for
    Reconstruction and
    Development) 149
economies of scale/scope 24, 166,
    175, 186, 197, 198, 238
Economist 4, 96

Editrice Co-operativa 220
EFIM 140, 141, 152(n20)
EFTA (European Free Trade
    Association) 150
EGAM 152(n20)
EIB (European Investment
    Bank) 142
emerging markets 55, 59–61,
    63(n21) 148
Emilia-Romagna 197, 225
employee buyouts 116
employee stock ownership 1, 7–9,
    28, 96–123, 203, 232
  company characteristics 105–6
  context (four major developments)
    96–7
  dimensions 103
  'failing firm' canard 105
  further research avenues 118–19
  impact on employees' attitudes
    and wages 114–17,
    119(n12–13)
  incidence 102–5
  legislation 105, 119(n8)
  'one-fifth of American adults'
    104, 119(n5)
  performance effects 109–14
  theoretical overview 98–102
  transitional economies 30(n1),
    159–80
  TVEs 159–80
employee stock ownership plans
    (ESOPs) 7t, 97, 103–4, 105, 109,
    111, 114–17, 119(n14)
  East Asia 204
employee welfare funds 171
employees 27, 61, 165, 170, 171,
    174, 185, 239(n5)
  attitudes and behaviour (China)
    161
  human resources 100
  JSCs 161
  knowledge workers 97
  mobility 81
  professional workers/staff 1, 107,
    218, 221
  workers 57, 96, 134, 182–3, 216,
    230, 233, 234
employers 103–4, 211

employment/job   110–11, 145, 149,
    154(n41), 170, 177(n1), 225
    creation   197, 210
    losses   213
    satisfaction   161
    security/guaranteed   217, 224
employment policy   203, 209t,
    231–5
employment protection   151(n6),
    235
Employment Retirement Income
    Security Act (ERISA, 1974)   50,
    51, 63(n10), 103
employment stability   117, 118
endogenous sunk cost   93(n15)
endowment funds   127, 131, 133,
    134, 136, 143, 144
ENEL (National Electricity Authority)
    152(n20)
ENICHEM   140, 141
Enron   60, 63(n27), 182
Ente Nazionale Idrocarburi (ENI, 1953–)
    133, 136, 140–1, 146,
    152(n19, n24)
enterprise ownership   viii–ix
    evolving diversity   1–35
    five unconventional forms   2
    hybrid forms   27
entrepreneurs/entrepreneurship
    70–6, 85, 88–9, 91
    cooperative   212–13
    opportunity costs   212
entry problems   203, 207t,
    209–13
equity   59, 96, 161, 163
ERM (Exchange Rate Mechanism)
    149, 153(n35)
Eroski (Mondragón retailing
    group)   230
Ersoy-Bozcuk, A.   63(n16)
ESOPs *see* employee stock ownership
    plans
Estrin, S.   57, 111, 172
Ettorre, B.   47
Europe   51, 87, 199(n15)
European Bank for Reconstruction
    and Development (EBRD)   149
European Commission   13, 130, 140,
    143, 148, 151(n14)

European Community (EC)   126,
    138, 141
    'upward devolution' of economic
        policies   129–32
European Community: Directorate for
    Competition Policy   140
European Court of Justice   141,
    154(n42)
European Economic Area (EEA)   149
European Investment Bank (EIB)   142
European Monetary System (EMS)
    12, 129–30, 137, 144, 148
European Monetary Union (EMU)
    12, 13, 129, 130, 143–5, 148,
    153(n35), 154(n43)
    benefits of membership   149–50,
        154(n41)
    costs of non-accession   150
European Recovery Plan   133
European Union (EU)   29, 97,
    124–58, 231
    applicant countries   149,
        153(n35–6, n40)
    institutional investment   39
    'upward devolution' of economic
        policies   129–32
Exchange Rate Mechanism (ERM)
    149, 153(n35)
exchange rates   130, 137, 154(n41)
Excite   92(n5)

Faccio, M.   54, 66
faculty self-governance   217, 231
FAGOR (consumer durables
    group)   222
Fehr, E.   199(n12), 234
Ferris, S. P.   63(n19), 66
Fiat   141
Fiji   237
finance   235, 238
finance and investment instruments
    203, 227–30, 240(n21)
    response of La Lega   208–9t,
        227–8
    response of Mondragón   208–9t,
        229–30
Financial Accounting Standards Board
    (FASB)   108
    Statement Number 123   108

financial
  contracting   74
  institutions   173, 236, 237
  instruments   183, 238
  intermediaries/intermediation
      209t, 227–8, 236
  markets   61, 144, 153(n35)
  statements   108
  system: decentralization   125
Financial Times Stock Exchange
      (FTSE) top 300 index
      companies   61
financing   74
  arm's-length   92(n4)
  relational   92(n4)
Fincooper   227–8, 240(n19)
FINEC (National Cooperative Finance
      Company)   228
FINMECCANICA   135f
Finsider   140
firms/companies/corporations
  antitrust policy   83, 144
  conventional   192, 198(n1),
      208t, 210, 212, 218, 223–4,
      239(n5)
  'degeneration' of cooperatives into
      207t, 214, 232, 233, 234, 236,
      239(n8)
  efficiency   22
  emerging markets   55
  employee-owned   235
  family   19
  foreign ownership   55, 56, 57, 59,
      60, 63(n22)
  four types of ownership
      (transitional economies)   55
  large   4–5, 8, 107, 219
  limited liability   171, 173,
      178(n3)
  market-taking versus
      market-making   23–4
  multinational   215
  new   235
  private   97, 136, 148, 150(n4),
      152(n22), 185
  public   127, 150(n3)
  size   81
  small   173, 208t
  survival   110, 118

firms: theoretical perspectives   18–26
  competition   21–3
  contract cost   19–21
  growth option   18–19, 31(n4)
  institutional change   25–6
  intermediation   23–4
fishing   178(n5)
fixed plan options   108
Florio, M.   153(n34)
fondi di dotazione (endowment
      funds)   133
foreign direct investment   227
former Soviet Union (FSU)   162
Fortune   4–5, 8
founder-managers   72
401(k) plans (KSOPs)   7t, 8, 97, 103–4
France   52, 54, 111, 210
Fraquelli, G.   146
fraternity/solidarity   212, 234,
      239(n5)
free-riding   42, 45, 62(n3), 100, 102,
      105, 182, 191, 196, 198, 236
Freeland (Hertzka, 1891)   193
Freeman, R.   115
Freundlich, F.   x, 239(n13)
Frydman, R.   55, 66
fund management   3, 4
Fuyang (Anhui Province)   163

Gachter, S.   199(n12), 234
game theory   102, 191–6
  coalition unanimity   192–3
  exclusive membership   192, 193
  league formation   193–4
  open membership   191–2, 193
  prisoners' dilemmas   198
Garaia (research complex)   227,
      240(n18)
Geer, C. T.   8
General DataComm Industries   112
Georgia (ex-Soviet Union)   55
Germany   41, 52, 53, 54, 96, 219
Gillan, S. L.   xii, 6, 37, 62(n9),
      63(n14, n27)
Giorno (newspaper)   152(n19)
Glass–Steagall Act (repealed,
      1999)   46
Gorton, G.   42, 43
governance codes   60

government 128, 147, 185, 237–8
  Basque 227
  central 14, 175
  Chinese 175–6
  city 14, 164
  coalition 149, 150
  communal 172
  community 28–9, 159, 165, 169, 171, 173
  Italian 126, 137–8, 140–5, 148, 151(n17), 154(n43)
  local 13–15, 28, 125, 126, 148, 161, 164, 168t, 171, 175
  national 28, 29, 125–6
  regional 197
  township 175
  village 163, 167, 175
government agencies 237
government intervention 170
Greenstein, S. 93–4(n15)
Grossman, S. J. 62(n3), 92(n7)
group incentives 100, 110
group system 99
growth options 18–19, 31(n4)
growth opportunities 27
Grundig (firm) 19
Gu, E. X. 173
Guangzhou 163
guanxi 19

Hansmann, H. 99, 105, 183–4, 210
Harrison, A. 153(n38), 154
Hart, O. D. 62(n3), 92(n6–7)
Hartzell, J. C. 43
Hausbank 52
Hawkins, J. 63(n14)
Hayek, F. von 22
Helsinki ii, x
Henggang Joint-Stock Investment Company 166
Hermes Focus Asset Management (HFAM) 51
Hermes Pension Management Limited 51
Hertzka, T. 193
hierarchical dependency 77
high-technology companies 8, 69, 97, 102, 107, 108, 111–12, 113
Hirschman, A. 40

Hong Kong 60
housing cooperatives 226, 237–8
huan gu yu min ('returning shares to original creators') 164
human capital 10, 18, 75, 90, 102, 172, 175, 176, 217, 228
Hungary 11, 55

IBM 9, 70–1, 82–3, 89
  System/360 73, 78, 82, 86, 87
'IBM model' 92(n2)
IBM–PC compatibles 86, 90
Ideko 208t, 221–2
Ikerlan (1973-) 208t, 221, 224, 227
Ilva 140, 152(n28)
incentive contract theory 101–2
incentives 87, 99, 150(n2), 176
  group 102
  individual 102
  organizational 233
incomplete contract approach 92(n7)
index funds 4, 38, 48
India 11, 60, 147, 203, 236
Indonesia 11, 60
industrial:
  cooperatives 181, 225
  districts 189, 199(n12, n15, n17), 222
  sector 143f, 162
  transformation 143
industrialization 127, 175
industry average performance bonds (proposed) 240(n21)
'inegalitarian' cooperative type (Meade) 193
inflation 129–31, 137–8, 144, 153(n39)
Inforco-op 220
information 10, 19, 41–2, 45, 62, 62(n8), 75, 99, 100, 170, 174–5, 226
  asymmetries 101
  imperfect 22, 37–8
  technological 72
information assurance policy board 229
information and communication industries 69, 73, 76, 82, 86, 91
information problems 20

information systems 87
information technology 9, 74, 80–1, 101, 228
information-encapsulation 70, 73, 85, 86
information-sharing 70, 73, 81, 83–4, 85, 86, 184
innovation 91, 102, 199(n11), 202, 209t, 223, 226, 235, 236, 238
  chain-lined model 85
  definition 238(n3)
  'gains from trade' 224
  Japanese chain-linked system 10
  labour-saving 225
  large 225, 240(n15)
  new product 113
  small 225
innovation commons 90, 92
innovation and technology transfer strategies 203, 208t, 225–7
  response of La Lega 226–7
  response of Mondragón 226, 227
insider trading 45
insiders 55, 57, 161
Institute of Corporate Law and Corporate Governance (Russia) 61
institutional investors/shareholders 1, 2–7, 9, 24, 108, 112, 165, 169, 172, 173
  activism 4, 45–6, 46–53, 62(n9)
  evolution 29–30
  fiduciary interests 47
  foreign 36, 38, 52, 57–8
  global perspectives 36–68
  as large shareholders 40–2
  pressure-sensitive and pressure insensitive 42–3, 47, 62(n6–7)
  rationale for involvement in corporate governance 39–46
  selling of shares 44
  voting turnout 50–1, 52
insurance 1, 228, 235
insurance companies 5, 55, 46
  pressure-sensitive investors 43, 62(n6)
Intel 83, 89, 93(n15)
intellectual property rights 70, 90, 91, 226

interest rates 152(n22), 154(n41), 240(n21)
interfirm alliances 203, 208t, 222–5, 236
intermediation perspective 23–4
internal accounts, individual 17, 31(n3)
International Accounting Standards Board 108
International Monetary Fund (IMF) 13, 29, 59, 126, 149–50, 153(n37), 154(n42)
  conditionality 149
Internet 86, 88–90, 103
investment 27, 134, 154(n41), 170–1, 196
  overinvestment 145–6
investment advisers
  pressure-insensitive institutions 43
investment companies 48
  pressure-insensitive institutions 43
investor ownership 100
investor protection 59
Investor Responsibility Research Centres 47
involuntary separation 185, 199(n7)
IPO (initial public offering) 88
IRI *see* Italy: Institute for Industrial Reconstruction
ISO 9000 certification 222
Istituto Co-operativo per l'Innovazione (ICIE) Institute for Cooperative Innovation 208t, 221, 224, 227, 240(n16)
Italian constitution: Article 49 (cooperatives) 205
Italy xi, 12–13, 54, 186, 197–8, 199(n17), 235
  Law on aid to southern regions (64/1986) 140
  Law on financial support to SMEs (317/1991) 140
  Law on the Fund of Innovation and Applied Research (46/1982) 140
  Law on tax relief to firms involved in M&A (4239/1989) 140
Italy: Economic Plan for Development (1966–70) 134

Italy: Institute for Industrial
    Reconstruction (IRI, 1933–)
    132–3, 135f, 136, 140, 141, 145,
    146, 152(n18–19, n21, n24)
  net income (1974–83)   136f
Italy: Interministerial Committee for
    Economic Planning (CIPE)   134,
    135f, 140
Italy: Ministry of Finance/Treasury
    133–4, 137, 140, 144–5, 152(n25)
Italy: Ministry for State
    Holdings   134
Italy: Public Holdings Ministry   140
  abolished (1993)   144
  see also north-central Italy

Jakobs, R.   199(n5)
Japan   41, 52, 53, 62(n5), 76, 87
Jensen, M. C.   62(n2)
Jiangsu Province   160, 161
John, K.   42
joint ventures   165, 185, 203, 208t,
    222–5, 236
  hypotheses   223
joint-stock cooperatives (*gufen
    hezuozhi*) (JSCs)   21, 160,
    177(n3)
  broad agricultural sector   166–7
  challenges remaining   174–6
  channels to raise capital and
      diversify risk   172–4
  community-based   163–5
  debt-asset ratio   160
  dynamics   162
  emergence   163–7
  enterprise-based   165–6
  features   161
  functioning mechanisms   167–74
  mechanisms to restrain insider
      control   167–9
  'most instructive lesson'   177
  performance (2000)   160t
  structures to avoid excessive cost
      of collective decision-making
      170–2
  urban   178(n6)
Jones, D. C.   101, 111, 119(n3)
Joshi, S.   x, xi, 191, 196
Journal of Comparative Economics   viii

Kahl, M.   42, 43
Kahn, C.   44–5
Kang, J. K.   40, 41
Kaplan, S. N.   40, 41, 69, 73–4, 76
Kardas, P.   116, 121
Karmin, C.   60, 63(n24)
Karpoff, J.   62(n9)
Kazakhstan   55
keiretsu   31(n5), 52, 229
Kensinger, J. W.   63(n12)
Kerala Dinesh Beedi cooperative
    network (India)   236
Keys, P. Y.   63(n19)
Khanna, T.   63(n19)
Khurana, R.   4
Klapper, L. F.   60
Kleiner Perkis   92(n5)
knowledge
  codified   72, 92(n4)
  tacit   71–2, 92(n4)
knowledge economy   217
Kornai, J.   124–5, 127, 148
Kremer, M.   184, 199(n9),
    239(n14)
Kruse, D. L.   xii, 109, 119(n5)
Kumar, A.   143–4
Kyrgyz Republic   55

*La Lega Nazionale delle Co-operative e
    Mutue* (National League of
    Cooperatives and Mutual Aid
    Societies)   28, 181, 185–6, 197,
    198, 198(n1)
  comparative case study   202–41
  cooperative adaptation and
      organizational innovation
      206–35
  key finding   17
  'new capital membership'   214
  nine dimensions of comparison
      203, 207–9t
  website address   238(n2)
La Porta, R.   52–4, 67
labour: skilled   230
labour disputes   238
labour force   199(n11)
labour market   130
labour overabundance   167
labour relations   184

labour-managed firm 232
neoclassical analysis 193
theory 119(n10)
Lagun-Aro (social insurance scheme)
208t, 221, 230
land 164, 167, 169, 175
land contract rights 166–7
Lanerossi 138, 140, 141, 152(n19)
Lankide (export group) 208t, 222
Lasfer, M. A. 63(n16)
Latin America 63(n20), 97, 204, 236
law 25, 56, 76, 140, 144, 152(n25),
204–5, 208–9t, 211, 239(n4)
cooperative legal reform (Italy,
1992) 228, 240(n20)
Spain 232–3
law enforcement 56, 153(n35–6)
lawcourts 25
layoffs 172–3, 183, 220, 230, 232
JSCs 161
Leal, R. 54
Lee, C. 92(n5), 94(n16), 95
Lefort, F. 63(n26)
legal environment 51–3, 60
lenders/lending institutions 41, 61
Lens Fund 47
Lerner, A. 31(n7)
less-developed countries 30
Lessig, L. 90
Letta, E. 154(n43)
leveraged management buyouts
119(n4)
Levine, D. I. 199(n4)
Li, W. 148
liberalization 125, 146, 148
Libertà, Uguaglianza ed Efficenza
240(n20)
Lifetouch 8
Lins, K. V. 55
liquidation rights 74
liquidity 44–5, 46, 52
litigation 140, 141
LKS (independent MCC cooperative,
1991–) 211–12
Lo Passo, F. 136, 146
loan back 17, 31(n3)
loans 133, 142, 150, 238
bad 149
syndicated 59

'logrolling' 218
Lopez-de-Silanes, F. 153(n34)
Love, I. 60

Maastricht criteria 149, 153(n35),
154(n43)
Maastricht Treaty (1991), 130, 144
Macchiati, A. 136, 146, 157
Mackin, C. 116
Majluf, N. 53, 67
Majumdar, S. K. 147
Malatesta, P. H. 153(n34), 155
Malaysia 60
Mallin, C. 50
management 3, 4, 38, 40, 42, 45,
47–8, 52–4, 55, 57, 63(n11), 99,
101, 171, 219
appointments 144
view of institutional investor
activism 63(n12)
management council 219
managerial
buy-out 174
discretion 145–6
myopia 43
managers 22, 27, 99, 107, 110,
124, 128, 133–4, 137, 146,
152(n21), 167, 169, 174, 185,
212, 216, 229
China 159
JSCs 161
manufacturing 108, 147,
199(n17)
market contracting 19–21
market economy 1–2, 124, 126, 148,
150(n2, n4), 235
market economy investor principle
(MEIP) 132
market imperfections 20, 127,
145–6
market information 23–4
market institutions 25–6, 31(n6)
market intermediaries 23–4, 172
market rates 233
market share 232
marketing 166, 167, 197, 222,
235, 238
markets: concentrated structure
93(n15)

Marschak, J.   83
Martin, J. D.   63(n12, n27)
Martin, S.   153(n34), 157
Martin, T.   x, 232
Maskin, E.   125, 128, 155
Maug, E.   44–5
Mayer, C.   63(n26), 92(n3)
McConnell, J. J.   43, 51, 62(n1)
McCormick, D.   199(n12)
Meade, J. E.   193
Means, G.   38, 40, 53
Meckling, W.   62(n2)
Mercer, W. M.   107
merger   207t, 213, 214, 219,
    222, 224
Mexico   60, 153(n34)
Mezzogiorno   186, 197–8, 211, 221
Microsoft   83, 89, 93(n15)
Milgrom, P.   93(n10), 101
Minton, B.   40, 41
Mitton, T.   60
modular parts: outsourcing   87
modular products   82, 83, 93(n15)
modular teams   98
modularization   76–90, 93(n9)
  architecture   76–8, 86, 89, 91
  coordination cost reduction
      79–82
  evolutionary formation of product
      system   89–90
  incentives   87–90
  informational arrangements   82–7
  innovation commons   90
  open interfaces and competition
      87–9
  option value   78–9
  parallel experiments   82
  research needs   91–2
  see also product systems
Moldova   55
Mondragón Co-operative Corporation
    (MCC)   xi, 185, 208–9t, 211,
    213–16, 218–22, 224–5, 227,
    229–30, 235, 238
  background (appendix available
      from author)   202
  inverted-pyramid nature   215
  key finding   17
  website address   238(n1)

Mondragón group (Spain, 1956–)
    x, 16–17, 28, 170, 172, 181,
    186, 197–8
  'colossal international
      reputation'   222
  cooperative adaptation and
      organizational innovation
      206–35
  comparative case study   202–41
  membership fee   233
  nine dimensions of comparison
      203, 207–9t
  open membership principle   193
  reorganizations   214, 222
  ten internal principles   205,
      206, 233
Mondragón University   221
monitoring   98–9, 101, 102, 146,
    164, 170
  centralized   98
  each other (workers)   99
  horizontal   98
  see also shareholder monitoring
Monks, R.   48–9
monopoly   148
Montedison   140
Moore, J.   92(n7)
moral hazard   124, 128, 134, 147,
    208t, 213, 228, 229, 240(n21)
Morck, R.   41
Morley-Fletcher, E.   240(n20)
Motta   135f, 152(n19)
multiple modules   85
multivariate analysis   119(n12)
Murphy, K. M.   48, 184, 199(n9), 201
mutual funds   6–7, 30, 46, 47, 55
Myers, S.   18
Myners Report   51

Nadvi, K.   187, 189, 199(n12)
NAFTA (North American Free Trade
    Agreement)   149, 150
Nakamura, M.   41
Nalbantian, H. R.   99
Nash equilibrium   191, 193, 195
National Association of Pension
    Funds (NAPF)   50–1, 63(n17)
National Center for Employee
    Ownership   105, 111

National Co-operative Bank (USA)
237
neoclassical economics 21, 193
Neoh, A. 60
Netherlands 54
network effects (general theory)
198(n3)
network externalities 181–201,
202–41
Newman, A. 199(n9), 200, 227
niche markets 71, 73, 227
Nigeria 11
Noe, T. 45–6
non-tariff barriers 131, 151(n13)
North, D. C. 25, 31(n6)
north-central Italy 225, 235,
240(n17)
Nuti, M. 184

oneri impropri 152(n25)
1/*N* problem 100, 102, 183,
187, 207t
open interface 87–9, 93(n15)
open membership principle 233
Organic Law of Villager's
Committee 165
Organisation for Economic
Co-operation and
Development (OECD) 3, 129,
136, 203
organizational
behaviour 204
capital 19
commitment and identification
115
exit 214
problems 220–2
Oswald, A. 151(n6)
outsourcing 87, 224, 225
owners 27, 45, 99

Pacific Northwest plywood
cooperatives 110
see also plywood cooperatives
Pareto, V. 20, 187, 191
Parker, D. 153(n34)
Parrino, R. 44, 62(n8), 67
partners (general/limited) 92(n3)
Patibandla, M. 105

pay-for-performance 43
pay-as-you-go (PAYG) 29
payoffs 192–5
Pencavel, J. 15
Pendleton, A. 115, 122
pension fund managers 43, 45
pension funds 4, 5, 30, 39, 46, 55,
63(n10), 161
corporate 47, 63(n17)
private 47, 48
public 47, 48
pension plans 3, 29, 97, 103
pension system 130, 138
pensions 96, 116, 117, 230
performance 56–8, 63(n13),
98–101, 106, 117–18,
127, 145, 147–8, 168t,
240(n21)
coworker 115–16
effect of employee share-ownership
109–14, 119(n9, n11)
financial and non-financial 74
high-performance workplaces 185,
199(n4)
JSCs 160, 162
pharmaceutical companies 108
piece rates 98
Pinto, B. 147, 157
plywood cooperatives 16, 21, 110,
213, 239(n6)
poison pill 49
Poland 55, 110, 147
political interference/pressure 134,
137, 146
political parties 140
politicians 128, 133, 134, 137,
152(n21), 154(n43)
party-political objectives 129, 143,
153(n31)
vote-seeking 129, 143, 145–6
pollution 175
Porter, M. 199(n17), 222
prices 23, 152(n22)
marginal cost pricing 151(n7)
principal–agent theory 98–100
private
funds 56–7
owners/ownership 147, 159
sector 59, 173, 185

privatization   11, 12, 13, 29, 39,
   55–6, 61, 97, 125, 132, 138, 141,
   144–8, 151(n5), 152(n28),
   153(n31, n34–5), 203
   attitude towards   161
   China   159, 160
privatization funds   56
process innovations   186, 199(n8)
processing   166, 167
product supply curves   119(n10)
product system innovation:
   institutional arrangements
   69–95
product systems   69, 77, 81–2, 85,
   86, 92(n1), 93(n9)
   ex post evolutionary formation
      89–90
   modular operations   89, 94(n17)
   partitioning   85–6
   research needs   91–2
   standardizing the interfaces   86
   see also modularization
production   166, 239(n11)
productivity   99, 101, 109, 110, 113,
   129, 136, 145, 224
products: high-quality   225
profit-sharing   105, 106, 116, 117,
   161, 215
profitability   134, 146, 152(n22),
   168t, 186, 224, 237
profits   90, 100, 127, 168t, 171,
   174, 178(n6), 182–3, 187,
   205, 227, 234
Promosviluppo (Development
   Promotion)   207t, 211, 221
property rights   1, 59, 74, 91–2,
   93(n7), 101, 161
Property Rights Regimes,
   Microeconomic Incentives and
   Development (UNU/WIDER
   research project)   viii, x
Prowse, S.   41
public
   funds   226
   procurement   143, 151(n13)
   sector   147
   transport   142
Publix Supermarkets   8
Putterman, L.   99

Qi, D.   57, 68
Qian, Y.   125, 148

Radner, R.   83
railways   142, 150(n2), 151(n17)
Rajan, R.   75, 93(n8)
Ramamurti, R.   11
rating services   61
ratios
   capital–labour   198(n1)
   debt–asset   160
   fiscal deficit/GDP   130, 139t,
      144, 151(n10)
   public debt/GDP   129, 130,
      138f, 144
Ravazzi, P.   142
Ray, D.   199(n9)
recession   212, 219–20, 240(n21)
regional aid   140, 152(n27),
   153(n30)
regional economic development
   131, 151(n10)
regulation   38, 46
Regulation Fair Disclosure   45
Relational Investors   47
relationship investing   42
rents (economic)   162, 172, 191
Report of Committee of Inquiry into
   UK Vote Execution   50
research and development (R&D)
   9–10, 43, 71, 73, 78, 79–80, 83,
   86, 87–8, 91, 108, 152(n27),
   208t, 221
research and development
   organizations   93(n13)
   activity levels of members   85,
      93(n14)
   hierarchical   84
   interactive   84–5, 86–7
   V-mediated information
      encapsulation   85–6
residual returns   100, 101, 119(n3)
resource allocation   138
restructuring   57, 137, 140, 141, 145,
   146, 148, 153(n34, n39)
   China   159–60, 170
risk   167, 168t, 182, 204, 216, 235
   diversification   172–4
   financial   118

job loss 230–1
  mitigation 203, 209t, 230–1, 236
  plant closure 230
  retirement income 230
Riva 152(n28)
Roberts, J. 93(n10), 101
Robinson, J. 234
Roe, M. 40, 52, 53
Roell, A. 54
Rogers, J. 115
Roland, G. 125, 128, 148,
  153(n40), 154
Romania 56, 147, 153(n39)
Romano, R. 47
Rondi, L. xii, 12, 13, 145–6, 155
Rosen, C. 119(n6)
Rosevear, A. 57
Route 128 firms 81–2
rules of the game 20–1, 25, 31(n6)
  enforcement mechanisms 25
  formal and informal 25
Russia 11, 28, 55, 61, 104, 125, 147,
  148, 203, 236
Rutgers University 104

Sahlman, W. 72
Saxenian, A. 73, 81
SBCS *see* soft budget constraint
  syndrome
Schaefer, S. 79, 80, 81
Scharf, A. 116
Schmitz, H. 187, 199(n12)
Schumpeterian creative
  destruction 22
Science Applications International 8
Seabright, P. 152(n27), 155
Securities and Exchange
  Commission (SEC) 45, 63(n10),
  104, 112, 116
Sen, A. 239(n5)
Sesil, J. C. xii, 9
Shandong province 161, 163, 166
Shanghai Stock Exchange 57
share blocking 51–2
shared
  capitalism 119(n4)
  rights of ownership 101
  values 186
ShareData 8

shareholder activism *see* institutional
  investors/activism
shareholder base 44
shareholder monitoring 36, 39–51,
  56, 58, 62, 62(n3–4)
  theory and evidence 42–6
shareholder protection 52–3,
  60, 61
shareholder returns 112, 113
shareholders 3, 5–6, 61, 63(n11),
  108, 128, 164–5, 167, 169,
  239(n10)
  minority 53–7
  outside 168t
  'party-political hidden' 134
  private individuals 57
shares 161, 165, 171, 173, 228, 231
Shenzhen 163
Shenzhen City: Henggang town 166
Shivdasani, A. 40
Shleifer, A. 37, 62(n4), 147
shocks 63(n26), 83, 110, 203, 231
Sigiani, M. 240(n20)
Silicon Valley (USA) 18
  institutional arrangements (product
    innovation) 69–95
  joint ownership and shifting
    governance 9–10
Silicon Valley model 70–3, 92(n2)
Silvestri, P. 136, 142, 155
Simon, H. 76–7
Singapore 60
Single European Act (1986)
  131, 148
single market 131, 138, 140,
  143, 233
SINNEA 208t, 220
Skillman, G. 99
skills 100, 196
Slovenia 110
SMAER 208t, 220
small investors 30
Smith, S. C. xii, 16–17, 196,
  199(n10, n12), 200, 224, 225,
  232–3, 239(n5), 240(n21)
soci sovventori ('capital memberships')
  228, 240(n20)
social capital 19, 176, 189, 235
social council 172, 219

social enterprises (Latin
America)   204
social insurance   236
social network   231
social security benefits   96
social services cooperative
sector   225
Socialist Party (Italy)   152(n24)
soft budget constraint syndrome
(SBCS)   124–8, 147, 151(n7)
China   151(n8)
cure   125
soft budget constraints   124–58
state ownership   126–8
software   74, 83, 108
South Asia   204
South Korea   58, 63(n19), 204
South-East Asia   91
Southern Italy   134, 152(n21),
153(n30), 211
sovereign rights   149
Spain   54, 153(n34), 216, 235
labour law   232–3
'splitting operator' effect (Baldwin
and Clark)   82, 94(n17)
Spulber, D.   23
Sri Lanka   237
Stability and Growth Pact (1997)   130
stabilization   125, 148
staged capital commitment
(Sahlman)   72
stakeholders   37, 128, 177
standard of living   96
Standard & Poor   4, 61, 112
Starks, L. T.   xii, 6, 37, 43, 62(n9),
63(n14, n20)
start-up costs   88
start-up firms   72, 92(n5)
going public   76
sale to larger firm   76
state aid   130–2, 141–3, 146,
152(n27), 153(n35)
private sector (Italy, 1987–98)
142, 142f
public sector (Italy, 1987–98)
142, 142f
state pension schemes   96
State Commission for Restructuring
the Economic System   178(n6)

State of Wisconsin Investment
Board   112
state-owned enterprises (SOEs)   1, 2,
11–15, 19, 28–9, 55–7, 124–5,
127–31, 151(n6–8), 152(n25),
153(n38), 172, 236
China   13–15, 148, 159, 161, 164,
167, 168t, 170
Italy   12–13, 29, 132–47, 149,
153(n35)
effect of European policies
137–47
macroeconomic channel (Italy)
137–8, 139t
microeconomic channel (Italy)
138, 140–3
privatization (Italy)   143–5
switch of budget constraint regime
(Italy)   137–47
usage   150(n4)
status   109
stock markets   58, 59–60, 97, 114,
150(n4), 177
stock options   8, 75, 97–8
stock prices   41, 44
stock purchase plans   7t, 8
strikes   115, 116, 119(n14)
Strömberg, P.   69, 73–4, 76
Stulz, R.   41, 58
subsidiaries   207t, 215–16, 225
subsidies   138, 213, 239(n8)
'substituting operator' effect
(Baldwin and Clark)   82, 87,
88, 94(n17)
Sun, L.   x, xii, 19, 148, 173
supermodular function   80,
93(n10–11)
supranational institutions   154(n42)
benefits of membership   149–50,
154(n41)
costs of non-accession   150
supranational pressure   12–13, 29,
125–6, 129, 140, 143–4, 147–9,
153(n35–6)
suriawase (tight coordination)   87
Sutton, J.   93–4(n15)
Svejnar, J.   29
systemic engineering environment
85, 86

takeover 61, 168t;
  antitakeover amendments 43, 49
Takizawa, H. xii, 10, 80, 81,
  83–5, 88
Tanzania 237
tariffs 131, 152(n22)
tax incentives 103
taxation 167
Taylorist (deskilled) production
  processes 205
Teachers Insurance and Annuity
  Association College Retirement
  Equities Fund (TIAA–CREF) x, 5,
  49–50, 59
team-theoretic framework (Marschak
  and Radner) 83
technology 196, 197, 226, 229
  transfer 223, 226, 235, 236
Telegdy, Á. 56
Texaco 49
Thailand 60
Tian, L. 57
time horizon problem 182,
  198(n1)
time inconsistency 124, 125, 127,
  128, 147, 148
Tobin, J. 113
Todaro, M. P. 199(n12)
Topkis, D. 80
total factor productivity 13, 148
township and village enterprises
  (TVEs) viii, 14, 19, 28, 29
  challenges 174–6
  definition 177(n1)
  growth 178(n4)
  mechanism degeneration 174,
    178(n8)
  mechanisms of employee stock
    ownership 159–80
  ownership categories (2000)
    177–8(n3)
  performance (2000) 160t
  restructuring 160n
  transfer to private ownership
    178(n4)
trade flows 150
trade unions 115, 116, 134, 209t,
  210, 224, 232
training costs 185, 199(n7)

transitional economies 11, 26,
  27–30, 38–9, 61, 97, 104–5, 110,
  148, 150(n4), 162, 172, 177,
  203–4, 235–6, 238
  evolving environment 59
  ownership 54–8
transparency 134, 138, 140,
  152(n26)
Travlos, N. G. 51
Treaty of Rome (1957) 130–1,
  151(n10)
trust 186, 235
tudi gufen hezushe (land share
  cooperative) 166
Turnbull, G. K. 102
Tuscany 199(n16)

Ukraine 55, 57, 147
Ularco (legal/administrative group,
  1965–) 208t, 221, 222
ULMA group 215, 222, 230
uncertainty 186, 192, 226
  marketing 88, 89, 94(n16)
  technical 88, 89, 94(n16)
unemployment 131, 153(n30), 197
  'biggest source of unhappiness'
    151(n6)
unemployment insurance 210, 230
unionization 106, 108–9, 113, 116
Unipol 228
United Airlines 8, 104, 116,
  182, 184
United Kingdom 54, 60, 149,
  151(n7), 153(n34)
  institutional investors 3, 50–1,
    63(n17)
United Nations 236, 238
United Nations University: World
  Institute for Development
  Economics Research
  (UNU/WIDER) ii, x
United Parcel Service 8
United States (of America) 41,
  45, 53, 54, 60, 76, 81, 87, 103,
  105, 204
  employee stock ownership 7–9
  equity ownership 96
  federal government 52
  institutional investment 39

United States (of America) – *continued*
  institutional investor activism
      46–50, 63(n12)
  institutional investors 2
  plywood cooperatives 16, 21, 100,
      213, 239(n6)
  voting turnout (by investors) 50
University of Southern California:
      Center for Effective
      Organizations 107
'upward devolution' 124–58
  definition 150(n3)
  macroeconomic policies 129–30
  microeconomic policies 130–2
  policy implications 147–50
urbanization 199(n12)
Urdangarin, C. 240(n22)
US Bureau of Labor Statistics 107
US Federal Reserve Board 107
US Labor Department 46, 47, 50,
      63(n10)
Useem, M. 48, 68
usus fructus 167

Valadares, S. 54
value added 199(n11), 240(n21)
Van Miert, K. 141, 145
Van Nuys, K. 48
Vanek, J. 193, 225, 240(n15)
'VC tournament game' 87
venture capital 161
venture capital contracts 70, 73–6,
      90–2
venture-capitalist mediated
      (V-mediated) information
      encapsulation 10, 85–6
venture capitalists 9–10, 70–6,
      85, 88, 92(n3, n5–6), 94(n16),
      168t, 211
'vertical competition' (Bresnahan) 89
vertical integration 24, 31(n5)
Villalonga, B. 153(n34)
Vishny, R. W. 37, 62(n4), 147
Vivendi Universal 52
voting
  heterogeneous voter problem 187,
      207t, 210
  majority 205
  outcomes 170, 171

procedures 170, 171, 183
rights 50–1, 52, 53, 54, 59, 74,
      103, 164, 228
voucher privatization 56

wages/pay 111, 118, 152(n22), 171,
      192–3, 209t
  automatic indexation (Italy),
      abolished (1984) 137
  and benefits 116, 117
  cuts 210, 233
  efficiency benefits 182
  variability 231
Wahal, S. 43
Waldmann, R. 240(n21)
Walker, E. 63(n26)
Wang (firm) 19
Wang, Y. 57
Ward, B. 193
Ward effect 232–4, 240(n21)
waterfall model (R&D
      organization) 84
Watson Wyatt Worldwide 112
websites 238(n1–2)
Weeden, R. 106–7, 123
Weijland, H. 199(n12)
well-being 151(n6)
Wenzhou (Zhejiang Province)
      163, 173
Whyte, K. 210, 239(n7)
Whyte, W. F. 210, 239(n7)
'Wintel' platform 89
Winton, A. 44–5
Woidtke, T. 48
worker cooperatives 21, 104,
      109–10, 119(n4, n10), 162, 181,
      182, 184, 198(n3), 203, 204,
      237–8
  economic advantages 15–16
  France 111
worker-investors 182
worker-managed firm, theory 231
working environment 118
works councils 219, 239(n10)
World Bank (author) 11, 199(n13)
World Bank (subject) 13, 29, 30,
      126, 149, 150
Worldcom 60
WTO/GATT 13, 29, 126, 149, 150

xiangban (township-run rural enterprise) 177(n1)
Xu, C. 125, 157
Xu, X. 57

yizi dailao (job opportunities) 166

Zarauz cooperative 214
Zhejiang province 160, 163
Zhidao yijian (guidelines) 178(n6)
Zhucheng city 166
Zibo City: Zhoucun district 163
Zingales, L. 18, 37, 75, 93(n8)